R. F. Burton

Lacerda's Journey to Cazembe in 1798

R. F. Burton

Lacerda's Journey to Cazembe in 1798

ISBN/EAN: 9783741141423

Manufactured in Europe, USA, Canada, Australia, Japa

Cover: Foto ©Thomas Meinert / pixelio.de

Manufactured and distributed by brebook publishing software
(www.brebook.com)

R. F. Burton

Lacerda's Journey to Cazembe in 1798

The Lands of Cazembe.

LACERDA'S JOURNEY TO CAZEMBE

In 1798.

TRANSLATED AND ANNOTATED

By CAPTAIN R. F. BURTON, F.R.G.S.

ALSO

JOURNEY OF THE POMBEIROS

P. J. BAPTISTA AND AMARO JOSÉ, ACROSS AFRICA FROM ANGOLA
TO TETTE ON THE ZAMBEZE.

TRANSLATED BY B. A. BEADLE;

AND A

RÉSUMÉ OF THE JOURNEY OF MM. MONTEIRO AND GAMITTO.

By DR. C. T. BEKE.

[*Published by the Royal Geographical Society.*]

LONDON:

JOHN MURRAY, ALBEMARLE STREET.

1873.

PREFACE.

THE interest excited by the recent letters of Dr. Livingstone concerning the country of the Cazembe and neighbouring regions of Central Africa, has induced the Council of the Royal Geographical Society to publish, for the information of its Fellows and the public, the present volume of translations of narratives of Portuguese journeys into those little-known parts of the African interior.

The first in order, and the most important, of these narratives, is that of Dr. de Lacerda, who led an expedition to Cazembe near the close of the last century. For the translation of this (copiously annotated), the Council are indebted to Captain R. F. Burton, who is so well qualified, by his great experience in African travel and his philological acquirements, for such an undertaking. The second narrative, the route-journal of the Pombeiros P. J. Baptista and Amaro José, who traversed Africa from Angola to Tette, and crossed, therefore, the recent line of march of Dr. Livingstone between Cazembe and Lake Bangweolo, has been translated by Mr. B. A. Beadle, Chancellor to the Portuguese Consulate in London, Captain Burton revising and editing this portion of the volume. Of the third narrative, that of Messrs. Monteiro and Gamitto, whose journey to Cazembe was undertaken in 1831, it has been thought sufficient to reprint a résumé that had previously appeared from the able pen of Dr. Charles Beke.

CONTENTS.

CHAPTER I.

THE DEPARTURE.

CHAPTER II.

THE MARCH FROM THE LUPATA DA JÁUA TO THE NORTHERN ARUANGÓA RIVER.

CHAPTER III.

THE MARCH FROM THE NORTHERN ARUANGÓA RIVER, TILL THE DEATH OF DR. DE LACERDA.

CONTENTS.

CHAPTER IV.

CHAPTER V.

CHAPTER VI.

The Return March, the Attack, and the Flight.

JOURNEY OF THE "POMBEIROS," FROM ANGOLA TO THE RIOS DE SENNA.

RÉSUMÉ OF THE JOURNEY OF MM. MONTEIRO AND GAMITTO.

INTRODUCTION OF DR. DE LACERDA TO THE PUBLIC.

BY THE TRANSLATOR.

OUR earliest authorities upon the subject of Africa, the classical and sub-classical authors, were followed by the Portuguese, who betimes, in the sixteenth century, established factories on both coasts, eastern and western: their traders crossed the interior from shore to shore, whilst their missionaries founded large and prosperous colonies, such as Zumbo in the east and São Salvador in the west, with cathedrals, churches, chapels, and stone houses. The explorers did not neglect either the Lake Regions of Central Intertropical Africa, or even the basin of the Zambeze River.

Foremost in the heroic band—whom of late years it has been the fashion to ignore—stands that "martyr in the cause of science," Dr. Francisco José Maria de Lacerda e Almeida. His family was Paulista, that is to say, from the city of São Paulo in the Brazil, a place whose name, however little known at present, will be famous for all time, a town of some 5000 or 6000 dauntless souls who explored and conquered the vast area bounded by the Amazon and by La Plata, and stretching from the Atlantic to the Andes.

It is doubtful whether Pará or Bahia was the birthplace of Dr. de Lacerda; he graduated, however, as an M.D. (doctor of mathematics) at Coimbra, and presently he was appointed astronomer to H. M. F. Majesty. He left Lisbon (January 8, 1780) in the *Coração de Jesus*, with the object of surveying and laying down the Western limits of the great Luso-American dependency. Whilst travelling from Barcellos to the capital of Mato-grosso,

he was attacked (September 23, 1781) by Indians, who wounded
him with an arrow: the carrapatos, or poisonous ticks, also
afflicted him with an unpleasant complaint, the well-known
"Sarnas." During 1784 he laboured in the interior with the
great Luso-Hispanian "Commission of Limits;" in 1786 he left
Cuyabá (Mato-grosso), and, ascending the Tiété River, reached
Porto Feliz, in the then captaincy, now the province, of São
Paulo. He passed a portion of 1788 near the lakes or swamps
of "Xaraes" (Xarayes): here he was hunted by, and sometimes
he hunted, the once formidable "Canoe Indians," or "Pay-
aguás," who call themselves Eijiguaijigi, and who, according to
some, gave name to the Paraguay river. He also visited the
Cayapós, a tribe not yet extinct, and other various clans of the
great Guaycurú or Aycurú race, whom the Spaniards term Cabal-
leros, or "Mounted Indians." Finally, he travelled amongst
the Moxos or Mojos, Indians of Bolivia, concerning whom
we have details in Trübner's 'Bibliotheca Glottica' (London,
1858).

In 1790, Dr. de Lacerda returned to Lisbon, and published
the results of his long and weary wanderings. His book, the
' Diario da Viagem do Dr. Francisco José de Lacerda e Almeida,
pelas Capitanias do Pará, Rio Negro, Matto-grosso, Cuyabá,
e S. Paulo, nos annos de 1780 a 1790,' was lately republished
at São Paulo—"Impresso por ordem da Assembleia Legis-
lativa da Provincia, &c.: na Typografia de Costa Silveira, Rua
de S. Gonçalo. No. 14. 1841." Yet it is not easy to procure
a copy, and I should have failed but for the kindness of my
excellent friend, then Deputy from Taubaté, and subsequently
President of the province of Alagôas, Dr. Moreira de Barros, of
S. Paulo. The work contains a valuable itinerary from Cuyabá,
and tales of jaguars, pumas and serpents, which, however mar-
vellous, may be taken on trust. One snake was so huge that the
slaves, fancying it to be an old canoe, began to burn it. Although
mere diaries, the records are remarkable for correctness: lati-
tudes, longitudes, and altitudes are duly chronicled, the breadth
of rivers is trigonometrically measured, and, in fact, all the
labours required from the latest travellers are regularly gone
through.

Returned to Lisbon, we find Dr. de Lacerda complaining that his slaves at São Paulo had plundered his property and had destroyed his valuable papers; hence the imperfections of the map which he presented to the Royal Academy of Sciences. I cannot discover the year in which he was transferred to Africa. We know that in 1797 he accompanied an expedition to explore the course of the Cunene River, which discharges itself westward into the Atlantic. There he failed: the recovery of his diaries, however, would interest geographers, as that intricate and confused section of African hydrography is still to be explored. A man of eminently advanced views, he returned with the mighty vision of a second and southern overland transit (viagem à contracosta) through Southern Africa, a whole generation before Lieut. Waghorn arose; whilst his proposal to erect a chain of presidios, or fortified posts, along the Coanza River, in order to explore the copper-mines of Angola, and to communicate with the Mozambique, was made before Dr. Krapf and the "Apostles' Street" were born.[*] The attempt was new though the idea was not. Fray Manoel Godinho, who travelled in 1663, describes an overland route from India to Portugal, and the literary Jesuit De Jarric declares that there was nothing to prevent our going from Monomotapa to Angola by land. These authors, however, bore the same relation to Dr. de Lacerda as the " Mombas Mission " to the first East African Expedition.

After this exploration, and certainly before 1708, Dr. de Lacerda addressed to the enlightened Minister of State, D. Rodrigo de Sousa Coutinho, certain memoranda touching an expedition from Angola to Mozambique. On March 12, 1797, he was appointed by Her Most Faithful Majesty[†] to conduct

---

[*] The Missionaries of Chrishona, near Basle, proposed twelve mission-stations along the banks of the Nile, from Alexandria to Gondar; whence other branch houses were to be established towards the South, East, and West of Africa, "as it shall please Providence to show the way, and to point out the requisite means." Each station, which is to be fifty leagues distant from the other, will be called by the name of an apostle—for instance, the station at Alexandria will be named that of St. Matthew: the station at Cairo, of St. Mark; at Assuan, of St. Luke; and so on.—*Dr. Krapf's Travels, Researches, and Missionary Labours* (pp. 183, 213), London: Trübner and Co., Paternoster Row, 1860.

[†] Donna Maria I., the daughter of D. José (Emanuel), born 1734, married in 1760 to her uncle D. Pedro (who died in 1786), reigned from 1777 to 1816, the year

the exploration, and Portugal has ever been generous to her
roving sons. Under D. Fernando Antonio Soares de Noronha,
fifty-fifth Governor of Angola, he was made Governor of
the Rios de Sena, in the Captaincy of the Mozambique. On
March 28, 1798, he addressed to the Minister another highly
interesting letter upon the subject of his intended march to the
capital of the African king known as the Cazembe, with depositions of certain backwoodsmen (sertanejos) who had volunteered
to accompany him; with oral information received from the
natives, and with copies of his orders to the expedition of which
he was in command. On July 3, 1798, he began his journey.
After opening up at least 270 leagues of new land he reached
his destination, and he fell a victim to his own exertions on
October 18, 1798. But he had marched to S. lat. 8° 15', and
the Portuguese were no longer in ignorance of everything north
of S. lat. 10° 20'.

The diary speaks for itself; it is a drama with the cata-
strophe of a tragedy. Well worth perusal, it is what every
African explorer should be taught to expect, and should learn
to thank his stars if he live to tell the tale. To one who has
undergone the ordeal it vividly suggests past horrors. Jeronymo Pereira, the then Governor of Mozambique, will not hear
the expedition spoken of in his presence, as too often happens
in this our day. The villainous Colonel of Maniça Militia
sells to the explorer bad cloth at the very highest prices. The
whites appointed to command the blacks are thoroughly disheartened and demoralised. They think only of "creature
comforts" and vile lucre, they refuse to lend any assistance,
and they privily tamper with the negroes, so as to ensure
desertion, which may shorten their trials. The slaves levied for
the Royal service fly from it in numbers, and the commander,
undefended by soldiers, is compelled to trust himself to wild
"Caffres," who throw down their loads, and without a word of
notice disappear in the bush. There are infinite intrigues and

---

of her death. In consequence of her insanity, the Prince of the Brazil, subsequently D. João VII., was made Regent on February 10, 1792, after which his
mother took no part in public affairs. It was therefore virtually under this prince
that the expedition was made.

quarrels between the whites, plots and battles between the blacks, and utter disunion between whites and blacks. The wild Maraves and Muizas plunder and threaten, and are ever upon the point of closing the road. Then come the usual fever-fraught anxieties, the sleepless nights spent in looking forward to hopeless days, the desperate determinations, the stubborn endurance, and the irritation, soothed only by the hope of being able to assert oneself at some future day. Presently, as the party leaves the coast and the coast-people, matters appear to mend; the subjects of the African despot are a distinct improvement upon the lawless republican neighbours of civiliza-tion, and one chief after another proves himself something very like a friend. But it is all too late; the excitement of the march is over, the traveller reaches his goal, he falls into the apathy of success, he sinks under the strong reaction, and—dies. Unfortunate even in death, he is exhumed when his companions are returning to their homes, the party is attacked in the bush, and the mortal remains of the unfortunate explorer are scattered upon the inhospitable African ground.

After Dr. do Lacerda's death, all, of course, went wrong. He had left orders for the chaplain, Fr. Francisco João Pintó, to command the rabble rout, and the ecclesiastic seems to have been wholly unequal to the task. He struggled, however, man-fully about sending men forward to Angola, and thus carrying out one object of the expedition; but here he was contending against a *force majeure*—African custom. His party rebelled spiritually and temporally, it refused to attend Mass or to be placed under arrest: finally, sundry members deserted, and on their home-march so conducted themselves, that the unfortunate padre narrowly escaped with his life. The ill-fated expedition left the city of the Cazembe, which it did not even name, on July 22, 1790, and reached Tette after four months (Novem-ber 22). Altogether it had spent sixteen and a half months on this enterprise, and the second in command soon followed the first to a place whence explorers, as a rule, return not.

Dr. de Lacerda was not only a scientific traveller, but also a sympathetic, zealous, and hard-working man. In his worst times of sickness he remembers his compass, he makes obser-

vations of longitude by Jupiter's satellites, and he remarks the
quality of ground, and its power of production. There is a
simplicity about his writing now unusual and, his Diary not
having been corrected nor prepared for the press, its style,
which scholars pronounce to be unclassical, lets us into the
author's heart. He "loves men," as the Arabs say of the benevolent, and he ever thinks of his party in the hour of hunger
and hardship. Though born when rational beings rarely doubted
the propriety of enslaving negroes, he is a kind of philanthrope,
and he avoids using harsh measures unless absolutely necessary.
Even when furious with his treacherous companions and his
false, cowardly friends, he speaks of the "lively grief caused
by the death of my beloved wife, whom God was pleased to take
to himself, in the flower of her age, on the first of April." He
is strong in hope, and is somewhat Utopian in his ideas of what
an African expedition and its leader ought to be; were his *sine
quâ non* made requisite, no party would set out for want of the
qualifications required. He has the habit of pious exclamations:
he begins his diary with "Dirige Domine Deus meus," &c., and
he thoroughly believes in the thraldom of Sathanas. He does
not, perhaps, quite come up to the serious and reverend spirit
which the 'Quarterly' finds in the 'Romance of the Nile,' alias
the 'Crescent and the Cross.' The fact is that his religiousness,
which crops out at times, is somewhat weather-worn by exten-
sive travel, and by the turn of mind philosophic and Plinian—he
quotes "Timor fecit deos "—belonging to the days of the Great
Revolution. He is characteristically loyal, like every Portuguese gentleman, especially in those pre-constitutional days,
when the king was to a great extent lord and ruler; and he
thinks of his beloved Queen, not of "Her Majesty's Government" nor, by way of climax, of "the Public." He moralises
much, and he is somewhat profuse in reflections, far more sound
than novel; whilst perhaps the first personal pronoun is made to
occur a little too frequently. He is grandiloquent as a Castilian;
he indites awfully long-winded sentences, and he drags in, like an
Anglo-Indian, breakjaw native words. Finally, he has not
forgotten his Hippocrates; and he is not ashamed to quote his
Horace.

The party which accompanied him must be briefly sketched. The African portion consisted of one "Chinimba" of the Muizu tribe, an envoy and servant (handasio) of the King Cazembe, and of "Catúra," a grandee of the same potentate's Court. These two high officers were accompanied by their spies, and this is a system of *haute* police in which, as I have elsewhere shown ('Mission to Dahome') Africa excels.* One *mouchard* died, the other, a confidential slave of the Cazembe, and sixteen-eighteen years old, accompanied the party the whole way, in order to look after his master's rights. Finally, there were 400 Caffre porters, a floating item in the caravan, as they seem to have deserted whenever and wherever they pleased.

The whites were much too numerous for marching without trouble or disunion. First, we have the inevitable chaplain, the Reverend Father Francisco João Pinto, brother of the Commandant of Tette, who afterwards succeeded to the command: he presently will speak for himself. There are two envoys sent to the Cazembe, No. 1 being Lieutenant-Colonel Pedro Nolasco Vieira de Araujo, chosen by Dr. de Lacerda to visit Angola, and to report success at home in Portugal. This gentleman with a name and a half is highly spoken of by both commandants; he behaved remarkably well during the dangerous retreat; he saved the poor Padre by his generosity, and he may be called the good angel of the party. No. 2 is the Lieutenant of Sena, José Vicente Pereira Salema, chosen by the priest, and also named as envoy to Angola, where he too did not go. He seems to have been a respectable man.

Besides what we may call the diplomats, there were three guides. The first was a Goanese, Gonçalo Caetano Pereira, popularly known as Dumbo-dumbo, or "the Terror":† his title

---

* So, in Abyssinia, governors of important towns are narrowly watched and reported on by paid spies.

† In 'Dr. Livingstone's Second Expedition' (chap. x. p. 205) we are told that Pereira, who gloried in being called "the Terror," was the founder of Zumbo, the latter being described as a Jesuit station; moreover that it was the departure point of two expeditions, that of Dr. de Lacerda and that of Monteiro and Gamitto. Zumbo, which has been conjecturally identified with the Ptolemæan Agysimba, was built by the Jesuits during the last century, and upon an island. According to Monteiro and Gamitto (p. 140) it had its church and church-bells, stone houses, and other commodities; it was the only inland town which can properly be so called south of Harar in Moslem Abyssinia, and here was discovered the

was Capitão Mór da Michonga, Chief Captain of the Bush. Like all men much acquainted with African travel, he was versed in every native "dodge," he was rendered independent by a troop of slaves as cunning as himself, and being an "old soldier," he preferred running to fighting. His name seldom occurs until after Dr. Lacerda's death, when the priest frequently mentions him; he ends by deserting his leader on the line of march, and by behaving much like a cur. No. 2 was Manoel Caetano Pereira, an African creole, and son of the former; he conducted himself badly, as regards the Chaplain-Commander, whom he also left in the bush. He had, however, the shadow of an excuse, the taste of a Muiza arrow. To these we must add the third guide, José Rodrigues Caleja, originally Chief Sergeant of Ordnance, and afterwards made Receiver of the Royal Treasury. Although highly recommended, he proved himself the hardest bargain of the little company. His name occurs with provoking constancy, his intrigues cut short the transit to Angola, and at last, after deserting the Padre, he does his best to compass his death. He is the bad angel, or devil, of the expedition, and every expedition of the kind has at least one.

The military commandants and the officers of the party were as follows:—

The Chief Sergeant,[*] Pedro Xavier Velasco, began well, but ended with "playing tricks on the clergy"; and, by putting himself unduly forward at Court, he became personally distasteful to the Cazembe. His slaves, also, seem to have been a "bad lot." Four years after the end of the expedition, in 1805, as senior survivor, he writes home to some Excellency, requesting to be rewarded for his exertions. The Captain João da Cunha Pereira, who, in his turn, became Receiver of the Royal Treasury, is described by Dr. Lacerda as a man of bad head and worse tongue. Presently he refused to be arrested by the ecclesiastical leader. He seems, however, after showing

---

celebrated Iberian of Frei Pedro,' mentioned in 'Dr. Livingstone's First Expedition' (chap. xxxi). Agysimba must probably be sought in the stone ruins of Zimbabye, lately discovered by Herr Carl Mauch. See the Diary, September 7, 1798.

[*] In the seventeenth century the Sargento Mór ranked before the Majors.

himself peculiarly seditious to have " turned over a new leaf," and to have ended tolerably well. Little is said of the commander of the troops, the fort-lieutenant, and notary of Tete,—Antonio José da Cruz, except that he preferred singing " comic," called by the priest " profane," songs, instead of hearing mass, and that he ran the party into danger by making fierce love to the Cazembe's wives. In objecting to be present at the "Sacrifice," he was joined and abetted by the ensign of militia, Vasco Joaquim Pires, who also placed his immortal soul in dire peril. He died on the retreat unsacramented—"unhousel'd, disappointed, unanel'd "—and he was " put to bed " in the bush, a palpable judgment and a pointing moral. We can hardly wonder at the poor priest taking such a view of the matter, when daily we see in the writings of our modern ecclesiastics the same presumptuous views of " miraculous interpositions," and the same spiritual pride which is perfectly conversant with the hidden designs of Omnipotence and Omniscience. The Lieutenant Manoel dos Santos e Silva was at first Receiver of the Royal Treasury, which office he lost in consequence of embezzling cloth and "cooking" accounts. He was the man who " wished to die," and almost every party has one. Finally, there was the commissary and fort-adjutant of Sena, José Thomaz Gomes da Silveira e Silva, he was a good man under Dr. de Lacerda, but the successor describes him to be a ruffian, as proud of his birth as he was vile and unworthy of it. He openly wished that the priest had been burned. Knowing most of the Caffre tongues, and easily learning others, he was a good linguist, and good linguists are often bad characters—mostly " too clever by half."

The other minor names which occur are "Caetano Fabião," the chief of squadron; the pilot "Bernardino," brought in case of boating being required; an unimportant soldier, "Antonio Francisco Delgado"; the corporal "Paulo da Silva," and the soldier "Caetano da Costa"—the two latter were left behind, in the vain hope that they might carry out the views of the Government, and reach Angola. Including all those above mentioned, the escort was composed of fifty men-at-arms, undrilled, unused to musketry, and badly provided with poor weapons and ammunition. They were, therefore, worse than useless.

The negroes must have thought those bastard whites a race baser even than their own. No wonder that such a party broke the hearts of two leaders. I seem again to see the scowling faces, and to hear the loud discordant voices of my *bêtes noires* of a decade and a half ago—Muigni Kidogo, the slave, and the Baloch soldier Khudabakhsh—la'anahum Ullah!

The Diary, as we are informed at the end, had been forwarded to Portugal before November 1805. The despatches were used by Bowdich when compiling his once popular volume on the 'Discoveries of the Portuguese,' &c. According to the "Geographer of N'yassi," these documents have been since published entire in a little Portuguese work, entitled 'Considerações politicas e commerciaes sobre os Descobrimentos e Possessões dos Portuguezes,' &c. Lisboa, 1830. By José Accursio das Neves. When at Lisbon, in 1865, I vainly attempted to buy the book, nor have I since been more fortunate.

Finally (November 5, 1844), the despatches were printed in the 'Annaes Maritimos e Coloniaes,' &c. (Imprensa Nacional, Lisboa), with observations upon the interior of Benguela, from a document communicated, June 2, 1844, to the Maritime Association of Lisbon, by its ex-president, the Viscount de Sá da Bandeira. That veteran statesman and venerable African geographer has also enriched the despatches with notes which I have been careful to retain.

If Dr. de Lacerda did not carry out his whole project, his partial success considerably increased our knowledge of the African interior. This is amply proved by the quotations from his writings, which occur in the pages of our best comparative geographers, and by the high esteem in which he is held by that conscientious student the late Mr. James Macqueen.[*] Indeed, the expedition of Monteiro and Gamitto, which in 1831 left Tete and reached the capital of the Cazembe, can hardly be said to have added much to what was noticed by the

* 'Notes on the Geography of Central Africa, from the Researches of Livingstone, Monteiro, Graça, and others.' By James Macqueen, Esq., F.R.G.S. 'Journal,' vol. xxvi., 1856.

energetic and courageous Governor of the Rios de Sena. It is time that his pages should appear in an English dress, more especially as they are now buried in a book become rare and becoming rarer. No time can be more opportune than the present for offering a translation to the public. Until Dr. Livingstone shall have returned from his third expedition, the writings of De Lacerda must continue to be our principal authority, and only from them the reader can at present learn where the English traveller is said to have been detained. Years ago I had translated the papers for my own instruction, and after reading Dr. Livingstone's last volume and hearing of his present journey and the latest reports, it struck me that the version might profitably be laid before the public. Since the visit of Dr. de Lacerda three Portuguese expeditions and one Arab have sighted the Cazembe. The first were the "Pombeiros," or native travelling traders (not "two black slaves"), Pedro João Baptista, and Anastacio José, sent in 1802 by Honorato da Costa, superintendent of the Cassange Factory. The second (1831–1832) was that of MM. Monteiro and Gamitto; it produced a large volume, which also I have analysed. Of the third I know nothing except from M. Valdez, who remarks (chap. vii. vol. ii., 'Six Years of a Travelling Life in Western Africa'): "I think the last visit of a white traveller to (the) Cazembe was in 1853, when my companion and friend Mr. Freitas was one of the gentlemen forming the expedition." The Arab journey is described in the Journal of the Royal Geographical Society (1854, vol. xxiv. p. 261) by Sr. Bernardino Freire and F. A. de Castro, and curiously mis-commented upon by Mr. Cooley.

I must own to having taken certain liberties with the earlier part of my text. The whole would hardly bear translation, on account of the many repetitions in a work evidently not prepared for publication, the triteness of the ideas, the diffuseness of the language, and the prodigious lengthiness of the sentences. In many parts the order of narration has been changed. An abridgment is therefore offered to the reader, but it is one of words, not of sense; the pith and marrow of the original have never been rejected; in no case has a difficulty of diction been shirked or turned, and the diary of actual travel is trans-

lated without curtailment. I have illustrated the obscure
passages by reference to other and later writers, especially
to the work of MM. Monteiro and Gamitto, ' O Muata Cazembe.'*
Finally, the reader must to a certain extent rely upon his
author, and allow due weight to the results of study and
experience. Had Dr. de Lacerda lived to print his book, he
would doubtless have explained the meanings of all the native
words scattered so profusely over the following pages. They
have given me considerable trouble, which has not always been
crowned with success.† After consulting the usual works, such
as the well-known 'Ensaios' of Captain Lopez de Lima,‡ I had
recourse to my "African" friends, and I desire particularly to
record my gratitude for the readiness with which Dr. John
Kirk, formerly of the Zambeze Expedition, at present of
Zanzibar, replied to my troublesome applications. May fortune
attend his next venture! there is no man who deserves it
better.

This journey of Dr. de Lacerda shows that the Portuguese
never abandoned the idea of a "viagem à contracosta," and we
can hardly characterise their claims to having crossed Africa as
"hanging on a slender fibre." Without mentioning the information given by Godinho and De Jarric, or the well-known
journey of the Pombeiros, we find that in 1845-47 the lands
of "Mwátá yá Nvo," on the highroad across the continent,
were visited by Joaquim Rodriguez Graça, and shortly afterwards by the late Ladislaus Magyar, if what he reported was a
fact. In 1854 the servants of A. F. F. da Silva Porto crossed
Africa in company with "three Moors," returning from Benguela. In the same year Mr. Messum wrote that he had heard
of a great lake in the interior from a Portuguese major whom

---

* 'O Muata Cazembe,' &c. 'Diario da Expedição Portugueza, nos annos do
1831 e 1832.' Lisbon, Imprensa Nacional, 1854.

† Such words, for instance, as "Racaja," "Calamanhas" (Collomanhas),
"Douros Sortidos," and "Cherves," have not been explained by me. I have in
vain turned over every dictionary in the College Library of S. Paulo, Brazil.

‡ 'Ensaio sobre a Statistica das Possessões Portuguezas na Africa Occidental e
Oriental,' por José Joaquim Lopes de Lima. Lisboa, na Imprensa Nacional, 1846.
I heard at S. Paulo de Loanda that several Portuguese officials had taken this
excellent book in hand with the view of bringing it up to modern wants, but that
all had died one after the other at the shortest possible interval.

he had met at Benguela, and who had crossed over from Mozambique. He is probably not the only one of these mute inglorious transitista. Captain Briant, employed by Mr. Brookhouse of Salem, Massachusetts, saw in 1843 men who had passed from shore to shore, and ascertained the possibility of establishing a profitable commercial intercourse; whilst in 1863 Captain Harrington, employed by the same house, proved that the only difficulty was a narrow strip of desert subtending the south-west coast. ('African Repository,' No. 12, December 1868, Washington.)

And now to enter into the middle of things. The first letter addressed to D. Rodrigo de Sousa Coutinho contains the preliminary remarks upon the expedition proposed by Dr. de Lacerda, showing his conviction that a journey intended to cross Africa should begin at Mozambique and end at Angola. The original memorandum—undated, but certainly written before 1798—is preserved in the library of the Count of Linhares, and it is offered to the "Associação Maritima," of Lisbon, by its ex-President, the Count de Sá da Bandeira.

In conclusion, I would warn the reader that the Notes are all written by me, except where otherwise specified, and that I, not my author, assume the whole responsibility of having written them.

PRELIMINARY OBSERVATIONS, &c.,[*]

DR. FRANCISCO JOSÉ MARIA DE LACERDA.

THE glory of the explorer, most illustrious and excellent Sir, surely transcends the fame of the conqueror, who is more often the bane of, instead of being a boon to, humanity. The memory of a Henry[†] laying at Silves the foundations of Asiatic discovery, which justified his noble motto, "talant de bien faire," is greater and dearer to us than the names of a Philip and an Alexander, who by intrigues and right of might forged the chains of slavery for Macedonia and Greece, and who usurped the proud title "Victor of Asia."[‡] These, spurred on by ambition, plundered fellow-men of their most sacred birthright, liberty. That most generous soul, not satisfied with the splendours of his own mental lights, cast them, like sunbeams, athwart the gloom of ignorance, promoted by commerce and agriculture the material prosperity of barbarous peoples, and introduced to them the knowledge of the True Faith.[§] It is evident whose name best deserves a niche in the Temple of Fame.

These thoughts, long brooding in my mind, were aroused by hearing the (to me) most gratifying intelligence that your Excellency, with the view of establishing land-communication between the Eastern and the Western coasts of Africa, and of cutting off the long and perilous passage round the Cape of

---

[*] This letter, without date, is addressed to D. Rodrigo de Sousa Coutinho, the Minister of State. The original MS. is in the library of the Conde de Linhares.
D. Henrique the Virgin, of whom our classic poet sang—

> "The Lusitanian prince, who, heaven-inspired,
> To love of useful glory roused mankind,
> And in unbounded commerce mixed the world."

[‡] The sentiment is amiable, patriotic, and good, but is it true? The answer will depend upon how we read history. To me Alexander is the first person of the triad which humanity has as yet produced; the other two being Julius Cæsar and Napoleon Bonaparte. Moreover, the earliest weapon of progress is invariably war, and whilst it is wielded progress must exist.

[§] In our days we should pass over these words. But the old Portuguese were earnest in their reliance upon propagandism, and this often unselfish motive runs like a thread of gold through the coarse web of their luxury, cruelty, and covetousness.

Good Hope, had proposed to explore the vast unknown interior, and the unvisited regions lying to the East of Benguela. The experience of years spent in travelling over those countries prepared me to expect great advantages from the undertaking suggested by your patriotism. I knew, also, that the enterprise had been planned by sundry generals and governors, the first of whom was the illustrious D. Francisco Innocencio da Sousa Coutinho,[*] Governor of Angola, whose prudence and courteousness, whose wisdom and integrity, will never be forgotten by those he ruled. Honour cannot but result to you from carrying out a project which has attracted the attention of your illustrious and excellent progenitor—a project right worthy of a minister who is actuated by zeal for his country's good, for the glory of his nation, and for the benefit of his sovereign.

These, Sir, are words from the heart, not from the tongue. These are the motives which induce me to place before a truth-loving minister the fruits of my long experience, in the humble hope that they will add a mite towards the success of the glorious design.

I now proceed to offer a short geographical description of the African interior, as far as is known to me, with a general notice of its natives—their customs, their character, their government, their religion, and their feelings towards the whites, whom they always regard with suspicion.[†] I would also record something of the many valuable productions of the soil, and the notable advantages which will accrue, from the proposed exploration, to our commerce and to the Crown. And, lastly, I will offer the most practicable measures for ensuring the success of the journey.

The great and fertile country known as Benguela[‡] borders northwards upon Angola, being separated from it only by the Aco River,[§] near the Presidio or fortified frontier-post, Pedras de Ponguandongo.[‖] To the south it extends to the country of the

---

[*] The forty-ninth Governor of Angola in 1764, one of the most active and practical of his order.

[†] Instinctively, as wild beasts hate their tame congeners.

[‡] The word is said to mean "the defence."

[§] Dr. Livingstone ('Missionary Travels in Southern Africa,' chap. xxi.) writes "Haco," after a branch of the Kimbunda or Ambonda family.

[‖] Dr. Livingstone (chap. xxi. p. 421) sketches and describes the column-shaped conglomerate spits of "Pungo Andongo"—the modern form of our text. Captain Lopez de Lima ('Ensaios,' &c.) also writes Pedras de Pungo Andongo. Usually the site is called the Pedras Negras de Pungo Andongo; and for a long time it was a kind of Botany Bay for political exiles. Mr. Cooley makes Pungo a Ndongo to mean the crest or impending heights of Ndongo or the Interior of Angola ('Inner Africa Laid Open,' p. 6). "Pongo," curious to say, is a word known in South America, e.g., Pongo de Mansericho; this, however, as De la Condamine tells us, should be "Puncu," a port.

Ovampos, beyond Cabo Negro.* Westward is the South Atlantic Ocean, whilst to the east it stretches nearly 500 leagues (1500 English geographical miles between 13° 24' and 37° east long. Greenwich) † to the coast of Mozambique. On both extremities, it contains much cultivated land, of which I will speak presently. The population is immense,‡ the tribes being under governments of different extent and authority, exercised by certain chiefs, called "Sovas," § and by their feudal vassals or dependent "Sovetas."

Unusually strong and large-framed—indeed, approaching the gigantic—these negroes are much more valued in the Brazil than those of Angola.‖ They are ready and dexterous in handling fire-arms, which we taught them to use; they have guns in plenty, and they can put in order and repair any part except the barrels. They would laugh to scorn our military expeditions, were it not for our field-pieces, of which they stand in great fear.

False and utterly treacherous, their friendship for the white man results from his importing articles now indispensable to them.¶ They never lose the chance of robbing and murdering a visitor; but, fearing the anger of the ruling powers, they confine these atrocities to the far interior, where the outrage cannot be punished. Even whilst plotting his destruction, they never drop the mask before the European, feigning entire subjection to him, and humbly addressing him as "Maneputo."** Cannibals

---

* Here Bartholomew Diaz placed his Padrão, or memorial pillar. It was in Lat. S. 15° 40' 42", and Long. E. (Greenwich) 11° 53' 20", between Mossamedes or Little Fish Bay, the Dizungo Ditiolo of the natives, to the North (S. Lat. 15° 13'), and Great Fish Bay to the South (S. Lat. 16° 30' 12"). According to the 'African Repository' (No. 12, of Dec. 1868, Washington), Little Fish Bay is called by the natives Gaconda, and Mossamedes was founded in 1840 by Major Garcia and three commercial houses of Loanda.

† In these papers the league is the smaller measure of 20 (not 15) to the degree, three English geographical miles. The larger league still used in the Brazil is four miles long. Monteiro and Gamitto ('O Muata Cazembe,' p. xxi.) count by the league of 8000 paces—a very short standard. Mr. Cooley makes the Portuguese league about = 20,000 English feet (more exactly 20,250 feet = 6750 yards).

‡ The population of Africa cannot yet be computed as our popular writers have done. Every traveller finds some thickly inhabited country, which statisticians have neglected to take into consideration. Thus, to quote no other authority, the late Mr. Keith Johnston's magnum opus, the 'Physical Atlas' (fol., 1856), copied in that excellent compendium, Mrs. Somerville's 'Physical Geography,' makes the 11,376,000 square miles of the "Dark Continent" inhabited by only 60,000,000. This is not half the area of British India!

§ Sova, Soba, or Sôva, is equivalent to Marquis in Angola: other authors translate it "chefe de uma ou mais povoações, regulo, chefe mais poderoso."

‖ In the Brazil and Cuba, a very offensive expression, M——a de Congo, is, or rather was, applied to most of the Angola Bozals (new importations).

¶ We can hardly wonder at their treachery if they are so "much valued as slaves."

** Muene (Malgni in Kiswahili), lord, and Puto, i.e. Porto, Oporto, Portugal,

all, especially the savage Ganguelas,* they devour those slain in their ceaseless, causeless wars; they kill for food the old and valueless captives, whilst the young are carefully preserved for sale. Such are their usual inducements to warfare: it brings them slaves, whose traffic enables them to purchase what they require.

All this vast country is, I have said, very populous. The traveller cannot cover a mile without passing some "Banza" or "Libata."† The climate ten leagues from the seaboard is benign and healthful as that of Portugal,‡ and the soil is so fertile that, despite the negligence of the cultivator, it produces a hundred-fold. There is an abundance of the larger and the lesser millet,§ here called Maçamballa (Masamballa), and Luco, also known as Moçango (Mosango), resembling the former, but a little longer in shape. All these afford well-favoured flour. It also supplies beans of sorts, twenty-four bushels (twelve guindas) being sold for a fathom of blue Indian cotton or dungaree (zuarte),‖ besides which there are peas, vetches, and lentils. Excellent wheat is grown, but only by the white and mulatto backwoodsmen (sertanejos),¶ who are settled for trade in the far

---

Europa. Primarily Puto means the King of Portugal or his governors; according to the Diary, Jan. 19, 1799, the title is given to the king nearest Angola; it appears also to be a name taken by certain African chiefs, e.g., by the son and heir of the Cazembe, as will presently appear (see Diary, Dec. 22, 1798). Finally, like "Sahib" in India, it is the title given to white men in Angola, and it corresponds with "Mfumo," addressed to a native. Monteiro and Gamitto (p. 413) translate it "Dono de espingardas," master of guns.

* A large tribe between the Gango River, a southern branch of the Coanza of S. Paulo de Loanda and the Cubango, the westernmost head-stream of the great Chobe. Sometimes they are called with the personal affix Mu-" Ganguelas;" they are said to be good archers and very ferocious.

† The "Banza" is a large, the Libata or Libatta a small, village; the "Ombata," is a single hut. The European reader must bear in mind that all the settlements cover much ground and contain very few inhabitants.

‡ This must be taken with many a grain, and it should be remembered that a Brazilian speaks. We may safely, however, assert that the interior is healthy, compared with the seaboard.

§ Maize is locally known to the Portuguese as "Milho Durro." The greater Millet (milho grosso) is the Jowarri, Durrah, Ta'ám, Btámé, or Holcus Sorghum. Monteiro and Gamitto, however, translate Milho Grosso by "Zea mais." The lesser Milho (milho miudo) is the Dajri or Panicum spicatum (Roxb.). I can only suggest that Luco or Mosango means either the Penniestum, or the East Indian Nagli or Nanchni (in Portuguese Naxenim), the Arabic Dukhno, the Kiswihili Uwimbi (Eleusine coracana).

‖ The meaning of "pano zuarte," according to Monteiro and Gamitto (Appendix D), is a blue cotton, the best being that of Jambaceira. In those days it was worth 2$ 400. The "panno" or "pano" generally is the "Tobe" of Zanzibar, two fathoms in length, or its equivalent.

¶ Sertanejo means a man of the Sertão (said to be an abbreviation of "desertão," desert), which, in the Portuguese world, usually denotes the far interior, where there is little population. It must not be confounded with "Sertanista," which is applied to an explorer of the Sertão.

o

interior. There is no want of water-melons,* melons, gourds, and pumpkins, of different kinds and sizes, sweet potatoes (batatas, the *Convolvulus batata*), manioc, and fine large sugar-canes. We find guavas, oranges, and lemons. The land will grow all manner of seed, and it would, if cultivated, produce the finest fruits.

Iron, which abounds in the interior, is an article that interests us not a little.† The negroes smelt this metal from the stones everywhere containing it, and, considering the absence of tools and labour-saving appliances, it is astonishing how well and how cheaply they make their assegais, chains, and similar articles. They have also, as I have seen, sulphur from the vast mines of Dombo da Guinzamba, a league and a half from Bahia Farta, on the seaboard. There is an even greater abundance of excellent copper, which they convert into ornaments, collars, wristlets, and anklets. The many kinds of useful woods equal those of the Captaincy of S. Salvador da Bahia in the Brazil. In its present state, their export commerce consists principally of slaves, ivory, and wax, which is sent out in quantities, despite the destructive style of collection, the hives being thrown into the fire, in order that the combs may be taken.

These blind barbarians recognise no divinity, nor do they show any remnant of true religion.‡ Superstitious in the

---

* When marching through East Africa from Zanzibar to the Lake Tanganyika, I found water-melons in many places; but, as a rule, they were hard, colourless, and wanting flavour.

† In a subsequent page of this Letter (195), Dr. de Lacerda thus reverts to this subject :—

"The iron equals the Swedish and the Biscayan; a Libambo, or running chain for twelve slaves, may be bought for two cloths, or a dollar and 200 cents. The Governor Continho judiciously built, in 1767, ironworks at the town of Oeiras in Golungo-Alto: they failed because each Governor—our Livy laments the fact in his 'Decades'—delights to destroy the labours of his predecessor. As our ships carry iron to Asia, this metal will give valuable results if prepared in the interior, and brought to the coast by the Cunene River. The same ships homeward bound can load with bars, which sell everywhere.

"Nor is the excellent copper, of which mines have already been discovered, less worthy of consideration. The negroes make of it their necklaces, manilhas (bracelets), and anklets ('vergas,' wires like carpet-rods, twisted round the legs and worn in many parts of Africa).

"There is also a great quantity of sulphur. I myself saw a large digging in Dombo da Guinzamba, five leagues south of Benguela, and one and a half from Bahia Farta on the coast.

"The timber of the interior is like that of Bahia in the Brazil, equally good for building and for other purposes. Can any one despise such sources of wealth, which will not only stimulate our commerce, but will also render us independent of other nations?"

‡ The great Kafir race ignores the idea of a deity. In the 'Lake Regions of Central Africa' (vol. ii., chap. xix.) I have attempted to account for this fact by their deficiency in the moral or sentimental development; and it is a question whether primeval man did not begin his worship of the ancestral umbra long ages

extreme, they hardly possess a worship to which we may apply the name of faith; their veneration, in fact, is confined to reverence for certain ancient Sovas or chiefs, distinguished by valour or justice. Without doubt some are baptized, but they behave like the other heathen, their ignorance of the mystery being extreme, and their contempt for all practical religion being consummate. They aspire, it is true, to baptism, as the means of cozening and deceiving unwary whites; in fact, they would assert that they are Christians, whilst remaining in their deplorable pristine state of no-religion, polygamy,* and barbarism.

Let us now specify the advantages which such an expedition would bring to commerce, to the Crown, and to the peoples themselves. It would extend our conquests over lands and tribes hitherto unknown. It would open a line of communication between the Eastern and the Western Coasts, which might thus mutually support each other; whilst in the case of one being attacked the other would offer a sure refuge to our colonists. Ships from Asia would discharge cargo at Mozambique, and goods could be carried overland to Benguela without the danger and the delay of doubling the Cape of Storms. Thus the Custom-house duty would increase, and the industry of the whites, as well as of the blacks, would be fostered. For better transport than the riding oxen (bois cavallos) now used, camels †

---

before the ghosts became heroes and gods, who could vindicate for themselves adoration.

* Yet the author tells us that they are a large-sized race,—polygamy therefore has not injured them physically. And if polygamous Africa is thinly populated, polygamous China swarms with the species man, whilst monogamous Iceland is sparsely populated and monogamous Cyprus is almost a desert.

† Note by the Viscount de Sá da Bandeira:—"In 1838, the Home Government imported into Angola camels from the Canary Islands; but the experiment failed for want of care. [The same has lately happened to Ceará in the Brazil.]

"The river transit of Angola, like that of Middle Brazil, is very limited. Yet steam communication has long been proposed between Loanda the capital, and the Falls of Cambambe, the highest point to which the Coanza River is navigable. From that place a road for carts or beasts of burden, might be run through Pungo-Andongo with depôts and markets on the way, to the uttermost Portuguese frontier. Thus there would be an easy exportation of ivory, wax, copper, and other licit articles, a traffic which would soon abolish the internal slave trade.

[There is now no want of energy in the colony. When I visited S. Paulo de Loanda in August 1863, surveys for a railroad between the capital and Calumbo on the Coanza River had been laid before the Government.]

"Angola, however, still suffers from an inveterate legal abuse [the 'begar' of India and Sind], corvée, or forced labour, a system which no longer prevails in Portuguese settlements, not even in Benguela. Men 'in libambo' (as the local phrase is), or with necks in running chains, were compelled, by blows and threats, to carry cargoes hundreds of leagues, for a few paltry reis. This process has depopulated the country, whose people have fled to the neighbouring regions, inflicting great loss of revenue upon the Portuguese Government. [Compare Dr. Livingstone, 'First Exploration,' chap. xi. Also M. Valdez, vol. II. chap. iv.]

o 2

might be introduced, and perhaps the zebra might be tamed."
Besides which there are thousands of negro-porters (carregadores),
each carrying, for many leagues and for small pay, a pack of
cloth worth $120.

The new possessors of Table Bay (the English) require careful
watching, or our want of energy will enable them to extend
themselves northwards.† Who will prevent these new colonists.
from selling the slaves of our southern interior, thus palpably
injuring our trade, which has already lost one-third of its value?
Similarly the captives of our northern interior are exported
viâ Ambriz and the ports lying to the north of Angola.‡

" The Governor-General D. Francisco Innocencio de Sousa Coutinho first prohibited, in 1764, this abuse, which was, however, re-established by his successor.
In 1791, another Governor tried to stop the cruelties inflicted by white merchants
upon their bearers, especially at the Fair of Cassange (Feira de Casanji). Antonio
de Saldanha da Gama (afterwards Count of Porto Santo and 56th Governor), in
1807, proposed a total abolition of the system to the Home Government. The
latter, in April 3, 1798, had already directed the Governor of Benguela to prevent
the traders forcibly taking men from the Sovas or native chiefs, unless by regular
agreement, and on payment according to the value of the loads. Finally, a Por-
taria (Royal Order) of January 31, 1839, abolished the custom, and allowed the
blacks to dispose of their labour like white men.

" Only time, however, can do away with the system. It is useless for the law
rigorously to suppress the abuse, when the local authorities are compelled to wink
at it. Without it, indeed, the natives will not work at all. The trader also finds it
a great economy. He pays, for instance, $4 to $0 per head of negro for long
journeys, and perhaps as much to the District Commander, if the latter be not
over-conscientious. It is evident that any other process would be impossible on
account of the expense." [Dr. Livingstone, 'First Expedition,' chap. xix., has
discussed the question, but we see how greatly he erred when he asserted, " This
system of compulsory carriage of merchandise was adopted in consequence of the
increase in numbers and activity of our cruisers, which took place in 1845."]

* This was written, N.D., long before the days of Mr. Rarey.

† Cape Town, founded by the Dutch in 1650, taken by the English in 1795,
restored in 1802, retaken in 1806, and given over to English possession ever since.
The prophecy in the text has been lately fulfilled, owing to the discovery of the
diamond diggings and gold mines.

‡ Note by the Viscount de Sá da Bandeira :—
" The author refers to the fact that, in his day, the greater part of the commerce of
the Portuguese interior profited only the strangers frequenting the ports of Northern
Angola. With respect to this old grievance there is a MS. memorandum of
J. M. Garcia de Castro Barbosa (dated 1772-1779), attributing this influx of
' interlopers' to the carelessness of the Angolan governors. These officers had
abandoned the Portuguese factories in Loango, Cabinda, Sonho, Ambriz, and
others south of Cape Lopo Gonçalves (Anglicé, Cape Lopez, lat. S. 0° 36' 10'', and
long. E., Greenwich, 8° 40' 0''), which commanded the coast and the rivers,
especially the great Zaire or Congo River.

" To keep off these interloping strangers, we built during the last century the
inland fort of S. José de Encóge (Presidio das Pedras de Encóge, on the Onze
River between the Bengo River and Ambriz), and on the coast at Novo Redondo
(lat. S. 11° 36' 42'') at Cabinda, and on the Loje or Ambriz River, which latter,
however, was presently abandoned. That of Cabinda, built in 1783, was
destroyed in 1784 by a French naval force, because it embarrassed French slavers :
hence the Convention of 1786 held between France and Portugal, whereby the
latter was limited to trade in the ports below Cape Padron (Cabo do Padrão, lat.

The cause of our trade's decay is simply this: the African has no objection to walking 150 miles if he can get for his slaves more and better cloth than can be afforded by our traders; whilst the latter here make smaller profits than their rivals. The proposed expedition would, doubtless, throw an obstacle in the way of the English, who, on their part, have offered considerable rewards for discovering and opening up the interior.

Moreover, the heart of the country, thus flanked on both sides by our possessions, will be more securely subjected to us, and the natives, knowing that Mozambique and Sena can aid Angola and Benguela, and *vice versâ*, will abstain from plundering and from ill-treating our now defenceless Sertanejos. Thus commerce will be free, and life and property will be safe. Unexpected assistance can also be afforded by establishing a few " Presidios," which have ever had the effect of repressing barbarous insolence.

I would now submit to your Excellency a thought which has long occupied my mind, and which, if confirmed, will produce incalculable advantages.

S. 6° 6' 0"), the southern point of the Zaïre River mouth. In the treaty of July 28, 1817, between Great Britain and Portugal, the latter is confirmed in possession of the coast and the interior, between 8° and 18° of S. lat., or almost as far as Cabo Frio (S. lat. 18° 23' 0"). England also recognizes the reservation of Portuguese rights upon Molembo (Malamba Bay, a few miles north of Cabinda) and Cabinda, or from 5° 12' 0" to 18° S. lat, which excludes Loango (4° 89' 30" S. lat.) but contains the mouth of the Zaïre or Congo River. This Zaïre, indeed, is specified by the Carta Constitucional as forming part of the empire.

" Angola is now in the same condition as when she found it necessary to build these forts. The Loanda custom-house suffers by ships discharging cargo at a distance to avoid dues. When the Lojo fort was built, the Sova of Mussul and other chiefs came to do homage at Loanda, whereby the revenue was increased. For this purpose, and to impede slave-exportation, the Home Government directed, in 1838, the Governor-General to found a presidio in Mossamedes, or Little Fish Bay (15° 13' lat. S.). This also was tried and succeeded. Others were afterwards ordered to be built at Ambriz, on the Zaïre, at Cabinda and at Molembo, with directions to admit foreign merchandise at moderate rates. The measure was not carried out, although it would have equally benefited Angola, by encouraging legal commerce, and the strangers who now suffer from the caprices of native chiefs.

" Such forts are necessary for the protection of national and foreign commerce in all the territories recognised as Portuguese, and extending from Loango to Cabo Frio. They will also prevent such disputes as have lately happened within the last twenty years between Portugal and Great Britain about Lourenço Marques Bay (near Delagoa Bay) and the Bolama Islands (near Sierra Leone); and with the French about the Sego Factory on the Casamanza River (near Gambia). Nor must it be forgotten that the French have lately taken one of the Comoro Islands (Mayotte), and another in the Mozambique Channel (Nosi Bé), besides founding two new factories on the coast of Minas and on the Gabão (Gaboon) River, although the latter is less than 2° north of Cape Lopo, and traded with our islands of Principe (Prince's) and S. Thome (St. Thomas)."

N.B.—The mouth of the Gaboon River is in 0° 30' 30" S. lat., and " Cape Lopez " in 0° 36' 10". Diff. 0° 5' 40" nearly 0 miles.

The Rio Sena* is celebrated for the volume and the magnificence of its stream, and for the wealth of its auriferous basin. We know nothing of its source, except that it rises in Monomotapa,† and proudly precipitates itself into the Mozambique Channel, where our fort Quilimane ‡ lies.

Now, in this part of Western Africa the most important stream between the Zaire (Congo R.) and the Cape of Good Hope is the Cunene, an African word meaning "great," or "grand."§ Rising in Candimbo, near Caconda Nova,‖ it flows to the south (-west?), and after absorbing the Cubango¶ and the Cutado ** Rivers, it passes, 30 leagues from its source, through the lands of the Sovas of Lebando and Luceque. Here it is already so considerable a stream that it cannot be forded, and the Chief of Luceque derives revenue from his ferry-canoes. Thence bending eastward, it reaches, after a total course of 50 leagues, the lands of Humbe Grande or Monomotapa,†† where it is 540 fathoms (600 tocas) broad. Beyond that point, nothing can be said of

---

* The river running past Sena, *i.e.*, the Zambese.

† Dr. Livingstone (First Exp., chap. xxx.) renders Mnene Mtapa, the "Chief Mtapa," headman of the "Bambire, a tribe of the Banyai." Of these more hereafter. The older Portuguese applied it to the whole extent of country lying behind the seaboard of Mozambique. The derivation is Mwene (or M'ana) and M'tapa, or Mutapa (the name of the head district), and thus the title is "Lord of M'tapa." The modern name is Chedima, and the king is known as Mambu-a-Chedima. It has greatly fallen in importance since it was the rival of "Monoemugo" (Unyamwezi), the Lake Empire to the north. An account of it is given in Monteiro and Gamitto (p. 83).

‡ A town on the northern branch of the Zambese Delta. The word is Killimani, "in" or "from the hillock," and the orthography greatly varies, as Quillimans, Quelimane, Quillimane, &c.

§ The English have injured it by their usual system of nomenclature. They miscall it the "Nourse River." The Portuguese also know it as Rio das Trombas (River of Rollers or Bar Swell), and lately as Rio dos Elephantes.

¶ There are two Cacondas. In 1864 the native Jaga, or chief, attacked the then now "Presidio" of Caconda (now Caconda Velha), built in a.d. 1682, murdered all the Portuguese garrison, and destroyed the fort and the church. The outrage was punished in 1685, the Jaga was imprisoned at Loanda, and the present Caconda Nova, to the south of the older settlement, was built and placed under a Capitão-Mór.

¶ This Cubango River must not be confounded with the stream passing by the district of the chief Cabango, Dr. Livingstone's Cuihombo. The Cubango is the westernmost head stream of the Chobe, a great feeder of the Zambese. Mr. Cooley throws his "Cobango" into the Lake Ngami; Mr. James Macqueen has placed it accurately. At the head-points the basins of the Zambese and the Cunene Rivers are separated by only a few miles.

** Can this be the "Quantanda River," the N. N. easterly influent of the Cunene?

†† "Humbe Grande and Monomotapa," says the Viscount de Sá da Bandeira, in his notes to Dr. Lacerda's letter, "being separated by a region 250 to 300 leagues broad, it is not probable that they are the same country as the author seems to believe." Humbe is the region lying to the north of and close to the central course of the Cunene. For a popular account of it, see 'Six Years of a Traveller's Life,' by M. Valdez, vol. ii. p. 355. The last traveller who visited it was M. D. T. Brochado.

the great and famous stream, save that it takes an easterly course.

Can this be the Rio Sena?* I am persuaded, by two reasons, that it is.† Firstly, after exploring part of this river, and consulting all the maps of the coast from the Adamastor stream to Benguela, I find none whose size entitles it to be considered the mouth of the mighty Cunene. Secondly, though the Rio Sena boasts of his auriferous sands, the Cunene is not on this point inferior. When accompanying the unfortunately abortive expedition which was sent in 1787 to explore the course of the Cunene, I myself saw a negress who had been captured in the lands of Acabona, three leagues from the Cunene, and limitrophe with Monomotapa. Her head-dress was composed of golden laminæ, about the size of ordinary spangles (lantijoilas), pierced with a few curly hairs, rove through and knotted for security. When asked whence these things came, she replied, "from a very large river not far off; that after rain a large quantity could be found, but that no one prized them."‡

What river can this be but the Cunene? And as it flows from Humbe towards the Mozambique coast, where our Sena, as we know, discharges its waters, the latter is, in my humble opinion, the same Cunene under a different name. Should this conjecture prove correct, and should the line be opened by Government, it will carry to Benguela cargoes landed by ships from Asia, and thus Mozambique as well as Benguela will become an emporium second to none. The inter-coastal and overland route once practicable, native guides will be forthcoming, and nothing will be easier than the exploration of the stream above mentioned. I leave the other advantages to your Excellency's consideration: let me now consider the means of connecting the eastern with the western shores of our colonies;

---

* I cannot understand why Dr. Livingstone will call the river "Zambesi." The orthography is distinctly "Zambeza." Mr. Cooley ('Geogr. of N'yassi,' p. 45), writes Zambezi, and translates it the "fish-river." But he derives the word from the Congoese and Angola "mbizo" and "mbigo" (Di'i), which mean fish. In another place he makes Zambesi the river par excellence, and its derivatives, Chambezi, Liambesi, and Yabonsi, to mean "river of meat," or "of animal food" ('Nature,' Nov. 18, 1869), going far too far for a derivation. Dr. Livingstone (First Exp., chap. xi.) informs us that "Leeambye" is the "large river," or the river par excellence, and that Luambéji (Luambegi), Luambési, Ambesi, Ojimbési, and "Zambési" are all dialectic varieties, "the magnificent stream being the main drain of the country"—which signifies nothing. The Rev. Horace Waller, F.R.G.S., makes "Zambesi" to mean "the Washer," hence its frequent recurrence under several forms in rivers liable to high floods.

† See the end of these observations for the note by the Viscount Sá da Bandeira.

‡ "They (Africans) always try to give an answer to please, and if any one showed them a nugget of gold they would generally say that these abounded in their country."—(Dr. Livingstone, First Exp., chap. xix.)

for which end it will be necessary to describe the terra cognita, that we may better understand how much of the incognita awaits discovery.

All the Nano* country between Caconda Nova to the north, and the Aço (Aso) River, is ruled by the four principal Sovas (neglecting the Sovetas) of Balundo do Ambo (or Hambo) of Quiaca, of Quitata, and of Gulangue.† The southern interior contains, besides the chieftains subject to those four, the powerful families of Quilengues, of Quipungo, of Gambos (Sambos ?) and of Avila. The latter is the formidable Canina, whose sway extends over the broad lands of the Cobaes, the Moconnhocas, and the Mococorocas of Cabo Negro, as far as the Hottentots: ‡ these, once a subject people, were enabled, by the carelessness of his great officers (Ambas), to shake off his yoke. Here are about 80 leagues, more or less, known and subject to the Portuguese Crown, north of Benguela, and crossing Balundo, viâ Quissangue, to the Aço (Aso) River. South of Benguela we have 100 leagues of safe country, held by our vassals of Quilomata, Lombimbe, Quilengues, Bemby, Quipungo, and Gambos (Sambos?), to the Humbe country, divided by the great Cunene River. Travelling eastward from Bengnala, by the road of Sápa-janjála, Caconda Nova, Monhembas, Galangue, and Obié, lands watered by the useful and well-known Coanza River, we have another tract of 100 leagues. There must be 80 leagues more from the Coanza to the Sova of Levar,§ a peaceful line lately opened by

---

* "Nano," "Nannos," or "Nhanos," is said to mean "high land," from the craggy mountains between Quillengues and Caconda Velha.
† A popular account of these and the other little-known districts is given in 1861 by M. Valdez, vol. II. chap. 9.
‡ Possibly the Kamakors or Bushmen east of the Cunene, as laid down in Dr. Livingstone's map.
§ Note by the Viscount DE SÁ DA BANDEIRA:—
"Levar is the 'Loval' of M. Alexandre José Botelho de Vasconcellos (the 6th Governor of Benguela, at the end of the last century), who places it south of the Molua country: it appears to lie to the south-west of the Cazembo's frontier. That author and Dr. de Lacerda both agree that the road to it from Benguela passes through Dalundo and Bihé, and crosses the Coanza River. But their distances greatly differ. From Benguela to the Coanza, Dr. de Lacerda makes 180 leagues; M. Botelho 148, and 191 to Quinhama, the headquarters of the Sova of Loval, a total of 339 leagues. Summing and dividing the two (viz. 180 + 148 = 328) we obtain from Benguela to the Coanza River 164 leagues, and from the Coanza River to Loval 193 leagues (160 + 339 = 510), a sum of 239."

Writing from S. Felipe de Benguela, on August 1, 1799, M. Botelho de Vasconcellos, gives the following account of the kingdom of Loval and its road from Benguela (p. 159, No. 4, 'Annaes Maritimos, 1844):—

"A Bahiano (Brazilian), José de Assumpção e Mello, guided by a native of Loval, travelled there twice with profit, but with some hardships and danger. On his third march he was accompanied by one Alexandre da Silva Teixeira, of Santarem, who afterwards related to me his journey as follows:

"They left Benguela with their stores on September 22, 1795, and slept at Catumbella (four leagues): the next stages, all in this Government, were Quis-

our traders, who, being hospitably received, might, if assisted, have gone farther. Thus, from Benguella, eastward, we have 180 leagues of well-trodden country, and about 50 west of Mozambique. Of a total of 500, but 270 remain for exploration.

As regards the *personnel* of an expedition we require a few educated officers, for the purpose of using instruments and field-pieces; and, at most, 400 well-armed men, who should be trained not to draw the sword except in the last extremity. I have learned from experience that presents and offers of our Sovereign's friendship manage barbarian insolence far better than blows and violence; the latter always make the people arm themselves against fancied conquest and captivity intended by white men.

This force should not demand much from the Treasury. Throughout the explored interior, on both sides, there are many white and mulatto traders, acclimatized and trained to travel. These "Sertanejos" might be induced to join the expedition by the gift of purely honorary titles, which, by the bye, they greatly covet, such as "Impacaçeiros," "Atalaias," "Aventureiros," and "Guerra Preta." * The leader of 20

---

ange (20 leagues), Quibulia ('Quibuile'? 24 leagues), Bailundo (35 leagues). Bihé (35 leagues), and the Quanza or Coanza River (30 leagues), a total of 148. Crossing that stream in the lands of Sova Angurucu, they made 86 leagues to Sova Angullo, and then they struck the bush to avoid certain barbarous chiefs whose jealousy would have stopped them from trading with others. After six leagues they crossed the River Cutla (an eastern influent of the Coanza), 12 fathoms broad; next at the same distance the Cioe River (Mr. Cooley makes it head the Coango), also 12 fathoms wide; then to the source of the latter, 17 leagues, to the Muchango River (13 leagues), to the head-waters of the Luena (28 leagues, Loena, eastern influent of the Leeba River?), and to the frontier of Loval (85 leagues), governed by the Soveta Caquinga. Hence they made (50 leagues) the Great Libata (settlement) of the Sova Quinhama, which is nearly on the eastern frontier of Loval, a total of 191 leagues from the Coanza River and 339 from Benguela.

* Loval is 60 by 10 leagues more or less, and contains many tribes. In front (east) it is bounded by the Sova-ship of Luz Amboolina, and on the right (south) by the powerful Amboolina chiefs of Bunda and Cananga; on the left (north) by lords, vassals to the great Sova of the Moluas (the Miluas, or people of Muátá yi Nvo), and in rear (west) by the Sovas Quiboqne and Dunda. The Rios de Sena of Mozambique (i.e., the Zambesi River, or its northern affluents) appeared to be near. The traders were hospitably received, business was prosperous, and they found less robbery than in our territory—the more we advance the less villainous are the people."

Thus we see the Portuguese, in 1799, pressing into the heart of the country visited by Dr. Livingstone.

* The "Impaçeiro" now generally written Empacaseiro, means, "not a sort of fraternity of freemasons," but a kind of militia, instituted in 1580 by Paulo Dias de Novaes, conqueror and first governor of Angola. The literal sense is "hunter of the Empacassa," the fierce wild cattle which extend down the west coast of Africa. Paul du Chaillu brought home a specimen from the Gaboon, where it is called Nyare. Mr. Cooley ('Inner Africa Laid Open,' p. 47) trans-

armed men might receive a captain's commission; of 30, that
of sargento-mór, and so forth, whilst a few chosen soldiers,
reliable in case of need, would complete the party. During
our war with the interior, in 1787, I saw 17 men and a field-
piece put to flight the Sova of Quiaca and his 12,000 negroes,
who dropped all the loot which they had just taken from the
Cobaca.*

It would be advisable to prevent the expedition being en-
cumbered by the presence of common negroes, who, slow to
attack and quick to fly, their sole object being plunder, disappear like lightning after the first shot. They often foment
and begin quarrels with the natives, besides which they are a
heavy burden upon the commissariat. But we might court the
company of the chiefs bordering on the Sena River, as they
would influence the other headmen. This might be done by
small presents which here, as amongst the Moors,† are indispensable. Perhaps we might thus induce some Sova to join
the expedition, or, at least, to supply provisions, guides, and
interpreters.

The presents to the Sovas and to the covetous Makotas, or
councillors by whom they govern, would consist of ankers of
rum, bales of the cloth preferred by the natives, and especially
false coral and beads of sorts.‡ Also we should want cloaks
of common broadcloth, trimmed with tinsel gold, large hats
similarly ornamented, and canes (bengallas)§ with heads of gilt
copper. Such a cloak, hat, and cane, with two ankers of rum

---

lates it "Gau," which is locally called Nhumbo. Dr. Livingstone ('Second Expedition,' chap. xi. p. 237) says, the Empacasso is the buffalo or gnu; and
in the same page we find the assertion, "no secret society can be found among
the native Africans." Every tribe that I know, from the Wanyika of Mombasah to the Camarones River, has its society built upon secret orders, in fact
a rude Freemasonry. The "Atalaia" is a sentinel; the "Aventureiro" a volun-
teer, and Guerra Preta (literally "black war") is a negro militia.

* This explains what we read in the old histories of Congo and Angola, where
thousands of negroes are defeated by dozens of Portuguese. The Bedawin of
Arabia were the same feeble fighters in the days of the Romans, and even
when Harthema wrote. After having armed themselves with matchlocks and
muskets they became "tough customers."

† In the original Os Mouros (of Morocco or of the East Indies?).

‡ In the text "Roncalha, Velorio, and other Missanga." Roncalha is explained
by Monteiro and Gamitto (p. 23) to signify "pedras brancas," i. e., white stoneware
beads. We also read (p. 189) of Roncalha Azul (blue Roncalha), and of "pedras
leite," or milk stones. Velorio or Avelorio, is also a large opaque porcelain bead.
Missanga, according to Vieyra is synonymous with "arranguem," glass beads.
Constancio explains it by a string of glass beads, the same as "Mites," which
Vieyra interprets a sort of porcelain bead, used as currency in Mozambique.
The word is mostly applied to the red glass or porcelains, and in the text to
beads in general.

§ According to Dr. Kirk, now of Zanzibar, "bengallas de abada" are canes of
rhinoceros horn. The Abada is called by this people Pembére, and by the Portuguese unicorn.

and a few strings of beads, would be a sufficient "dash" to the most powerful Sova.*

Cattle, which abound in the interior, might be bought by way of rations. When these fail, powder and ball would supply the camp with meat of elephants, rhinoceros, wild cattle (empacássas), zebras (impalancas?), quaggas, wild goats (gamos), and various antelopes (veados), all of them good eating.† I well remember that our army, campaigning between 1774 and 1779 against the Spaniards on the River S. Pedro,‡ lived entirely on meat and enjoyed excellent health.

The choice of season is a vital condition of success. The best time to set out would be in May, during the cloudy but dry weather, locally called Caçimbo, and corresponding with our winter. If the journey is not concluded, as it ought to be, with September, when the wet season begins, the expedition should turn into some winter quarters where provisions are plentiful. The rains come on very suddenly, and a body of men compelled by unexpected downfalls suddenly to halt, and to go into winter quarters, would be exposed to great discomforts and lose many of its members.

Perhaps the Mozambique and the Rio Sena would be better starting-points than Angola or Benguela. The region to be explored is nearer the eastern coast, and the oriental negroes are more civilised and better fighters. Moreover the explorers would thus be better able to meet difficulties and to make head against the enemy than if, weary and broken-down, they had marched all the way from the western coast across Africa.

I now pass to the most important consideration—the kind of person to manage so delicate a mission, which could hardly be re-attempted should the first trial fail. The commandant must be a man of patience and probity, fortitude and prudence, healthy and vigorous in frame, accustomed to the country, and acquainted with the manners and customs of the people, sober and modest, grave and continent. Barbarians expect from the white man truth, good faith and honesty in the matter of payment; they are extremely jealous of their women, and evil would result, not only from violence, but even from seduction. The leader should personally set the example of total absti-

---

* A considerable miscalculation, as will presently appear.

† I have always found game in Africa and in America, northern and southern, the most heating, and, being destitute of fat, the least nourishing of meat. Moreover such a diet, except to those who have become familiar with it, leads to diarrhœa and dysentery. Finally, it is over-sanguine to expect so much game, and the author does not see that all the time would be wasted in hunting. The densely forested and swampy regions of Intertropical Africa could hardly supply four, much less 400 men, with regular rations of meat procured by the chase.

‡ Alias Rio Grande do Sul, in the Brazil.

nence in this matter, and enforce it upon his followers, under
the promptest and severest penalties. He must be invested
with the power of punishing offences,* and, if prudent and cir-
cumspect, he would temper justice with kindness and humanity.
He should not be placed under governors or generals; these,
on the contrary, should be peremptorily ordered to lend him
their aid. Hitherto the authorities have ever succeeded in
thwarting all such undertakings which were not directed by
their own orders.†

Finally the leader, ambitious only of glory, should be ani-
mated by true patriotism, an essential to success. Unhappily,
the best prepared African expeditions have mostly failed from
the vile interestedness of the commandants and from their bad
example. Thus the name of the sovereign becomes odious,
the sacred rights of truth and justice are violated, and to fill up
the measure of disgrace, merited punishment is avoided by
cunning subterfuge.

First impressions generally decide the part which we take,
and men are mostly governed by what strikes their external
senses. The barbarians, appreciating the good conduct of the
leader and his party, will easily infer the pacific and benevolent
intentions of those by whom they are sent. My personal
experience of the people assures me that, under such circumstances, success is certain.

Display not being wanted, the luggage should be as light as
possible: articles of constant want should be so packed as to
ensure mobility, whilst the usual impediments of boxes, tables,
bedsteads, crockery (loiças), and cloth-bales should not be admitted. If the leader be a true soldier, he will carry no more
kit than can be conveyed by one negro.‡ Thus he will be
willingly obeyed, and his party, seeing the example of their
superior, will learn to endure hardships without murmuring.

In case of accident to the commander, a second in command,
chosen with the same regard to fitness, should be duly appointed
to take charge of the expedition.

These, Excellency, are my views upon the subjects of exploring the vast regions of Inner Angola, and of establishing

---

* Punishment, again, is impracticable where desertion is so easy and so disastrous to an expedition.

† And not only amongst the Portuguese. I found this to my cost in exploring
the Somali country, wherever the influence of the British authorities of Aden,
Colonel Coghlan and Captain Playfair, unhappily extended.

‡ This assertion beats even the celebrated order of my old chief Sir Charles
Napier—the soldier and his "bit of soap." It is always my practice to carry
with me as much, not as little, as possible; at the same time, when the necessary
moment arrives, I am ready to limit luggage to a pair of saddle-bags.

land-transit between the Eastern and the Western Coasts of
Africa. My familiarity with the country has given birth to
them: zeal for the welfare of my native land, for the glory of
my race, and for the interests of my sovereign, has induced
me to expose them. After weighing my opinions in the
balance of your strong intellect, adding, diminishing, and alter-
ing as may seem fit, you, and you only, can give to us the
hope of seeing this important and glorious undertaking brought
to a successful issue. Such are my hopes: such is my only
ambition. The pleasure of knowing that I have lent my aid
to the furtherance of the project, is my sole intention in thus
addressing you, and with our Horace, in the dedication of his
poems, I can truthfully assert,—

> " Enough of glory, 'tis for me to boast
> I loved my native land and nation most." *

---

* A somewhat (of late years at least) hackneyed quotation from Camoens :—

> " Eu desta gloria só fico contento,
> Que a minha terra amei e a minha gente."

Note by the VISCOUNT DE SÁ DA BANDEIRA.

" The following are the objections to this theory. The Cunene, we are told by
the writer, is 540 fathoms broad at 50 leagues from its source. Subsequently Dr.
de Lacerda measured the Zambeza, in Jan. 1799, a short way below Tete, and
found its width hardly 450 to 500 fathoms. Lower down, in the broken gorge of
the Lupata mountains, its flood was only 180 to 200 fathoms wide, and the waters
fell four hands breadth whilst he was on the river, rendering it necessary to unload
the canoes.

" Were the Cunene and the Zambeze the same streams, the length from the
source to Tete would be 300 to 400 leagues. After such a drainage, the volume
of water should be much greater than at 50 leagues from its source, whereas in
the Lupata Gorge it is less. And as the channel of Mozambique receives nothing
larger than the Zambeze we cannot admit that the mouth of the Cunene River is
to the north or to the south of it.

" The opinion that the Cunene discharges its waters into the Atlantic Ocean is
more plausible. On March 31, 1794, a Governor-General of Angola named, in
order to prevent smuggling, a captain or chief over the ferries of the Rio Trombas,
subject to the Capitão-Mór of Casonda Nova. The Governor of Benguella, Ferreto
de Vasconcellos, wrote, in 1799: 'The Cunene falls into the sea at Cabo Negro,
and forms before reaching the mouth three islands; it has a very heavy bar
swell.' This cape is in S. Lat. 13° 46' 0" (15° 40' 7" Raper), and still further
south an English ship found, about 1824, in S. Lat. 17° 15' (17° 25' Raper;,
the mouth of a considerable stream, to which it gave the name of ' Nourse
River.' In the following year Captain Owen, R.N., then surveying the coast, met
with no signs of an embouchure, within 30 miles north and the same distance
south, of the place laid down as its mouth. But many African rivers, *e.g.*, the
Rio das Mortes (of murders), in Mossâmedes Bay, are absorbed in dry weather by
the sand.

" Although it seems probable that the Cunene falls into the Atlantic, there is
a third theory which deserves consideration. This river may serve to feed a great
lake in the very heart of the continent, as the Asiatic streams supplying the
Caspian, the Aral, and the Baikal, and as the African lose themselves in the Lake
Tchad (Chad), and in a basin which exists south of the Rios de Sena. This lake

is called in maps* 'Maravi' and 'Zachaf' by P°. Manoel Godinho, who says ('Viajem da India por terra à Portugal,' 1663) that two streams issue from it to the Zambesi, and who considers that it would facilitate land transit between Mozambique and Angola. Meanwhile, Captain Gamitto, in his interesting diary of a Portuguese expedition sent, in 1831, from Rios de Sena to the capital of the Cazembe (it afterwards appeared under name 'O Muata Cazembe,' Lisbon, 1854), asserts that the name of Maravi is wrongly applied to the Nhanja Grande,† which falls into the sea near Zanzibar Island.

* *Translator's Note.*—The political necessity of concealing discovery, and perhaps a something of official incuriousness belonging to tropical climates, have hidden many of the Portuguese discoveries from the world, and thus in this nineteenth century we have carried off part of a glory due to them. Dr. Livingstone's prodigious labours on the Upper Zambesi about the Nyassa and Shirwa Lakes, and in the country of the Casembe, may well

" Obscure the glory of each foreign brave."

But it is too much to assert that his predecessors ignored the course of the Zambese, the Shire, and the Nyassa Lake, which under the name of Zaflan (1623) was known centuries ago. We cannot accept the assertion that "beyond the great and little swamps (on the Shire River and called Nyanja) Portuguese geographical knowledge never extended. Dr. de Lacerda will prove that before 1799 the Portuguese settlers at Tete had begun to trade with the Cazembe in S. lat. 8° 15' (not S. lat. 10° 20'), and that in 1825-27 a colony was established on the banks of the (Southern) Aroangoa River, distant but 1° from the south-western end of the Nyassa. The great traveller unconsciously proves to us how well this water was known. In his 'First Expedition' (chap. xxxi.) we find that Sr. Candido (José de Costa Cardozo, the Capitão Mór?), had visited Lake Maravo, 45 days N.N.W. from Tete. In chap. xix. we read that an Arab had been living for fourteen years at the "Katanga's, south of Cazembe's," where malachite is dug; that he was acquainted with the drainage of the Nyassa, and probably with that of the Moero Lake, which is described as "flowing out by the opposite end to that of Nyassa"—that is to say, northward—a very fair "piece of Arab geography." So in chap. xxv. we are told that the Arab Ben Habib, whom the traveller met at Linyanti, in 1855, had been taken across the Nyassa.

We may thus resume the question treated above, with the assistance of that eminent statesman, geographer, and savant, the Viscount de Sá da Bandeira. ('Notes sur les Fleuves Zambesi et Chire, et sur quelques Lacs de l'Afrique Oriental.' 'Bulletin de la Société de Géographie.' Série Vme, tome III. p. 361, and tome iv., 390.)

1. The Chire (Anglicè, Shire) was navigated by the Portuguese in the sixteenth and seventeenth centuries.

2. The Nyanja-Mucuro, or Great Lake, in the Marave country, had been visited by them in the eighteenth century.

3. They had laid down the positions of the lake and the Chiro (Shire) River in maps.

4. They had often crossed the Chambeze, or Northern Zambeze, in their journeys from Tete to the city of the Cazembe.

5. "Sr. Candido had visited the place where the Chire (Shire) leaves the lake." N.B.—This place, called by Dr. Livingstone Murombo, is changed by Mr. Cooley to "Pa-Marombo"—place of junction, viz. of the Nyassa with its lake-like drain.

6. Dr. Livingstone, by visiting the Upper Zambese, the Chire River, and the Nyassa Lake, and by determining certain points astronomically, and by describing the country, has added much to our knowledge of this part of Zambesi.

† Monteiro and Gamitto (1831-32) make this Nhanja-Mocuro (Great Nyanja), nine leagues (Portuguese?) broad. The last African expedition led by me, in 1857-59, showed that the confusion caused by this generic word "water" for sea, lake, pond, river, had thrown into a great central sea the Nyassa (not Nyassi) of Kilwa; the Nyanja lately established to the west of Mombasah, and the (Victoria)

"In confirmation of the Lake theory we have the following fact. In 1801 two Dutch Commissioners, Fraier and Somerville, left, on a cattle-purchasing expedition, Cape Town for the interior. After passing northwards of the Orange River into the before unvisited lands of the Batlapi, their linguists told them that all the territory to the north and the north-west were Bechwana, that is to say congeners of the Batlapi, and speaking Sechwana (Sitlapi) with various dialects. The country consisted of vast dry plains, with a great lake to the north-west; this, according to the Commissioners, would be on the confines of Benguela. Dr. de Lacerda makes the Cunene to run east; it may find its way into that lake.

"This interesting point must soon be decided. Of late years many Protestant Missions and Moravian Brothers have settled in the Bechwana country; moreover Cape merchants have penetrated 300 to 400 leagues into the interior. They find this travel easy, for three reasons—the hospitality of the people, the being able to employ Cape waggons, and the general use of the Sechwana language, of which there are English and Dutch grammars, and which is cognate with the Bunda of Angola.

"Moreover, since 1836, some 80,000 Boers have fled from the English rule. This extraordinary exodus of families with flocks, and universally recalling to mind the Hebrews' flight from Egypt, went eastward; and part settled in Natal, whilst some reached the Lourenço Marques Bay and the Inhambane. In 1844, we are told, part were still wandering; haply they may turn to the Portuguese possessions north-west and discover the mouth of the Cunene.

"The glory of exploring the Cunene should be ours. No other nation has such opportunities of discovery, and we are the most interested in opening up a stream which, as its breadth of 500 fathoms argues, is probably navigable, and which, provided with properly-placed Presidios, would become an important centre of trade.

"Mossamedes Bay (so called from Baron Mossamedes, Governor-General of Angola, who explored the country) is the best starting-point for an expedition which, marching upon Huila, would strike the Cunene and trace it down to its mouth. If our Government resolved to undertake this fine exploration, it might easily be carried out by young naval and military officers, and the advice of our author upon the mode of travelling might be adopted as the counsel of experience and of good sense. Those should be preferred who have completed a course of polytechnic study. They must be able to lay down their longitudes by Jupiter's satellites, as did Dr. de Lacerda, determine altitudes by the barometer, and register thermometric and magnetic observations. A naturalist and a good draughtsman would complete the personnel. The road-book should be kept with care, and plotted off without delay, whilst interesting geographical notices and minute memoranda describing the country, the people, the languages, and other points of interest, should not be omitted."

Since this highly interesting note was written (in 1844, it must be observed, before the "Mumbas Mission" had taken up its abode on the coast, and a year before its excursions began) much has been done. Fraier and Somerville's lake has been determined to be the Ngami or old Mampur Water, 14° or 840 miles in direct distance from the Nyanza Lake. The Batlapi have been visited by many English travellers, and Dr. Livingstone includes them amongst the Balakahari or western branch of the Great Bechwana family, once an "insignificant and filthy people," but much improved by "trading, peace, and religious teaching" (Dr. Livingstone, 'First Expedition,' chap. x.).

Dr. de Lacerda's error about the course of the Cunene, making it flow eastward instead of westward, is the rock upon which many African inquirers split, forgetting that it is impossible to determine the direction of streams or the lay of mountains except by ocular inspection. The mouth, said to have been discovered by "L'Espiègle" in 1724, and passed by Captain Owen, November 28, 1825, is

Nyanza Region discovered by Captain Speke, sent by me for that purpose. The Nhanja Mucuru, or Great Water, is called "Elephant Marsh" by Dr. Livingstone, and his map shows it in S. lat. 16° 20'. The Nhanja Pangono, Little Water, is transferred to S. Lat. 17° 10'.

partially intermittent, as was wrongly reputed to be the case with the Juba
River, and rightly with the Webbi Gamana, the Nile of Makdishu (Magadoxo', or
Haines River on the East Coast of Africa. Captain Owen believed that the rains,
beginning with the year, open the Cunene's mouth, and that during the dries a
strong south-west wind and furious breakers, especially on the southern point,
called in old maps Cape Ruy Perez, heap up a sandbank which seals the embouchure.   •

The Nhanja Grande is partly a confusion of the Nyassa Lake, between 11°
and 14° 25' S. lat., and a flooded morass, or rather a lake region to the north
of the Zambeze in S. lat. 17° 10'. The Zambeze expedition found that
both drain, as the chaplain of Dr. de Lacerda's party had asserted, into the
Zambeze River, not into the Zanzibar Channel, as Captain Gamitto had supposed.
" Zachaf" is evidently the Nyassa Lake.

INFORMATION TOUCHING

THE PROPOSED "CAZEMBE EXPEDITION,"

AND INSTRUCTIONS ISSUED TO ITS PARTY,

BY DR. FRANCISCO JOSÉ MARIA DE LACERDA.

SECTION I.

RESPECTING the important enterprise, most illustrious and excellent Sir,* with which Her Most Faithful Majesty has charged me, namely, to discover or to confirm the feasibility of overland transit between the Eastern and the Western Coasts of Africa, I have the honour to report to you, for the information of the Sovereign, that whilst preparing to carry out with all despatch the commands of Her Majesty, though doubtful as to what measures would produce a happy result, being ignorant of the route to be taken, I heard with pleasure that an old backwoodsman, Gonçalo Caetano Pereira† by name, had arrived at this town. In the days of my predecessor he had explored the lands of a king called Cazembe, dwelling near Angola, who, having been sent by his father to make conquests in the interior, now rules, as an independent prince, the Muizas, ‡ and

---

* This letter, dated Tete, March 22, 1798, is addressed to the same Minister, D. Rodrigo de Sousa Coutinho, and furnishes all the preliminary information collected by Dr. de Lacerda concerning the march to the Cazembe's country. The paper is reprinted from a manuscript in the library of the Count de Linhares, and was offered to the Maritime and Colonial Association of Lisbon, by its ex-President, His Excellency the Viscount de Sá da Bandeira.

† This is Dr. Livingstone's " Pereira " (see his ' First Expedition,' chap. xxix. p. 587). The traveller gives a curious account of " Dr. Lacerda's expedition," and tells us that his papers were " lost to the world." Moreover we find that he considers the " real negro " to be only the anthropoid " north of 20º."

‡ Also termed Moizas, Movizas, Invizas, and Aizas. Dr. Livingstone writes à la Makololo Abisa, or Babisa, the Kisawahili Wabisa or Wabisha. The learned Jesuit de Jarrio (ii. 163) calls them Ambios or Imbies. Das Noves (p. 397) prefers " Vaviza " and Vavua, " the rich people " (Vavua in Kisawahili, the plural of " M'vua," would mean " hunters " or " fishermen "). Dr. Livingstone (chap. xix.) confounds the tribe with the Wanyamwezi, misled by Mr. Cooley (' Geog. of N'yassi,' p. 17), who tells us that they are "similar in physical character and natural marks." Of these marks I shall have something to say on a future occasion. The " Muizas " originally lived on the west of the Nyassa, extending to the Tanganyika Lake. According to Monteiro and Gamitto, they were expelled

D

other Caffre (Kafir) tribes. The chief had sent two envoys to
visit me, and from them I took down the following depositions.
Having obtained this information, I will delay no longer than
is necessary to hire the 300 Muizas who escorted my informant
the son of the said Gonçalo Caetano. So many slaves have
lately deserted and died of famine, that, without such aid, I
hardly could have obeyed Her Majesty's orders. Yet I am
aware that even under these favourable circumstances, full
confidence must not be reposed in the Muizas and in the
Cazembe.

I have made every arrangement that is here possible. A
company of fifty soldiers with officers has been recruited, to
assist me in carrying out the measures which their knowledge
of the country suggests. Want of time prevents my applying
for aid to the Mozambique, nor do I regret it. The Governor-
General there informed me that, though ready to assist in all
requisites, he did not wish to know or to hear a word about my
undertaking.

I have the honour, &c.,

(Signed)   FRANCISCO JOSÉ MARIA DE LACERDA
E ALMEIDA.

SECTION II.[*]

Before entering upon this deposition I will briefly state that,
about forty years ago, Gonçalo Caetano Pereira came from Goa,
and made his livelihood, as do all the colonists, by gold-washing
and trading with the Caffres of the interior.[†] Thin of frame
and high-spirited, his generosity and courage have made
him loved and feared by all the knights of the interior, and
they, as well as the Portuguese, nickname him "Dombo-
Dombo," meaning "the Terror."

---

their territory by the Muembas or Moluanas, and they have since been much
scattered. They are now great travellers and traders, and they have approached
the northern banks of the Zambeze River—Dr. Livingstone met them near the
Loangwa stream, bringing English goods from Mozambique. They are acute as
Levantines, and are well known at Zanzibar: I have found several of them
reduced to slavery in the Brazil.

* The deposition of Manoel Caetano Pereira concerning his journey in company
with his father, Gonçalo Caetano Pereira, to the city of Cazembe, the king nearest
to the Portuguese possessions on the West Coast of Africa. In Monteiro and
Gamitto's Expedition of 1831 (p. 129) we read that they found Manoel Caetano
Pereira, a Capitão-Mór of the interior, and his brother, Pedro Caetano Pereira, in
the lands of the Chévas north of the Maraves.

† The Portuguese apply the word Caffres (Kafirs) generically to the heathen of
the inner regions, and especially to slave porters. According to Dr. Livingstone
("First Expedition," chap. x.), the Caffres consider the name Caffre an insult. So do
"niggers" at Sierra Leone and convicts in Australia.

Years ago the Muizas, in their tradings with the Mujáo,[*] heard that this man was working at, and dwelling near, the mines of Java (Jáua), beyond the Zambeze River, some five days' journey from this town. In 1793 they came to trade with him in ivory, and they informed him that their lord, the Cazembe, desired his friendship. He entrusted to these Muizas, without other security but their word, a little cloth, which sold well; and afterwards he sent to the king, with the like success, two of his trading slaves (Muzambazes).[†] Desiring to benefit the colonists—a rare idea in these regions—Gonçalo Caetano Pereira informed them of the new opening for commerce, and some of them resolved to send up their slave-porters in charge of his son Manoel Caetano Pereira, a young man, going for the first time to manage his father's third venture.

In May 1796, Manoel, accompanied by his own slaves and by the Muizas, who, the year before, had brought down the Cazembe's ivory, set out for Marenga[‡] (Marengue ?) land, three days' march from Tete. The first regions which he traversed were those of the Marave[§] kinglets, called Dive, Vinde, Mo-canda,[‖] Mazy, and Mazavambu; and he secured free passage by presenting a little cloth to the most powerful He was forty-five days in reaching the banks of the Arangôa River, which falls into the Zambeze near the town of Zumbo.[¶] The Portuguese,

* This is the Portuguese form adopted by Dr. Livingstone ('First Expedition,' chap. xxxi.). In Expedition No. 2, he calls them Waiao, Waiau, or Ajawa, and he records a fight with them. The Wamwahili prefer "Mhiáo," in the plural "Wáhiáo." The once powerful tribe has its habitation on the north and east of the Nyassa Lake. Some authors confuse it with the Angúros. The women, like those of the Marave, distend the upper lip.

† Also written Mozimbazes and Musambazes. It means "commerciantes ambulantes dos Sertões," native itinerant traders, the same as the Pombeiros of the Western Coast, who take their mongrel name from the Angolan Pombo, a path, with the Lusitanian suffix -eiros.

‡ In some of the Zanzibar dialects "Marenga" means water.

§ Of the Marave more anon. It is a powerful tribe, and hostile to strangers, living between the Zambeze River and the lands to the south-west of the Nyassa Lake, hence the water for years has been known to Europe as the "Marave Lake."

‖ In Monteiro and Gamitto (p. 448) we find that the lands travelled through by them between Tete and the Cazembe's country were governed by three great chiefs. These were—1. The Unde of the Maraves. 2. The Mucanda (Mohanda) of the Chévas; and 3. The Chiti-Muculo, King of the Muembas.

¶ Of the Southern Aruangoa, the stream here alluded to, more will be found in a future note. The Northern Aruangoa, Loangwa or Roango, is made a northern influent of the Zambeze, 180 direct miles west of Tete : it was first crossed by Dr. Livingstone on December 14, 1855. The map of his Second Expedition lays down for its upper branches a course very different from that of the first and, agreeing with Portuguese information, it is probably more correct. We can hardly understand how the traveller, after seeing a stone church and other such signs of civilization at Zumbo (the old mission town on the right bank of the Zambeze and the left of the Loangwa), could persuade himself that the Portuguese never travelled up the Zambeze Valley.

however, had not reached the place where he crossed the
stream. The Maraves, professed robbers, fearing the number of
his party, allowed him transit for small payments; nor did they
annoy him with their "Milandos"* or palavers, by means of
which they mulct the traders in cloth, to the great injury
of commerce. A dog entering a hut or chasing a hen; even
the trader's slaves appearing in a village without warning; in
fact any trivial pretence of the kind, becomes a crime, which
can be expiated only by cloth. We are weak, so we must suffer.
But, if I return safe from Western Africa, these bandits shall
be punished.

Throughout the Marave country millet (*Holcus sorghum*)
abounds; there are also beans, seeds of different kinds, and live
cattle. The travellers saw no sheep, goats, or pigs. The
Cazembe alone had a sow, sent from near Angola by his father,†
and now, his only hog being dead, he is sending there for some
couples.

Leaving slaves to treat with the neighbouring Caffres, Pereira
Junior crossed the Aruangôa in ferry-canoes, for which he paid a
small sum, and 'reached the Muizas, who begin beyond the
northern bank. He halted there awhile for necessaries; then
marching, according to Caffre caprice, four or five hours a day,
after twenty days he struck another river, which the people
called "Zambeze." ‡ From their information I venture to say

---

* The term "Milandos" means charges brought against travellers for the
purpose of plundering them: in fact, the "palavers" of the West Coast. I shall
have more to say about this word, which is constantly re-occurring.

† "Father" here means "liege lord" and "son," often "subject," whilst
"brother" is any man of the same tribe. The Matiamvo, Matianfa, Muata-
Yambo, Muata-Ilianvo, or Muáta yá Nvo, was visited by Joaquim Rodrigues
(Iraça in 1847: he is the paramount Chief of Londa (Lunda) and of the Alunda,
Varunda, Aronda, or Alonda tribe, the Balonda of Dr. Livingstone.

‡ Dr. de Lacerda's Zambeze divides the Muiza country from the dominions
proper of the Cazembe. In the map of Dr. Livingstone's Second Expedition we find
a "Zambesi eastern branch" in lat. 8. 11° and W. long. 28° to 31°. It thus
became a headwater of the stream, concerning which the canoe men sing,—

"The Lecambye! Nobody knows
Whence it comes and whither it goes."

('Livingstone's First Expedition,' chap. xxvi.)

And, finally, Mr. Cooley has distorted it in a special manner, which will require a
future notice. Dr. de Lacerda's assertion, touching the non-identity of the two
streams, has been verified by Dr. Livingstone's third and latest expedition. The
traveller, in February 1867, crossing the "Zambesi eastern branch," which he calls,
like all the Portuguese travellers, Chambeze, clearly a dialectic variety, found it
flowing to the left hand (from east to west), and forming the Lake Bangweolo.
This water lies at the northern counterslope of the Muchinga Mountains, and
drains through the Lakes Bangweolo, Moero (Livingstone, September 8, 1867), and
Ulenge or Kamalondo, to an unvisited lake further north. I have given my
reasons for believing that this great valley communicates with the north-western
branch of the mighty Congo. Dr. Livingstone (addressing Lord Granville from

that it is not our Zambeze, nor any of its influents from the Xire (Shire) River * upwards. The Zambeze of the Muizas flows to the right hand of those crossing it from Tete, and it falls into other streams, of which I shall presently speak.

The Muizas were found to be a kindly and commercial people. A little cloth was "dashed" to the chiefs, who, conquered by the Cazembe, pay tribute to him in stuffs, for which he always returns ivory. The dry goods hitherto imported into this country have been bought by the Mujao (Wahiáo), indirectly or directly, from the Arabs of Zanzibar and its vicinity.† Hence these people receive all the ivory exported from the possessions of the Cazembe; whereas formerly it passed in great quantities through our port of Mozambique.‡

The Cazembe declines to take cloth from his subject chiefs, who bring it cut up and high priced. He wishes the Portuguese to send him bales, "as they come from afar."§ Our trade would soon supplant that of our rivals, the Mujao, if we could import a quantity of cloth; and if we are rightly informed, a matter into which I will look personally, the Cazembe does not buy goods: perhaps it would not be held dignified for him

---

Ujiji, December 18, 1871) now derives the "Loeambye," or Upper Zambezo, from "Palmerston's Fountain." Of this curious theory a few words have been said in the Introductory Remarks.

* The Missionary Luis Marianno ('Lettere Annue d'Etiopia, &c.,' Rome, 1627) well knew that the Cherim (Shire) flows out of the Maravo Lake (Nyassa), and that its bed has rapids. Fray Manoel Godinho (1663) makes the Chire River drain the "Zeabaf" Lake. Mr. Cooley ('Geog. of N'yassi') thus comments upon the old explorer: "With respect to the River Cherim, said to flow from the lake, it is evident that Mariano had in view a River Querimba, that is to say, a river entering the sea somewhere opposite to the Querimba Islands." And this is what is called Comparative Geography! The supposed "Querimba River" is not even traced in Mr. Cooley's map. Dr. Livingstone ('First Expedition,' chap. iii.) tells us "we could not learn from any record that the Shire had ever been ascended by Europeans" (before his first journey in January 1859). He forgot that the missionary João dos Santos, who had resided in the country eleven years from 1586 to 1597, mentions, in his 'Æthiopia Oriental' (Pinkerton, vol. xvi. p. 337), the great river Chiri navigated by the blacks and colonists of Sena. The Shire is now unhappily well known as the quarters of those murdered men, the first University Missionaries.

† Through Kilwa, which, when I visited it in 1859, had a large trade with the Cazembe's city: many Arabs were engaged in it. From this point started the late Dr. Roscher, who reached the Nyassa Lake two months after it had been visited by Dr. Livingstone; and he was followed part of the way by the late Baron von der Decken.

‡ The European establishments at Zanzibar have, of course, increased this evil to the Portuguese. Unfortunately, however, the Wahiáo tribe has been so favoured in the slave-market that it is now nearly extinct. I have discussed the subject in 'Zanzibar, City, Island, and Coast' (London, Tinsleys, 1871).

§ That is to say, "whole," uncut. This general want of African accounts for the negroes' desire to trade with the white man face to face. The King of Dahome, like the Cazembe, does not buy or sell: it is a cunning African "dodge," by which he gains greatly.

to trade; they must be presented as "dashes," or free gifts
(siguate),* and he makes a return in ivory. Clearly this king,
though in the heart of Africa, is not the barbarian whom closet
geographers (geografos de vidraças) describe. The Caffres are
in some points like the Mexicans and the Peruvians, who were,
in my opinion, more civilized than their Spanish conquerors.†

Beyond the influents of the (northern) Zambeze River begin
the lands of the Cazembe, conquered by his father Muropéo‡
(sic), as those of the Muizas have been by the Cazembe himself.
The party travelled thirty days from the river to the king's
capital, crossed some deserts, saw wild beasts of different sorts,
and spent a day fording a lake waist-deep. This body of water
is drained by two channels;§ according to the Caffres, one feeds
their Zambeze, the other goes to the Murusura River, upon
whose banks is the royal residence.‖ This Murusura passes

---

* Dr. Livingstone ('The Zambesi and its Tributaries') calls this "Seguati,"
and explains it well.

† This assertion should hardly pass uncriticised. In Mexico, as in Peru, a won-
drous physical civilization, chiefly shown by public works, monuments, and roads,
a despotism which secured life and property, and a religion which annually slew
its hundreds of human victims, was summarily destroyed by a band of Conquis-
tadores—men who in the present days would be looked upon as barbarians. But
these men had, those people had not, the material of true progress within them.
Peru has now her Blakeley guns and her railways; she would not have had
them under the Incas or their descendants.

‡ More generally Murúpée or Murópúe. Ladislaus Magyar declares that this
title given by the Portuguese to the Muátá yá Nvo is unknown to the people
of Lunda or Londa. The following Diary (January 16, 1799, and elsewhere)
shows that it is applied to a neighbouring king, and here too we find "Sana
Muropue" the title of an officer.

§ Poor Dr. de Lacerda never knew what a "row" such a statement would
now excite in the geographical world: we are still disputing about "lakes with
two outlets."

‖ Murusura is called Hemosura by Father Luis Marianno, called by Mr.
Cooley "Luigi Mariano," the Sena Missionary, who published in 1627; and he
makes, as I have said, the Shire River flow from it. It is therefore a synonym
of the Marave Lake, Dr. Livingstone's Lake Nyassa. In this century, Mr.
Cooley has actually confounded it with the River Luapula, the Mofo Lake, and
the Tanganyika Lake. He makes "Hemosura" a mistake for "Murmura,"
meaning "the Sea" (p. 17), even as Moçuro is a rivulet, and Roçuro grande a
large body of water. In my 'Report to the Royal Geographical Society' (vol.
xxix. p. 272) I have explained these words (note on Diary, Sept. 10th). Dr.
Livingstone ('Second Expedition,' chap. x. p. 214) says, that the Bashukulu
(Zulus?) are known to geographers, who derive their information from the Portuguese, as "Murusuros." Mr. Cooley suggests that "the Portuguese call them
Moairuro, meaning perhaps, M'zariro, the name of a powerful chief on the
River Save." This is mere conjecture.

According to Monteiro and Gamitto (p. 349) Lunda, the Cazembe's capital, is
on the southern or south-eastern edge of "Mofu, Grande Lago." Mr. Cooley has
lately placed the Cazembe's city on the north-east bank of the Mofo, a lakelet
2 or 3 miles broad, and not connected with "Lake Moeri." In Mr. E. G. Ravenstein's map, this Moro (Mofo) drains into the Zambeze basin, which also receives
the waters of the Tanganyika, by means of the Luapula River (compare note
on Diary, June 6, 1799). In Monteiro and Gamitto's map, the "Guapula

behind the Murimbala* Range, near Sena. Some of our people call it Nanjacjá Matope (Nyanja yá M'tope), others "Shire."† Travellers making the Cazembe's city cross it in three days, nighting on islands. They also say that their Zambeze falls into this stream far below (south of) the city.‡

The Muizas are a mercantile tribe, who have penetrated into those countries, and who have at times brought down their ivories to Quilimane§ (Kilima-ni). Possibly they may tell the truth respecting the Xire (Shire) River; but if we compare its mouth with the width of the stream in the Cazembe's country, there appears to me a contradiction. The former, however, is confined by mountains; the latter flows through immense plains (Dumbos), which begin upon the Aroangôa River;‖ hence,

---

River" three days' journey, or 30 direct miles, from the capital of Cazembe, flows to the northwest. I have long ago recorded the Arab opinion that the Tanganyika Lake has at the south an influent, the Runangwa or Marungu River, not an effluent as Mr. Ravenstein. Dr. Livingstone ('Second Expedition,' chap. xxv,) says: "Flowing still farther in the same direction (to the west) the Loapula forms Lake Mofuo or Mofa, and after this, it is said to pass the town of Cazembe, bend to the north, and enter Lake Tanganyika." In chap. xxviI. the traveller bears this from Babisa tobacco dealers, and says, "this is the native idea of the geography of the interior." Dr. Livingstone's Third Expedition, however, sets all right, and gives us the first correct view of the country. The Cazembe's town is placed north-east of a diminutive basin called Molo or Mofwe, which connects, through the Londa (Loapula) River with Lake Moero, the centre of three fed by the northern slope of the Muchinga range.

* Dr. Livingstone ('First and Second Expeditions') describes Morumbala ("the lofty watch-tower") near Sena, to be an oblong, wooded mountain-mass, "probably 3000 to 4000 feet high," and, as its hot sulphurous fountain on the plain at the north-eastern side (northern in 'First Expedition') would show, of igneous formation. In his map there is an island in the Nyassa Lake called "Murumba Hill," which has disappeared from the chart of the 'Second Expedition.'

† This is clearly a confusion between the Lake Nyassa and the two Nyanjas (to the North Mukulo or Mucuro, "the great," and to the south Pangono or "the small"; on the road from the Zambeze River to the Nyassa Lake. It must again be observed that in the Zangian tongues, Nyassa, Nyanza, Nyanja, and other forms, all signify water. M'tope is a mud, the Portuguese "Lama," in Monteiro's map "Dambo Lodoso."

‡ M. Ravenstein makes both streams, "Loapula" and "Schambose," fall into the Chaia Lake (Portuguese, Chover, to rain?). This is Dr. Livingstone's "Shuia," which has three outlets. I called it, in 1859, the "Chama Lake," from the district which it occupies.

§ So in 'Annaes Maritimos' (p. 291). I am at pains to know why Mr. Cooley ('Geography of N'yassi' p. 17) should translate this passage, "The Movira, being great traders, go a long way into the country, and even penetrate at times to Lulibim" (for Kilima-ni on the coast). He adds, "In this name it is easy to recognise the Portuguese abbreviation of Lukelingo," which (p. 13) he calls the capital of Iáo.

What a confirmed confusion! Lunkeringa (not Lukelingo) is the name of a station on the way from Kilwa to the Nyassa Lake. "Iáo" (for Uhyáo) is the land of the Wahiáo, who, I have said, are now nearly annihilated by the slave-trade. Their "capital" is on a par with the "town Zangallon," west of the Tanganyika Lake. Dr. Krapf ('Travels,' &c., p. 419) mentions "Keringo," a station in their country; but he knew too much of Africa to talk of a "capital."

‖ From Tete to the Cazembe's country the traveller crosses two streams of

perhaps, the difference. Or it may be the Lucunse River, *
whose mouth is near Quilimane, but whose upper course is
unknown—a doubtful point which I hope soon to resolve.
Perchance, again, it may be some other stream which discharges its waters into the ocean between Mozambique and
Quilimane.

The Cazembo evidently desires intercourse with us. After
vainly attempting to detain Manoel Caetano Pereira, with the
assurance that he would send his own ivory-porters to bring up
more cloth, he unwillingly dismissed his visitor, and only
on express condition that the latter would return; and he
threatened, if deceived, to slay all the Portuguese in those
parts and to seize their property. During the six months of
Manoel Caetano Pereira's stay, the king made him many presents, amongst which was a large farm of manioc—there the
staff of life. He promised restoration of stolen goods, with
profit to the injured person; and gave him and his followers
immunity from the laws to which his vassals are subject, such
as cutting off the ears, hands, and pudenda of adulterers. They
witnessed an instance of the latter amputation, and similar
pains and penalties.

This king, our good friend, is proud of intercourse with us.
Shortly after the arrival of Manoel Caetano Pereira he sent a
message to his father, the other king (Mwátá yá Nvo), that as
the latter had his . . . . ,† meaning sons of, or born under,
water, so he himself had been visited by whites from the other
shore. It is this boast,‡ combined with want of cloth, which
makes him so much desire our friendship. He sent to me, as

---

nearly the same, and possibly quite the same, name. The southern is the Aru-
ingoa, Aroangôa, or Arangôa, which falls into the Zambeze about the Kebrabasa Rapids, and upon whose banks a Portuguese colony was built: the northern
is the Arangoa, or Loangwa, the head-water of the Roango or Loangwa, which
falls into the Zambeze at Zumbo.

* In Dr. Livingstone's map we find the "River Licuare," alias Likuáre
(' First Expedition,' chap. xxxii.), a northern influent of the Quilimane mouth of
Zambeze; but it appears to be an insignificant stream.

† A word is here omitted in the original—in Kisawahili it would be "Wáná
Máji." The negroes of the interior look upon the whiteness of European skins,
and especially the straightness of hair—of which they sometimes say, "it is the
mane of a lion, and not hair at all," and "only look at his hair! it is made quite
straight by the sea-water"—as the effect of marine or submarine life. The old
Maharattas also regarded the English as an amphibious race.

‡ In my 'Mission to Dahome' I have shown that a similar vanity exists, and
that its result is a modified form of human sacrifice. King Gelele, wishing
to send a message to his father, summons a captive, carefully primes him with
the subject of his errand, generally some vaunt, adhibits a bottle of rum, and
strikes off his head. If an important word be casually omitted he repeats the
operation, a process which I venture to call a postscript.

envoy, the son of a Muiza chief, whom he had conquered and put to death. This messenger brought in his train one Catára, a grandee of the Cazembe's kingdom, and two spies (sôpôzos), to see that neither I nor their master were deceived by him in the matter of my reply.* Of these, one died; the other, a youth of sixteen to eighteen years old and a confidential slave of the monarch, survived. The envoy and Catára both informed me that the Cazembe, or his ancestors, coming from about Angola, which they pronounced Gora,† overran his present territories; that from his capital to the small kingdom of Morópoe is a journey of sixty days, or somewhat less for white men;‡ and, finally, that canoes from Angola and its vicinity came up to fetch slaves. On the way between the two countries are four rivers running to the left (south-west), and therefore falling into the Atlantic; and one is so broad that it takes a day to cross. May this not be the Cunene, or, as it is called in some maps, the Rio Grande? From the Morópoe's kingdom to the Cazembe's country pass cloths, and the "notions" (trastes) common on the western coast, as mirrors, tea-things kept for show, plates, cups, beads of sorts, cowries,§ and broadcloths of various kinds. I myself saw a scarlet "durante" (a narrow woollen stuff without nap) which the king had given to a Caffre slave of Manoel Gonçalo Pereira.

The Cazembe sends his chattels to his "father," who remits them to Angola, taking in barter broadcloths, as baize, durante, fine serge (serafina), and the articles specified above. They do not sell their captives to the Portuguese, who hold them of little account compared with ivory. The latter article, however, would be much more lucrative if transported by water, instead of the present tedious and expensive land-journey.‖ The Cazembe's country abounds in manioc, white gourds,

---

* This system of spies and of duplicate officials is quite African, as I have shown in the ' Story of a Mission to Dahome.'

† From Monteiro and Gamitto we learn (p. 498, &c.) that the Alundas call the lands of the Murópue (or Mwáta yá Nvo) " Angola " or " Gora; " the latter evidently a European corruption of " Bunda Ngola " in full A-Ngola, the land of (the chief) Ngola.

‡ The direct distance from the capital of the Cazembe to Kabebe, the capital of the Mwáta yá Nvo is from 4 to 5 degrees = 240 to 300 miles. This place is built near and north of the Luiza River, supposed to be an eastern branch of the Great Kasai. According to Ladislaus Magyar, the Portuguese call this capital also Lunda. The four rivers running, as was formerly supposed, to the south-west, will re-occur in the course of these pages.

§ Caurim or Cauril, plural Cauris. The popular word is " buzio," from which the French in the Brazil coin " des bougie." In Angola it is Zimbo, and it has a different name amongst every tribe.

‖ The only cheap way of exporting ivory from the heart of Africa is upon the shoulders of slaves, the latter being of course sold on the coast.

ground-nuts,* "jugo," a small haricot like the ricinus,† white sugar-cane, the sweet potato (*C. batata*), and the Dendé, whose fruit makes oil.‡ Between the lands of the Cazembe and Moropoe there are many deserts wanting supplies. Our traveller found provisions deficient amongst the Muizas when taking on his return a different road (the westerly?), nor did he reach the lake above alluded to. The cows are the king's private property :§ only his dignitaries may herd black cattle.

The entertainment of the Cazembe is magnificent. He has a number of domestic slaves, and he carefully preserves his many wives, who are allowed to speak with his confidants only. His usual dress ‖ is a large silk sheet (tobo) wound around the middle and girt with a bandoleer: it is plaited and folded above the girdle after the fashion of the Cabindas. He wears a cap ornamented with red feathers, and his legs are adorned with cowries, large white beads (velorio), the pipe-shaped beads (canutilho),¶ much valued amongst them, and beads of sorts.**

The Cazembe rarely appears in public, the better to preserve

---

* In the original "amendoim," which does not mean almonds, of which the Persian variety, or "bidam" (a Starculia), is found upon the Zanzibar coast, but never far in the interior. Monteiro and Gamitto, however, say (p. 163) that on the banks of the Northern Aruāngoa River they observed "amendoeiras das que dão as amēndoas chamadas duzarias em Portugal." Here it is the *Arachis hypogæa*, the Pistacho of old and the Arachide of modern French travellers, the pea-nut of the Northern United States, the Pindwa (a Loango word) of the Southern States and the Ginguba of Angola.

† Especie de feijão carrapato. M. Constancio's Dictionary explains Carrapateiro as Palma Christi, the castor-oil tree, from the resemblance of its fruit to the cattle-tick (carrapato). The vulgar Portuguese name of the shrub is "mamona."

‡ The Dendé, or Dendem, in Africa and in the Brazil, is the *Elæis Guinēensis*, or palm-oil tree. I found a species on the Tanganyika Lake which produced good oil, but the fruit was a bunch like grapes, not a spike, as on the West African Coast and about Bahia.

§ The same is the case in Benin city. (See my 'Visit to the Renowned Cities of Wari and Benin,' 'Fraser's Magazine,' February, March, and April, 1863.)

‖ So MM. Monteiro and Gamitto describe the Cazembe's dress as a waist-cloth or swathe, called Mocenzo, with one end made fast below the waist by a little ivory arrow to the body-cloth, and the whole wound round the middle in short, regular folds. A leathern belt, known as "Inalpo," supported the garment. Their frontispiece, "O Muata Cazembe vestido de grande Galla," shows this swathe and its bandoleer. The chaplain of Dr. de Lacerda's expedition will presently describe it in these pages.

¶ M. Constancio derives this word from the French "canutille," meaning "purl," "filum argenteum vel aureum," the gold or silver wire, tubular and spiral, used in embroidery. In MM. Monteiro and Gamitto it is a bead material. They make it (p. 181) a synonym of "Dorūru," a pipe-shaped bead, or rather bugle, one inch long by four to five lines in breadth. In p. 189 we read of "Canutilho de todas as cōres." In Venice "canutilho" is called Piplotal.

** In the days of MM. Monteiro and Gamitto (1831-1832), the beads for Quilimane were white, black, green, and grey; for Sena, white and black; for Tete and Sofala, large white, black, and brick-red; and for Inhambane and Lourenço Marques, of all colours.

the respect of his people. He receives his nobles sitting behind
a curtain, and presents to them, not tea, coffee, nor chocolate,
whose equipage is always displayed, but millet-beer (Pombe),*
and the wine (Sura) of the Mediuca palm.†   The courtiers
drink only what the king portions out to them, for fear of
intoxication, which is an offence severely punished by its own
peculiar judge.‡

The Cazembe has a number of well-disciplined troops, whose
chiefs every night bring him the news, and receive his orders
and the watchword (Santo),§ which they pass like civilized
nations.   There are different corps de garde, patrols and rounds
to keep the peace and to repress disorders and drunkenness.
The city is surrounded by a deep ditch, said to be several
leagues in length:‖ during war time the vassals are lodged
within the enclosure, so as to be out of danger, but it does not
appear that any neighbouring king claims superiority over, or
even equality with, him. The offensive weapons are spears
6 feet long, and shorter assegais for throwing, with broad-
bladed and well-worked viol-shaped and pointed knives (Pocué),
whose short neck acts as a handle.¶   For defensive armour
they have shields, flat parallelopipedons, externally of light
thin tree-bark, large enough to defend the whole body : the
inside is strengthened and kept in shape by neat wickerwork,
and before battle these defences are soaked in water. The
soldiers do not use bows and arrows, but the Muiza archers
skirmish in the van of the army, which is formed in three lines.**

The Cazembe prescribes the seasons for amusement, lest

* Pombe is a word generally used throughout Zanzibar and the Sawáhíl.
The kings of Yoruba also affected, like the Cazembe, to conceal themselves from
public view, especially whilst eating, drinking, or snuffing. When the King of
Dahome drinks, a curtain is held before him by his women.

† My friend Dr. Kirk informs me that the date-palm is there called Jindi.
The Devil's-palm (Raphia vinifera) is that most used on the East African Coast.
The best liquor is drawn from the oil-palm, but it injures the tree; the cocoa-nut
also gives, on the Western Coast at least, a first-rate wine : I do not like that
drawn from the date. Monteiro and Gamitto (p. 403) mention a wild palm which
the natives know as "Mediqua." It is evidently that of the text.

‡ In Dahome the punishment for drunkenness is very severe : it is regretable
that such is not the case throughout West Africa.

§ So called in Portuguese, because it is or was generally the name of some
saint.

‖ This style of defence is also African ; the text would well describe Abookuta.
The curious reader may consult the first of my volumes on Abeokuta and the
Camaroues Mountains. Agbome, the capital of Dahome, is girt by a fosse, but it
has no walls.

¶ These short handles, unfit for the European grip, remind us of the swords
and daggers of India and Abyssinia.

** Like the Roman hastati, principes, and triarii. I have described a similar
organization amongst the Watuta of the African Lake Regions. ('Lake Regions,'
&c., vol. ii. p. 77.)

there should be no work and all play, which would breed
troubles amongst his subjects and demoralise the soldiers.
Ivory selling is a royal prerogative, and only the nobles can
dispose of small quantities with his express permission : hence,
as I have said, all the cloth is presented by the traders to the
king.   He has copper and iron mines, and he is now at war
with a chief whose country produces tin.*   I showed our Caffro
visitors gold, which they recognised, calling it in their tongue
" money ; " all declared, however, that there was none in their
lands.   Perhaps they do not know how to extract the precious
metal, or it lacks value amongst them.   His officers are me-
chanics, workers in cloth and in iron.†

There is a great difference between the modest deportment,
the way of eating (comedimento), the songs, the dances, and
the drumming of these Caffres and those of our black neighbours
near the Rios de Sena.   A messenger from the kingdom of
Baróe,‡ whom I saw at Sena, harangued loudly for a good half-
hour, with immoderate gesticulation, in order to give a short
message.   On the contrary the Cazembe's envoy spoke little,
with great civility, and so softly, that not much was heard.
Before the latter addressed us, his interpreter, a Caffre slave of
Gonçalo Caetano Pereira, collected with his fingers, as is their
custom, a little earth, with which he rubbed his breast and
fore-arms, and this ceremony was repeated after he had translated the message.§   Our negroes drum a horrible thunder-
storm, and he plays best who beats the hardest : besides which
both men and women dance with extreme indelicacy.∥   The
drums of our guests are tapped like zabumbas (tomtoms) gently
and sweetly : this serves as an accompaniment to their songs
and dances, which are as graceful and decorous as can be
expected.   The chief did not honour me by dancing before
me : Catára and his spy did so before delivering their message.
After this the people came to compliment them, some em-
bracing him ; others touching with their little wands, in token

* In the original "latão," which the dictionaries explain "brass, a mixture of
copper and calaminaris stone "—but from African hills we do not dig brass.
There is probably antimony, and Monteiro and Gamitto twice mention tin
(estanho).   Dr. Kirk suggests that "latão" may signify "pewter," but it cannot
have that sense here.   I have alluded to antimony near Mombasah in ' Zanzibar :
City, Island, and Coast.'

† So in England, Wayland Smith, the blacksmith, was once adored.

‡ Probably the Barue of Dr. Livingstone (to the west of Sena and north of
Manica), the Dambire, or people of Barue.

§ This earth-rubbing is general amongst the more ceremonious tribes of
Africa, as those of Benin, Dahome, the Congo, &c.   Of course it is a token of high
respect.

∥ Again showing that the interior peoples are more civilised than the
maritime, who, from foreign civilisation, pick up only the vices.

of their inferiority, the lance or spear which they held in hand.

The Muiza jag the sides of their teeth, making them resemble those of a saw.* It must be hard work, without files, thus to spoil the work of Nature: they effect it, however, making the patient suffer severely, by means of a bit of iron, which they promised to give me.† I greatly admired their head-dresses (toques). The Cazembe's vassals proper, so to speak, neither chip their teeth nor use the toques, being soldiers, who have no leisure for such coquetries.

With regard to religion, we could only learn that the Muizas and the Cazembe's people have hollow idols (fetishes?)‡ in which they store their medicines before drinking them. A Caffre of this country, being at a house in Tete where some Muizas had danced, and where they had been rewarded with cloth and beads, invidiously remarked that they had consulted their wizards. The Muizas (I must observe that here both whites and blacks understand the strangers) indignantly rebutted the accusation, telling the man that they had no such habits. They do not affect the ill-omened "palavers" (milandos negregados§): in war time, when compelled by hunger, they are cannibals.

Catúra and another, his slave or his companion, declared, on being shown the compass, that they had seen that thing in "Gora." When asked how far it was from the Cazembe's country to Angola, they answered, with a vivacity which ensured

---

* I have stated ('Lake Regions of Central Africa,' vol. ii. p. 150) that, according to the Arabs, the Wabisha (Muizas) do not file their teeth nor raise a dotted line on the nose. Mr. Cooley, in his 'Review,' (Stanford, London, 1864), objects to my making the latter assertion. Did it never suggest itself to this writer that African tribes, especially the wandering and commercial, often change their customs, and that what was the fashion in 1832 is not so in 1859? Thus the Wanyika, behind Mombasah, gave up tattooing after the missionaries had lived amongst them for some years, and used to say, "Why should we spoil our skins?" I fear, however, that this is an amount of progress not to be expected from the obstinate advocate of the Central-African "Sea."

† A common bit of hoop-iron is generally used: the enamel must be removed by it from the sides of the teeth, but decay does not follow.

‡ Meaning that they have no God. All anthropologists are agreed upon this peculiarity of the Kaffir race. So in the tongue spoken about Tete, and understood by the Maraves and Chévras, "Murungo," the word generally translated "God," means thunder: Dr. Krapf ('Travels,' p. 168) gives the same signification to the Mulungu of the Wanyika race. So Dr. Livingstone ('Second Expedition,' chap. xxiii.) makes the people confound God and thunder in "Morungo."

§ Monteiro and Gamitto ('O Muata Cazembe,' pp. 7 and 91) tell us that Milando means a debt, an obligation contracted but not satisfied, a theft, a murder, a "pleito" or question, e.g., "Milando do Pombo," a process on account of adultery. The word appears to be the South African "Molatu," as given by Dr. Livingstone, chap. xviii.—"I have no guilt or blame (Molatu)."

my belief, that black men took three months and whites a little less. They also mentioned the Lucuale River, which, according to some maps, is an influent of the Cuanza (Coanza).

Gonçalo Caetano Pereira, knowing my wish to cross Africa, offered me his escort. I accepted it willingly, as he is the only trustworthy person; and, in the hope of promoting the work with which Her Majesty has honoured me, I made him Capitão-Mór of the Bush (Mixonga). He thanked me thus—"If your Excellency desires to visit Angola, you need not trouble yourself with these questions and with writing down answers: cross the Zambeze, trust yourself to me, and I will see you to the end of your journey, at my own expense if I could afford it." Such is the good effect of a measure which costs nothing but care to employ it at the right time. The Africans and the Americans would do good service to Her Majesty, if their rulers would bestow honours upon those deserving, and not disgust the people by selling them to the worthless.*

Before arriving at Tete, and examining these people, my intention was to set out from Zumbo, our westernmost settlement. I soon found that in Quilimane and Sena, as at Mozambique, people knew nothing of what had happened since 1793, and that their information could not be relied upon.† Therefore, I did not bring from Mozambique certain necessaries, such as white soldiers, good ammunition, arms, and similar supplies, of which nothing but the worst is here procurable.‡

(Signed)   D. Francisco José Maria
Tete, March 22, 1798.   DE LACERDA E ALMEIDA.

---

* These are memorable words, coming from a Brazilian.

† The same proved to be the case at Zanzibar: what these affirmed of the interior these denied; many misled me through ignorance, some for their own interests.

‡ The following is the official Act :—

"On February 27th, 1798, in this town of Tete, at the house and in the presence of His Excellency the Governor of the Province (Rios de Sena), Dr. Francisco José Maria de Lacerda e Almeida, and all the citizens and inhabitants of the same town, appeared the Envoys of the King Cazembe, to salute His Excellency the said Governor on the part of his master, and to offer friendship and trade to him and to them. On his side he promised that, in case of the road being stopped, or of merchants being plundered by any neighbouring chief on the way, his lord the King would send a force to clear it, we also sending our forces; that the Portuguese would be allowed to build a settlement, and to plant manioc near the Arangúa River, and that they should not send their goods one at a time but all together. [In fact, to form a caravan was a desideratum in East Africa.] This proposal was unanimously accepted, and a resolution was passed that the inhabitants would be guided by His Excellency the Governor, who took so lively an interest in the public good. Having thus agreed, they bound themselves in a bond before me the writer and signer of this instrument.

(Signed)   "José Sebastião d'Athaide,
"Public Notary."

Section III.

Deposition of the Bandazio* of the Cazembe, sent by his Mambo or liege lord, and then lodged in the house of Dionizio Rebello Carvo.

The above declares that, when sent by the Mambo Cazembe his master to the Kinglet (regulo) Muropoe,[†] during three months' march, he crossed in small canoes four streams like this (southern) Zambeze. The first was the Roapura,[‡] the second was the Mufira,[§] the third was the Guarava,[|] and the fourth was the Rofoi.[¶] In this distance, where the land belongs to the Varunda nation,** there are but four settlements, one on each

Here follow the signatures of those present, twenty-four names :—

José Sebastião d' Athaide (writer and signer of the document).
Dionizio de Araujo Bragança.
José Luiz de Menezes.
Manoel José Cardoso.
Pascoal José Rodrigues.
Placido José Rebello.
Joaquim José d' Oliveira.
João de Sousa.
Victorino José Gomes de Araujo.
José Francisco de Araujo.
João da Cunha Pereira.
Ignacio Gomes dos Santos.

Sebastião Rodruinho Mascarenhas.
Luis Nunes de Andrade.
Jose Luiz Rodrigues.
Caetano Bomedicto Lobo.
João Joaquim de Mattos.
Leandro José de Aragão.
Dionizio Rebello Carvo.
João Baptista Octaviano dos Reis Moreira.
Manoel Antonio de Sousa.
Gonçalo Caetano Pereira.
Nicolão Pascoal da Cruz, and
Sebastião de Moraes e Almeida.

---

* Monteiro and Gamitto (p. 14) explain " Bandazo " to be a domestic slave.

† This is the usual African style of exalting the master at the expense of truth.

‡ This stream has been before alluded to, under the name of Luapula. It was found by Dr. Livingstone to connect the Bangweolo, or Bemba, with the Moero Lake.

§ All African rivers have half-a-dozen names. We must, therefore, not be surprised if we do not find these words in other travels. The only check upon this march is that made by the two Pombeiros, sent in 1802 by Sr. Francisco Honorato da Costa. The Mufira, alias Rufira, Luvira, or " Luvivi," is a stream 12 fathoms wide, and laid down as an affluent of the Buapura or Luapula, crossed by Pedro João Baptista on the 35th day. According to Mr. Cooley, it is the great river Luviri, called by the Arabs Lufira, which flows into the Luapula about 100 miles S.W. or S.S.W. from the City of the Cazembe. Dr. Livingstone first throws it into the Tanganyika Lake; he now makes it rise, under the name of Luviri, on the western watershed of Conda Irugo, to the south of which is Lake Bangweolo: it thus takes the name of Lufira (Bartle Frere's ' Lualaba ') and falls into Lake Ulenge, or Kamalondo.

| This Guarava is evidently an influent of the great Lulua, or Lualaba, a stream 50 fathoms wide, and formerly laid down as one of the head waters of the Loeambyo or Upper Zambeze. It was crossed by Pedro on the 41st day of his march, and he found a large settlement there.

¶ The Rofoi must be another eastern feeder of the Great Lulua or Lualaba. We find in Dr. Livingstone's last labours a Ropneji influent, crossed by the Pombeiros.

** Pedro calls these people Viajantes Arundas and Viajantes da Alundas. Bowdich terms them the nation of the Varundas. Mr. Cooley, with extreme error, explains, by the Congo languages, Alunda or Arunda—elsewhere he tells us that the Alunda never pronounce the letter R—to mean mountaineers or bushmen. It is clearly Alunda, Dalunda, or Walunda, according to dialect, the great nation

river; and the people live on milho burro, maize (Zea Mays) and
manioc. From the lands of the Maropoe to those of the Mueneputo (a chief so called from the Portuguese), either on the east
or on the west, it is one month's journey, and whites (Muzengos)*
come up with their slaves to purchase ivory and captives. The
sea is large and salt, and from the sun-dried water they derive
the salt brought for their Mambo.† On the other side of this
sea-arm also appear large masted vessels, and houses as big as
ours. The further bank of the river (Zaire or Congo) is occupied
by the Congo kinglet,‡ a neighbour of the whites. Whatever
cloth he receives from them annually he divides with the
said Mueneputo and the Maropóe.

And the deponent further states that, after leaving the
Cazembe's country en route for Tete, he passed the first night
at the village of Muenepanda. After travelling through an
uninhabited country and canoeing across the Ruena River,§ he
spent the second night at Caunda, and the third day's journey
brought him to the house of Maruvo. The next stages were
Capangara, fourth day; the bank of the Mamuquendaxinto
(Mamukwend-ashinto or -achinto) stream or streamlet, fifth
day; Chydeira-majepo, sixth; Chipaco, seventh; Chiuheme-
apes, eighth; the bank of the Roarro Grande,‖ a river which
he crossed in a canoe, ninth; the Zambeze Grande (River
Chambeze), also requiring a ferry, tenth; Mugruva, eleventh;
Camango, twelfth; Xiárá (Shiyárá), thirteenth; Caramuga,
fourteenth; Macatupa, fifteenth; Parusoca, sixteenth. He
passed the night of the seventeenth on the bank of the Ruanga

ruled over by the Muáta ya Nvo: hence Lunda (Mr. Cooley's Roonda), the city of
the Cazembe. (See Dr. Livingstone's first map.)

* Muzungo is the Mundele, or Mondele, of the Congo, hence Dr. Livingstone's
"Dahindole, or Portuguese" ('First Expedition,' chap. six.). That traveller
uses "Bazunga" for Portuguese, and mistakes it for "half-castes;" whilst he
calls Englishmen Makoa (sing. Lekie). Muzungu is the general East African
name for a white man, Urungu being the land of the white man. Mr. Cooley
('Inner Africa Laid Open,' p. 35) explains Muzungu to mean "properly, wise
man:" at Zanzibar I have heard this derivation. Dr. Livingstone ('Second
Expedition,' xvi. p. 831) takes it from "ranga," to visit or wander, perhaps a
little too fanciful.

† Many African tribes (e. g., the Bube of Fernando Po) hold salt to be a bad
substitute for salt water. I have seen sea-water drunk even in the Cape Verde
Islands.

‡ The great and powerful Manicongo (Lord of Congo) was certainly not tributary to the Maropóe; nor have his smaller successors ever been dependent upon
the latter.

§ Luena, or Ruena, appears to be a general term for river in that part of
Africa. This one is the Loena of Monteiro and Gamitto. Mr. Ravenstein writes
Ruana and causes it to fall into the Luapula. Dr. Livingstone's first map makes
it a widening of the river south-west of the Cazembe's city. His last journey
makes it an eastern influent of the Luapula.

‖ Probably the Roaneze of Monteiro and Gamitto, a northern influent of the
Chambeze.

(Northern Arangòa) River, which is also passed by boats. During these days his only food was raw millet and beans of sorts. At the Ruanga River ends the nation of the Vaviza (Muizas) and begins that of the Marave.*

Through the Marave country the stages are. 1, Capangára; 2, Ruminda; 3, Mazanba; 4, the Jungle; 5, Chenene; 6, Inharuanga; 7, Caperimera (this is also found in Monteiro and Gamitto); 8, the Jungle; 9, the Sansa River (Sanhara of Monteiro and Gamitto?); 10, Mucanda; 11, Pasnicheiro; 12, the Dua rivulet, crossed on tree-trunk rafts; 13, the settlement of Carnore; 14, the Roven River,† also passed on tree-trunks; and 15, the Bar de Java (Jáua) where the Portuguese work gold.‡

(Signed)   DIONIZIO REBELLO CUNVO.

Tete, *March* 12, 1798.   Public Notary.

Deposition of a Muiza Caffre, touching the Roads to Angola.

From Tete to the Arangoa River the people are Maraves, and hostile to us. From that stream to the Cazembe's country live his subjects the Muizas. It is a march of two moons thence to the lands of his father Moropóe, through a country mostly waste. Settlements are not found, except on the banks of four distant rivers, which are crossed in canoes, there kept for ferrying purposes. From the Maropóe, after one moon and a half, we strike Angola, at a cove or bay, where are ships larger than the largest houses of white men here. The most inland nation is the Cabinda:§ it reaches as far as the Muropóe and the Cazembe, who, when they want slaves, attack it, and send the captives to Angola.‖

(Signed)   SEBASTIÃO DE MORAES E ALMEIDA.

Tete, *March* 10, 1798.

P.S.—It is probable that this Caffre speaks the truth. When

---

* The native thus acknowledges only two tribes, north the Muizas and south the Maraves. Monteiro and Gamitto (chap. iv.), insert between them the Chévas (Shevas) and the Macmbas. Mr. Cooley makes Anahera (plural of M'shera) to mean " the strangers or foreigners."

† Probably the Buia River of our modern maps, which receives the Arangòa, and which falls into the Zambeze at the Kebrabasa Rapids.

‡ In the text "o é llar em que mga os miners a nossa gente." "Ilar" means a gold-washing place. Dr. Livingstone ('First Expedition,' chap. xxxi.) says " when many masters united at one spot it was called a ' Bara.'"

§ The Cabindas of the Coast assured me that they extend but a short way into the interior. But there may be two " Cabindas." In the Brazil we find a tribe called " Cabundas," who are probably Angolese. Dr. Livingstone (' First Expedition,' chap. xix.) mentions a place called Cabinda, near Golungo Alto.

‖ Our first ocular information touching these countries was given by Pedro the Pombeiro, who travelled in 1806, and who returned to Angola about 1814. This is sixteen years after the date of the above documents.

E

asked if he knew the name of any stream in or near Angola, he
replied that there was a river called (Coanza) Quanza.

(Signed)   DR. FRANCISCO JOSÉ MARIA DE LACERDA
Tete, March 19, 1798.   E ALMEIDA.

SECTION IV.

*Instructions issued to the Members of the Cazembe Expedition by the Governor
of the Rios de Sena, Dr. Francisco José Maria de Lacerda e Almeida.*

Her Most Faithful Majesty—whom God preserve!—in her
Royal Letter of March 12, 1797, commanded me to ascertain
without delay if Central Africa contains any mountains capable
of sending forth the Cunene River, which falls into the Atlantic
a little below Cabo Negro.   I am also ordered to see whether
a short and easy communication for commerce between Portugal
overland to these Rios de Sena be possible: to report concerning the advantages of the country and the industry of the
peoples, and especially to seek the means of bringing these
infidels into the bosom of the Church—the principal motive
which urged Her Most Faithful Majesty to so costly an undertaking.   I now proceed to execute these orders.   And as, in
case of any accident happening to me, the Expedition might,
to the detriment of the service, be broken up for want of
instructions, I issue these directions, holding every one responsible for their being obeyed:—

1. The senior superior officer will command; but when
counsel is needed, all the members will assemble, and each will
be heard.

2. An account will be written daily, after each march,
recording and describing all adventures and occurrences; the
quality of the soil, productions, mines and villages; the manners
and customs of the people; the breadth, depth, and direction of
the rivers, relative to one travelling from these parts; the fittest
articles for barter; and, finally, everything seen, even though
it appear trivial—diffusiveness being preferable to over conciseness.

3. Arrived at the (lower) Aruângoa River, the party will
select a proper site* for the settlement desired by the Cazembe,
and will carefully note the advantages to be derived by it from

---

* In 1824 a colony was founded at this unpropitious spot, by Colonel José
Francisco Alves Barbosa, Governor of the Rios de Sena.   The land was bought
from the Mambo Muáine, and in 1827 a small force of soldiers was sent there.
These were withdrawn after two years, and the colony was allowed to go to ruin.
We can hardly, therefore, say that the Portuguese have not explored these parts,
which are about on a parallel with the northern part of the Nyassa Lake.

trading with the Muiza tribe which there begins. The Lieutenant of Sena, José Vicente Pereira, will descend that river in the best canoe procurable, to trade with the Caffres. He will keep a journal, like that recommended in No. 2, and he will avoid disembarking at populous places, lest he be insulted by the barbarians, of whose dispositions we are not ignorant, and lest we lose the results of a valuable discovery. He must register all such important information as the number of days spent in making Zumbo, and the approximative total of leagues from his point of departure to the end of the voyage whence he will regain his post. His Diary will be forwarded to the Commandant of Tete, who will transmit it to the Governor of the Province, and supply a copy to his Excellency the Governor-General of Mozambique. It must also be shown and another copy must be supplied to the chief Captain of Zumbo. It is not supposed that he will require to purchase provisions, as a few days will probably place him at our colony of Zumbo; but should he want anything, he must put on shore two or three Caffres to buy necessaries in the villages, and be careful on no account to land. If the river called by the Muizas "Zambeze," prove navigable during the dry season, and flow to the right of one marching towards the country of the Cazembe (i. e., from north-west to south-east), the party would do well to descend it; and in so doing they will pay due regard to all the directions given above, and register whatever occurs to them as likely to benefit the Royal service. That river is, they say, the Shire, or a branch of it which falls into our (i. e., the southern) Zambeze a little below Sena. If not, it must be the stream which discharges itself into the ocean a little north of Quilimane. From that point he will transmit to the Commandant and to the Governor-General a copy of his Diary, together with all the information which he may have collected touching the transport of such goods as are procurable amongst the Muizas and in the African interior.

4. Should the said Zambeze prove to be not navigable, the lieutenant will send his Journal when he reaches the river upon whose banks is founded the city of the Cazembe. This, the Muizas assort flows to the right (south-east) and receives their Zambeze.

5. But, if the said river of the Cazembe flow to the left (south-westward), and if it may possibly be the Cunene or another and a branch stream, then Captain João da Cunha and the pilot Bernardino shall descend it with the compass and sextant, Crown property. They will learn the use of these instruments on the march, and they must trace the river according to the method taught to them. They will keep a

E 2

detailed Diary, noting the number of leagues daily navigated; the respective distances of Caffre villages on its banks, and whether the natives know of the Portuguese or any other white nation. In so doing they will take every precaution against being insulted. Arrived at the mouth of the river, they will observe what sized vessels it can admit; they will sound the bar, survey the channels, prospect the port establishment, and take the latitude with other necessaries, remembering that Cape Negro is in S. lat. 10° 8'.

6. Having examined the river mouth, they will await favourable weather for running up the coast, as far as Benguela, in rafts or in any craft that may be procurable; a voyage which may be accomplished in two or three days. Thence they will pass to Angola, and report their good service to His Excellency the Governor-General of that province, who will doubtless lay the names of the Captain and the Pilot before Her Majesty. Intelligence of the movements of the Expedition should also be sent by land to His Excellency. Should the two travellers be unable to go up the coast by want of a vessel, they will return by the same road; and, after reaching the city of the Cazembe, they will make a full report to His Excellency the Governor-General of Angola, that Her Majesty may receive information with the least delay.

7. They will perform their land-marches under the safe-conduct of the country Caffres, who are said to be peaceful, and to trade with the Portuguese. Their expenses will be paid by what they take with them, and if that be not sufficient, by the Royal Treasury of Benguela or of Angola.

8. This undertaking being of the utmost importance, all members of the Expedition are hereby ordered to lend it every aid in their power, and will be held personally responsible, should it fail by any fault of theirs.

9. The chief sergeant, Pedro Xavier Velasco, and the Lieut.-Colonel Pedro Nolasco Vieira de Araujo, shall also be despatched to Angola. Thence the latter, being the fittest person, shall proceed to Lisbon, and shall report to Her Majesty the details of their journey from Tete to the country of the Cazembe, and from that point to Angola. And I leave to His Excellency the Governor-General of Angola the choice of sending to Portugal with the said Velasco (Nolasco) the above-mentioned chief sergeant. One of them must return here with a full Diary.

10. But if the river in the Cazembe's country flow to the right, then the members of the Expedition will advance as far as they please, and will carry out these orders by descending the first stream which flows to the left. The branch expeditions concluded, the remainder will return to Tete, and

there report themselves to the Governor-General of Mozambique.

11. The greatest care will be taken to economise Crown property, and detailed accounts of receipts and disbursements are to be laid before the Junta or Council.

12. The quantity of Crown cloth required for the return march will be calculated, and the remainder will be bartered for ivory. This, on arrival at Tete, must be handed over to the Junta, which will determine what is to be done with it.

13. They will enter into a friendly alliance with the Cazembe, and settle and sign with him the terms of a commercial treaty as favourable as possible to ourselves. They will repress all disorderly conduct, robbery, and violence on the part of the troops and the Caffres of the Expedition, lest they lose the favour of the king, who might treat them as enemies, and prevent their passing on to Angola.

14. The better to obtain leave to make this journey with the necessary help, the king should be assured that our thus opening communication by land or by the Cunene River will be to his benefit as well as to ours. His ivories must be sent for sale to those Rios (de Sena) where they fetch the highest prices. The Western Coast will afford a better market for his copper, his "latão,"* and his slaves.

15. The Expedition will act upon two well-defined principles. Firstly, it is Her Majesty's desire that an easy line of communication should be traced between the two coasts, and the best is, of course, *viá* the rivers. Secondly, they must do their utmost to discover, for the readier exploration of the interior, some stream flowing from the Cazembe's country into our Zambeze, or falling into the sea between Mozambique and Quilimane. And I expect from men who are ambitious of the glory which must result from such a feat, that they will set the best example to their inferiors, and will supply all deficiencies found in my instructions. The land is a *terra incognita*, and my experience in Mato-Grosso of the Brazil has taught me how little reliable is information collected under such circumstances. I, therefore, cannot trust to the depositions of Manoel Caetano Pereira, who thought of nothing but of his trade.

16. In the various councils of the Expedition the members will commit to writing the orders which I leave them, the difficulties which may prevent these orders being executed, and the reasons of those who are of different opinion; so that, after the papers shall have been placed before Her Majesty, merit

---

* This word has before been explained.

may be rewarded, and disobedience, cowardice, and remissness
may be punished as they deserve.

And, as it may happen that I have not time to correct these
orders and instructions, I direct, in the name of Her Most Faithful Majesty, that this rough draught be held valid.

(Signed)   DR. FRANCISCO JOSÉ MARIA DE LACERDA

Tete, June 18, 1798.   E ALMEIDA.

(55)

CHAPTER I.

THE DEPARTURE.— THE TRAVELLERS REACH THE LUPATA DA JÁUA.

"Dirige, Domine Deus meus, in conspectu tuo viam meam."   "Ut cognos-
camus in terrâ viam, in omnibus gentibus salutare tuam."

PSALMS v. 9; LVI. 8.

ON March 12, 1797, Her Most Faithful Majesty—whom God
defend!—having commanded me to ascertain the possibility
of overland transit between the eastern and the western coasts
of Africa, I sought at Mozambique, Quilimane, Sena, and Tete,
for information touching those hitherto untrodden lands. But
all was in vain. Those consulted concerning an enterprise not
yielding in importance to the discovery of Asia, only represented to me its impossibility; their reasons were those of men
who choose the Royal service rather as a profession that pays
than of men who love glory, and who would be useful to the State.
I had resolved, in the present year, to visit Maniça (Manisa),*
as the Crown had ordered, and then to make Zumbo our
westernmost settlement, where possibly satisfactory notices concerning the best and safest route could be procured. This
failing, I should next year have pushed on to the interior with
good guides, and by the shortest paths, making astronomical
observations, and thus I should have done my best to carry
out the Royal commands, either pacifically or, if necessary,
by other means.

But Providence smiled upon the righteous and benevolent
intentions of our august Sovereign. Thirty-three days after
my arrival at Tete, I was visited by certain envoys from the Court
of the King Cazembe in the distant interior, one Chinimbu
(Chinhimba), a Muiza, and the other Catára of the same race as
the Cazembe, namely the Arunda.† I took down their depositions, and they are given above, together with those of a native

---

* A country lying to the N.W. of Sofala. Dr. Livingstone erroneously writes
it Maniça (Manika), and in his 'First Expedition' informs us that it lies
three days N.W. of the Gorongozo Mountains, and that it is the richest gold
country known in Eastern Africa. At Sofala, its nearest point, pieces of wrought
gold have been dug up (they say) near the fort and in the gardens. Hence it has
been identified with the ancient Ophir—a point, however, upon which opinions
greatly differ. The "Ophir literature" would fill volumes; and we have not yet
heard the last of "Gold in South Africa."

† Vulgarly Londa; the word has been discussed in the preceding pages.

of these parts (the Rios de Sena), and what I could obtain from
other strange Caffres who were lodged in the houses at Tete.*

Short was the time for organising an expedition, or for finding
good porters, trustworthy soldiers, ammunition, and country-
money, Caffre cloth (fato Cafral), beads, and other necessaries;
yet I resolved at once, and at all risks, to carry out the Royal
orders. In one point I was fortunate; three or four hundred
Caffres were expected at Tete, some composing the escort of
Chinimbu and Catára, others bringing their own ivories, and
others carrying tusks presented to certain Portuguese inhabitants
of the town.

On March 10th and 12th, I wrote officially to the factory and
commandants of Sena and Quilimane, directing them to purchase from the resident merchants all that could not be obtained at our ill-provided factories in Tete. I offered to repay the
loan in kind by drafts upon the Royal treasury at Mozambique.
They refused, however, and nothing was to be done without
compulsion, a proceeding of which the Crown could not have
approved. The Colonel of Maniça (Menisa) Militia, Jeronymo
Pereira, who passes for the most respectable man at Sena, proved
himself a knave, not only by taking exorbitant prices for his
cloth, but also by supplying this primary necessary in Caffre
travel of so wretched a quality that it was well-nigh useless.†
Certain capotins,‡ sent from the Sena factory, were equally bad,
and of 440 only 175 bore the Royal mark. Those whom I consulted assured me that, when cloth for the Treasury is bought at
auction from the lowest bidder, the sellers send in superior
samples and make the bad pay for the over-good.

As time pressed, and I could not procure the necessary cloths
and Ardeans,§ I resolved to punish the knavery of Jeronymo
Pereira by directing the Factor of Sena to take from his warehouses the best cloth, to be repaid in kind from Mozambique.
I also warned him that he himself should be at the expense of
sending back his vile stuffs to Tete.

Although, however, the supplies from Sena and Quilimane
were repeatedly ordered up in time for me to set out about

---

* Often written Tette. Dr. Livingstone prefers Tette, and explains the word
('Second Expedition,' chap. xxiv.) to mean "a place where the water rushes over
rocks," in fact, the Brazilian "Cachoeira."

† A footnote informs us that a complaint against this man was written; but that
this document with two other papers, besides a map and a second diary, were
lost.

‡ The Capotim, according to Monteiro and Gamitto, is a blue stuff, valued when
good. Dr. Kirk informs me that it is "two fathoms, a common measure among
natives in their bargains." Dr. Livingstone ('Second Expedition,' p. 57) says that
two yards of cloth, the fathom, were once worth sixpence.

§ A blue stuff like "Zuarts," but differing in size.

May 25th, they were delayed by the river-floods, by the loitering of the unsuperintended Caffres, by the indolence of the whites, and by other hindrances.   Doubtless, my outfit would have been cheaper if brought from Mozambique, and I should, if allowed to go there, have found better soldiers than Caffre porters, who are more used to the bow than to the gun.   But this would have involved a delay of two years, before transport could have been sent down to me by the Cazembe; whereas, my orders were to set out at once after arrival.

I assured myself that the ivory formerly carried by the Mujáo (Wabiáo) to Mozambique had greatly fallen off in quantity, from being sent to Zamzimbar * (Zanzibar Island and coast): and as all or most of it comes from the Cazembe's country, I saw that it would be better for him if he sold it to us, not to the Caffres.   This could be done only by availing myself at once of the king's kind intentions, and by showing him that we can afford to pay more than the natives, who give only a little cloth, and that cut up; whereas, as his message shows, he wants "whole cloth, as it comes from afar."†

On the other hand, I saw that, despite the favourable accounts of trade brought by Manoel Caetano Pereira, our people would do nothing to win the good opinion of the Cazembe; and this, too, at a time when we were about to visit him.   I knew that he, being suspicious, like other Caffres, would prefer the certain to the uncertain, and still sell to the Mujáo—a practice which would injure us, if at any future time we wished to trade with him.   Moreover, a Moçambaz, or slave-factor of D. Francisca Josefa de Moura e Menezes, who, after delivering a harangue from his mistress to the Cazembe, had reached Tete on May 13th, informed me that he had found a good market for buying ivory, copper, and slaves.   I therefore issued a proclamation, from which, as may be seen in Compendium G,‡ nothing resulted.

I soon found myself in fresh difficulties.   An exact muster proved that, of the 300 or 400 Maizas, at most 100 were avail-

---

* Mr. Cooley, who appears to have read some of these papers, asserts—"In 1831 there were no trading routes to the Cazembe but those from the West and South. There was no road Eastwards." It was to close this Eastern road that both the Portuguese expeditions were made. "Mponni, near the Querimba Islands," means the Zanzibar Coast, as Mr. Cooley might have found had he taken the trouble to read my reports. This name also occurs under the form of Impoáne in Monteiro and Gamitto (p. 300), who, however, did not quite understand the word.

† This was especially impressed upon me during my first visit to Dahome. Those who know the practices of the coast tribes acting as "middlemen" cannot wonder at it.

‡ These two documents are lost—possibly stolen.

able as porters, the others having died or disappeared, whilst
some refused to carry packs. The Sena Caffres had also fled
without a cause, and I expected those of Tete to follow their
bad example, because their masters were frightening them. As a
last resource, I made the owners responsible for their slaves.
There was no chance of my collecting more porters. The first
levy had been raised with moderation and impartiality, yet,
though many of the masters owned more than 200 "captives," *
and some held valuable Crown lands, they thought much of letting
me have ten or fifteen, begging me to be content with fewer as
the men leave labour to the more industrious women.

In these straits, I had recourse to the heroine of these
lands, D. Francisca Josefa de Moura e Menezes, widow of two
officers who had held the captainship. Her boats, and other
possessions, are ever at the service of the Crown, and she takes
a pride in the Royal service. She replied that, to her legal
share of forty, she would add sixty, and retain only those absolutely necessary; also, that the negresses, who were her chief
stock, were scattered, and working at the mines of Maxinga,†
where I should pass, and where the rice for our journey was
stored.

As the sixty men did not appear, I asked D. Francisca if, in
case of need, I could use negresses; she answered, that they
would serve me as well as, if not better than men.‡ Availing myself of the opportunity, I told her that if she could
supply the necessary number of negresses, it would be duly
reported as a great service to the Crown. This request the
lady granted with certain remarks, which must be reserved for
an especial report. She at once despatched her freedmen
(Butongas) § with her negresses, and even her house attendants,

---

* A salve for the conscience of Roman Catholics, who never bought slaves, but
ransomed prisoners of war. Protestants have until lately found gold the best
salvo. It must be noted that the levies in the text were legal from persons
holding Crown property, the "captives" being required for the public service.
† Serra Maxinga (Mashinga), five short marches N.N.E. of Tete. Monteiro
and Gamitto do not explain the word. Mr. Cooley (loc. cit., 43) says "Mashinga
means' the lash' an appropriate name for "a slave depôt." But it was not a
slave depôt; and, firstly, the name is Mashinga, not Machinga. Secondly, Mashinga does not belong to the tongues of the Eastern Coast (in Kisawahili it is un-
intelligible), but to the Western or Congo branch. The negroes in Brazil still
threaten one another with "Machinga no Malako,"—i.e., fustigation on the seat of
honour.
‡ The Donna was quite right, as I recorded in 'First Footsteps in East
Africa.'
§ Negroes who live on, and work in, Crown property. The Butonga are probably some conquered nation: the boatmen on the Lower Zambeze use Bororo and
Batonga to express north and south. The holders of "prazos" are generally
called "Colonos" or tributary native landholders, who do all the cultivation, and
who pay rent in kind.

to distribute amongst the sixty Caffres and their wives, the rice
and the loads lying at Tete.

THE JOURNEY.

July 3, 1798.—Fearing delay from other troubles, I set out
for Nhaufa Fatiola, an estate lying north of the Zambeze River,
and distant about three-quarters of a league from Tete; where
we had been stationed since the end of June. Our general
direction lay north, through Sonte and Cube—Crown properties*
like Nhaufa—and through the estates of Caboamanga, Pequizo,
Condo, and Chibanbo, to Mitondo, our nighting place.† Beyond
Sonte there is broken ground, and the path winds up narrow,
hill-girt valleys. Our day's march lay through troublesome
thorns, and over lands left incult by want of hands, or by the
laziness of their owners; the only clearings and signs of population were about the huts of the estates above alluded to.
The Caffre men rarely touch the ground, and their women sow
but little. Part of the crop goes to the lord of the manor,
part is made into their bread, a kind of dough (massa) like the
Angú, or porridge‡ of the Brazil, and the rest is brewed into
a beer (pombe), with which they intoxicate themselves, and of
which much is wasted in their funeral superstitions. I wondered
not a little at the universality of these death offerings, which
Captain Cook found in the islands lately discovered by him,
and which I myself observed amongst the Roman Catholic
"Indians" of the Spanish province of Moxos.§ It is likely that
this tribute to the departed ‖ is the result of the fear of death
instinctive to the uncultivated, and is, in fact, a propitiatory
offering, for, as Pliny said, "Timor fecit Deos." This waste and
indolence explain the yearly famines to which the Caffres are
subject, even in fertile places.

Some porters deserted, kindly leaving upon the path their
packs, which were carried by the bearers of our hammocks

---

* The Prazo fateosim (emphyteosis) is, in Mozambique, land held on condition
of making certain improvements.

† These are names of estates often varying. Mitondo is doubtless the "Ma-
tando" belonging to D. Filippa Maria de Moura Meneses, mentioned by Monteiro and Gamitto.

‡ A stirabout made of Fuba (maize-meal), and much used by Brazilians. It is
the Ugali of Unyamwezi, where "sitting upon Pombe" is equally well known.

§ Or Mojos, west of the Rio Grande, one of the headwaters of the Great Rio
Madeira.

‖ The traveller speaks of Almas, in Portuguese souls or ghosts. His explanation is sound and philosophical without the customary shallowness and tradition.
Dr. Livingstone ('First Expedition,' chap. xvii.) unconsciously explains the negro
belief when he says "they appear to imagine the souls to be always near the
place of sepulture."

(Manxilas). Such flights are fatal to progress, and are the
worst of examples. I am in constant dread of fresh cases being
reported to me.[*] We could not reach the place where the
cooks had been ordered to await us on the second day; consequently our suppers and beds were such as the reader may
imagine. This had, however, one good effect; it was well that
certain of the party, who were used to every comfort, should at
once see the giant's finger, so as not to find the figure, when it
might chance to appear, over-gigantic.

July 4th.—We were thrown into confusion by the sudden
flight of more than thirty bearers, who left Crown property
to be plundered.[†] Upwards of twenty belonged to D. Paulina
Anna do Sousa Bragança.[‡] This lady, when her quotum had
been fixed, showed herself so recalcitrant, that I had sent the
Reverend Father Francisco João Pinto, then staying with his
brother, the Commandant of Tete, to declare, *in verbo sacerdotis*,
my unwillingness to punish her, but my determination to carry
out the Royal command. D. Paulina yielded, but with delay
and bad grace. This desertion, which seems to be an old practice amongst the Caffres attached to Crown property, compelled
me to go a little more than a league further on to "Inhacengeira," where the Expedition was expecting me. Thereon I sent
Captain João da Cunha Pereira to Pequizo, where D. Paulina
was living, with directions to show that I had ordered the
Factor of Tete to sell her lands by public auction, if the
twenty fugitives were not forthcoming. I sent the same order
about a man who had not supplied his share of four slaves.
"Inhacengeira" is the last of the Crown lands to the north
of the Zambeze River, and here we enter the Marave tribe.
The valleys are rich, and the occupant (foreiro) [§] might, with
industry, which, however, he wholly wants, make it one of the
richest establishments near Tete.

5th.—As sailors in a terrible storm throw cargo overboard
to lighten the ship, so we reduced our goods to the most
needful. I began reforms at the provisions, and divided our
salt amongst the soldiers and porters, reserving a little for
general use; when it is finished we must do without it, as they
say "hungry men want no mustard." A box of tea was distri-

---

* There is no African explorer who will not feel the full force of this sentence.

† The traveller carried with him a trading outfit of about 6000 cruzados or
700l., partly Crown property and partly belonging to the Portuguese merchants of
Sena and Tete.

‡ Montoiro and Gamitto (p. 438) explain how it is that these estates called
" Prazos da Corôa " are held principally by women, and they justly term the thing
an " Instituição pessima."

§ One who pays a quit rent to the Crown.

buted to the officers, also a case of spirits: I remained without
any, as, despite the cold weather, I cannot touch strong liquor.
Besides other things, two kegs and a large pot of vinegar remained behind—acids disorder the stomach, and roast meat
is meetest for health.* Seeing my party downhearted, I represented to them the honour and glory of our undertaking,
and concluded by saying that anyone who liked, might return
home. They then recovered some spirit; but only four
members of the Expedition betrayed no weakness, namely, the
chaplain, the chief-serjeant, Pedro Xavier Velasco, the lieutenant-colonel of militia, Pedro Nolasco d'Araujo, and Antonio
José da Cruz, fort-lieutenant of Tete.

We spent the day "subsisting" the people; like a spirit
I was everywhere, working hard as an example to idlers. In
the evening the abandoned loads were brought up by the
Caffres whom I had sent back. Lastly came the captain, with
a report that D. Paulina, terrified by my threats, had gone to
Tete, in order to send her negroes at once. We shall see the
result.

6th.—I spent a sleepless night, thinking of and fearing desertion, and so it again came to pass—thirty-four more porters
fled. My foresight and firmness prevented despair getting
the better of me. To the Caffre care-taker of the Crown property
I entrusted the least valuable objects which were to be brought
on by the slaves of D. Paulina and her brother—the proud
fool at Sena of whom I spoke in the other diary.† I left some
personal effects, as justice should begin at home, and I looked
forward to reaching Maxinga. My firm resolution to push on,
despite the lateness of the season, calms my mind and enables
me to endure these vexations, as the storm-tossed mariner
consoles himself with exaggerating the pleasures of the port.

Disgusted with the place, I marched on till we entered the
lands of the Marave,‡ our false friends and fast foes, whose only end
is to fleece us of cloth. We passed three little villages, where
the males, old and young, stood scattered, and without showing
fight; but each armed with his bow and arrows.§ Caffres,
from their childhood, never even visit a neighbour without
these weapons. What a well-made, finely-limbed, graceful race
it is! I was never tired of looking at them.

---

* This merriment is "não canny"—of course it is the result of excitement.
The traveller was unwise to leave behind such "medical comforts," and to load
himself with cloth. But it is the error of almost all young African explorers.

† It was lost or rather stolen, because it reflected upon the people.

‡ Of this celebrated tribe it is here sufficient to remark that the name Marave
or Maravi is properly the title of the numerous petty chiefs.

§ I have described an exactly similar scene amongst the Wazaramo of East
Africa ('Lake Regions,' vol. i. chap. iii. p. 71).

Some elders came up to beg presents,—the tribute paid by Portuguese travellers, and which is regulated by the quantity of goods and by the strength of the party. Thus little can be gained by the poor beginner going to a distant but good market; he must, *nolens volens*, pay blackmail in cloth to a swarm of Fumos, or district-chiefs,* for the reputed "avanies" ("palavers," Milandos) of their subjects.

The soil appears excellent; it is a plain, or rather a prairie, abounding in streams of the purest water, and from afar we sight hills higher than those of Tete. Who would credit, without seeing it,† that our colonista, having such fine lands, with slaves and vassals (Mossenses) annually paying tribute of everything, must yet, at the end of the year, buy grain from the Maraves? Had it not been for this resource, and for the supplies of Sena and its dependencies, Tete must have been ruined by the famines general of late; the Marave lands however, being cool and fresh, always produce something, even when the rains are wanting.

But Tete appears an infant colony in almost everything. It cannot even tan leather, and it ignores soap-boiling and sugar-making. These articles we might supply to Mozambique, instead of importing them from Goa. And they often fail, as during this and the last year, when there was no leather even for heel-pieces; the expense also greatly increases—so soap, whose ordinary price is $8 to $10, has risen to $18 milreis fortes.‡ Who would expect the sugar of Mozambique to come from Rio de Janeiro and Batavia?

By way of shaming these people, I manufactured three pounds of soap: the bad lime and ashes gave it a black colour; still, it washed as well as any other. I also made a little indigo. As the year was very rainy, and sugar-cane is planted by them in damp ground, it was necessary to defer, until late in the season, ex-

---

* The word is properly written Mfumo.

† "Vêr para crer" is an idiomatic Portuguese saying, mostly said with an *arrière-pensée* of Saint Thomas.

‡ Per arroba of 32 lbs. I presume. In Monteiro and Gamitto (p. 2) we find that $40 000 milreis fortes (strong) are equal to $100 000 milreis fracos (weak); the former therefore (= 4s. 2d.) contains 2½ of the latter, each equal to 1s. 8d. In 1852, by order of Government, $100 000 milreis (fortes) of Portugal were worth $410 000 milreis fracos of Mozambique. The latter currency was wholly abolished by the home authorities in 1853, but it is not so easy to alter the customs of a distant colony. Dr. Kirk informed me (1865) that the coins of Mozambique are still of different value, at different times, in different places, and that in his day 280 reis of the province were valued at 20 reis of Lisbon. Thus $1 400 provincial would be equal to 100 reis (= one testão = 6d.) at the capital. The Madeiran milreï fraco is = 4s. 2d, and the milreï forte is 20 per cent. more. At Cape Verde the milreï forte contains 225 reis, equal to 1000 fracos, and the dollar (4s. 2d.) passes for 920 reis fortes.

tracting the molasses (melaço or melado), which is used for sweetening tea and coffee and for coarse confectionary, not eaten in public. They boil down the juice until it assumes a certain thickness, in little copper pots, having none larger; and, after whipping it to the consistency of sugar, they use it without other preparation. Unable to remain at Tete whilst this stuff was being made, I resolved to see what could be done with irrigated cane. The season, however, was exceptionally wet, and when arrived at Sonte, I found, to my astonishment, water flooding the fields. Of four little loaves which I had manufactured, one only retained a small quantity of coagulated sugar, almost all of which escaped through the orifice of the loaf-mould. This remnant I clayed, and had the pleasure of seeing that, although there was not time enough for purifying the whole, it produced two finger-breadths of good sugar.

These digressions are not unnecessary. Amidst the multiplicity of my engagements, many things run the risk of being forgotten. The Crown, however, must see, not only that the reports about Sena are greatly exaggerated, not to say false, but also that the colony, if provided with able handicraftsmen, and at a certain expenditure of money, will in time become valuable.

I posted sentinels, with orders to hail one another every five minutes, and thus to scare away Marave thieves. The people cannot be trusted, and mine must learn the duty. Were they soldiers, our danger would be less; enough to say, that when they were firing two volleys at Tete, my heart sank within me—the greater part, dreading the recoil, remained with their guns at full-cock, whilst the others did not know how to load. Such is the state of the soldiery in these provinces, and the officers are as good as the men.[*]

7th.—The porters set out at sunrise, I at 7.30 A.M. Half-an-hour after noon, we awaited at a brook those who were behind. Later in the day, the lieutenant came on, and reported that all the porters had halted near a rivulet, distant three-quarters of a league from this place, and that when ordered to advance, they had flown to their inevitable bows and arrows. I neither wondered at, nor cared for, the flight of five Caffres who, shortly after starting, left their loads, including my clothes-box. My mental anxiety is that, to-night, despite all our vigilance, they will disappear in a body. In order to remedy this evil, should it befall us, we must leave early for Maxinga, and thence despatch the necessary aid.

---

[*] African travel repeats itself. This scene is a counterpart of one enacted by the Baloch mercenaries before our march from the Kaole village on the Zanzibar coast.

To-day we passed only two small villages of Maraves. Others are probably off the road, as I often saw men standing by the wayside, and looking at us. According to the interpreter, they were surprised to see me riding in a small palanquin, declaring that the Dive, their king, though a great man, never travels in a house, as they call my conveyance.

8th.—At 2.30 P.M. I reached the Muxinga estate,* at the beginning of the valley ending with the Lupata (gorge). Here the negresses of D. Francisca, and a few others belonging to two Tete men, were digging for gold. My multitudinous and ever-growing perplexities made me at once send all the Caffres who were found ready, to aid those left behind. Happily they were not required; and on the next day, the whole party arrived safe. I chose out two hundred able-bodied women, but, for reasons aforesaid, I could not visit the mines.†

10th.—Despite my care to feed the Caffres, who are not supposed to fly from work or blows after meals, last night fifty-two of them deserted. When thrown into bitterest perplexity by the news, I was informed that thirty-seven more had fled. Those who know my activity and zeal for the service of the Crown will appreciate my affliction: yet they will do me the justice to believe that I was resolved to push forward at all risk, and never to return until absolutely necessary.

I sent forward the chief captain of the bush (Mixoaga), Gonçalo Caetano Pereira, with as many Caffres as could be raised, to prevent the carriers deserting on the line of march, which, however, many did during these three days. They walk like cattle, but even in a more straggling way. The reinforcements from Tete have not arrived; the season advances. I fear that fatigue and anxiety of body and mind will induce sickness, so to-morrow we leave this place.

14th.—"Qui confidit in Deo non confundetur," saith the Psalmist. As I was mounting my palanquin at 11 A.M. some twenty-three Caffres arrived with the loads left at "Nhassengeira" ("Inhacengeira," July 4th). I was as joyful as if they had been twenty-three thousand. I sent with them our necessaries, reserving a few bearers for the loads abandoned by the party of Gonçalo Caetano Pereira. At one mile and a half beyond Maxinga a faithful Caffre slave of the chief captain was waiting to inform me that in a neighbouring Marave village lay thirty loads without porters. I sent there the Lieutenant

---

* The latitude of Maxinga as laid down by the traveller is S. 15° 19' 15", about the parallel of the Shirwa Lake. He gives the variation N.W. 22° 50' 40".

† This also alludes to some papers now lost. The negroes of this part of Africa will not be looked at, during work, by any except the owner of the mine. The stranger's eye, they say, makes the gold disappear.

Antonio José da Cruz and the adjutant, with the few remaining
negroes; and presently arrived the medicine-chest, one of my
clothes-boxes, a little tin case, containing four flasks of coffee
and butter, and two canteens of wine, bought for my especial
use. I could here dilate, were time at my disposal, upon the
insolence of these slaves, who rely for impunity upon a multitude of neighbouring chiefs, ever glad to receive them, however
numerous; upon the easy flight to Crown lands, whose occupants
welcome them, and, finally, upon the mismanagement of the
Caffre trade. None but a company, aided by good chiefs and
soldiers, can prevent these kinglets, especially those subject to
the Imperador,* from plundering and encouraging desertion.
But what manner of man must the Governor of Tete be? I
know him not. I can only say that he must be active, wise,
prudent, and gifted with all good qualities.

15th.—The Maraves came for their loads, but seeing my
position they would not carry them till paid. After long
haggling, I gave to each a capotim (two blue cottons), with the
chance of losing all by desertion that night; this, however, the
Caffre of Gonçalo Caetano Pereira assures me they will not do.
Other Maraves being persuaded to join by these good terms, I
divided the remaining loads between them and the Tete Caffres,
of whom three had fled during the dark hours. Nothing now
remained but a box of crockery destined for the Cazembe, and
three arm-chairs, for which he had applied, a case of kitchen-
butter for immediate use, and a barrel of gunpowder. I did not
regret the loss of the latter, for, though bought by the Crown
at the highest price in Mozambique, it was not worth its
carriage.

Giving orders for these stores to be forwarded, I left Maxinga.
After marching two leagues, we arrived at the largest village
yet seen, and there I was surprised to find the people who had
been sent from our halting-place on the 12th instant. The
soldiers declared that the Caffres had refused to advance, and
that on the same day, after marching only half a league, they
had insisted upon halting at the village, threatening the guard
with their arrows if compelled to proceed. That was credible,
as the same had lately been done to the officers. Present
punishment would only frustrate my plans: it must be deferred
till after our return to Tete.

I cannot wonder at the porters, whose nature is such. As the
Caffres are the slave factors, whom their masters send to the
lands of these chiefs, and are here lords of their own liberty,
they march when they like, they carry many women at their

* Meaning the "Unde, Imperador dos Maraves."

F

employer's expense, and finally they do as they please. I
summoned the head men of the porters (mucazambos),* and
harangued them, after which they promised more activity.
But a short experience has taught me that those men, of
vicious nature and uncurbed by law human or divine, make
and break their promises at the same moment. We shall see if
I am mistaken as to the result of my sermon.

16th.—The Maraves ran away, and, unluckily for them,
one was captured. This they say will be the source of quarrels
and of serious "palavers" (milandos), as the father and relations
of the prisoner must turn against the runaways. Although all
are born thieves, robbery amongst themselves is severely
punished, though I know not if a general plundering is held
to be a crime. Happily appeared other Maraves, who agreed
to receive their pay at Java (Jáua).

At 8.30 A.M. I set out, when certain Maraves, standing by the
wayside to see our large party pass by, seized and carried off two
boys. The negresses screamed, my people rushed to the noise,
a soldier fired in the air, and the two little negroes (here
called bichos) † thus escaped captivity amongst the Caffres. I
halted at a village (Jáua) a little before coming to the Lupata.‡
This is the name of a place where the mountains almost meet,
forming a valley which we entered when arriving at Maxinga,
and which ends with the said mountains. The plain near the
highlands is sufficiently fertile, and a large brook of excellent
water and smaller streams course through it. At the Lúpata §
ends the district of the kinglet (regulo) Bive, subject to the
" Unde," or Marave Emperor.¶

---

* Sometimes written Moruscmbos and Moazembos; they are the servile head-
men of slave parties, not to be confounded with the Moçambazes (Mussambazes)
or Pombeiros.

† According to Monteiro and Gamitto (p. 14) a slave generally is called " Bixo "
(Bicho)—worm or beast, a word of general application: I have heard it facetiously
said of a locomotive engine. Muleque (fem. Muleca) is a slave-boy for the house.
" Ladino " (a dodger) is an old slave; Burro (an ass) is a newly-caught or " green "
chattel.

‡ Lupata is translated by Monteiro and Gamitto (p. 28) a " col," very im-
properly by Mr. Cooley a " glen." Do Couto (Dec. IX. chap. 23) says that the
Lupata or Gorge of the Zambezo River gave its name to the district. Dos Santos
(' Ethiopia Oriental,' part 2, fol. 726) describes the Zambeze rapids as being in
" the Lupata, where there are great ridges." Cacian Charpy (' L'Histoire de
l'Ethiopie Orientale ') mistranslated Dos Santos, and hence arose the epithet " Great
Spine of the World" (Espinhaçao do Mundo). Botelho (' Memoria,' &c., p. 812)
tells us that " Lupata touches the skies, and is covered with perpetual snow."
At last Dr. Livingstone visited it, and described it intelligibly: in his ' Second
Expedition' he called the northern continuation " Kirk's Mountains." The older
Portuguese may have prolonged it westward to the great and lofty Serra Muxinga.

§ There are several Lupatas in these hills, Matantora, Chindundo, and others.

¶ His village, we are told by Monteiro and Gamitto (p. 53) is called " Muxinda
a Unde." Probably of this tribe Dr. Livingstone (' Second Expedition,' chap. ix. p.

17th.—All the Caffres assembled and declared their intention
of spending the day in the large village; such was the result of
my sermon. I told them that being ill we would halt at noon,
but the brutes were unmoved. Dread of their desertion made
me dissimulate, and the better to hide my displeasure I gave
them some beads (velorio) to buy beer. They were delighted,
whilst I, having noted the four most maggotty heads of the
party, took thought how best to repress and punish such
disorders.

I gathered the opinions of sundry of my company, especially
of José Rodrigues Caleja, who, by the by, had been represented
to me as a ready man, well versed in native habits. I blamed
their invariable answer to all my perplexities, "We must do
what your honour orders us to do." Finally, it was agreed to
put up with the porters' insolence till one or two stages after
Java (Jáua), then seize their bows and arrows, and burn these
weapons in the presence of their tied-up owners, who would, if
properly guarded, march as I might direct.*

---

198) says: "Formerly all the Manganja were united under the government of their great chief, Undi, whose empire extended from Lake Shirwa to the River Loangwa; but after Undi's death it fell to pieces, and a large portion of it on the Zambesi was absorbed by their powerful southern neighbours the Banyai." Mr. Cooley explains them "Manganja," who thus hold all the country north of the Zambesi from the Shirwa to Zumbo, as "obviously an ordinary variation of Moagaza, the name given by the Jesuit missionaries to the hill-tribes called Mongazi or Mongazyi, the Portuguese Munhae, rendered in the plural, by "the Makololo" and Dr. Livingstone, "Banyai."

* I also had resolved to disarm my Baloch in the Mountains of Usagara, but I was too much invalided to carry the thing into execution.

CHAPTER II.

THE MARCH FROM THE LUPATA DA JÁUA TO THE NORTHERN ANUANOÒA RIVER.

July 18, 1706.—Being this subject, for a time, to my porters, I left the village at 8 A.M. It was impossible, despite all commands, to secure on the line of march order and readiness enough to defend ourselves from the pilfering Maraves, who carried off a black boy belonging to Lieutenant-Colonel Pedro Nolasco, and the load of a second, the property of a soldier. My directions to fire at the legs of any negroes found stealing were obeyed at length, but though the soldier missed—here no new thing—the Marave dropped the load, together with his bow and arrows. Leaving the village we made for the mountain-chain on the East, which I named Cordilheira Marisana, and that on the West, Joanina, in honour of our most august Sovereign (D. Maria I.) and most serene prince (D. João), who created this expedition. When near the highlands, we skirted them, travelling over the plain before mentioned.

10*th*.—The Marave porters who had received hire refused to leave the village where we nighted, despite my threats of not paying the cloths which, according to agreement, they were to receive at Java (Jáua). I vainly sought substitutes, till, seeing that none were procurable, and that we must either lose that day or abandon necessaries, I resolved by contrivance to gain the cause and to show them that we will not timidly endure the insults which they heap upon the feeble traders. Seeing the sudden action, all the villagers fled, but they stopped on hearing that we had no quarrel with them. The Fumo—however small the village, it has always a chief so called—after viewing the cloth for which I sent, the only reason which they understand, prepared Maraves, who soon became too numerous. After marching three-quarters of a league, we entered a large opening in the Cordilheira Marisana, and, after a gentle ascent, we advanced over the champaign ground between the ridges which, running together, form a group of highlands, divided by fertile and populous valleys.

We halted at the largest stream yet seen, and bearing the name of Carozissira. Here I heard news of a faction-fight between the Caffres of D. Francisca and the few men of Captain

João da Cunha Pereira, fomented by this man of bad head and worse tongue. The facts, as recounted to me by Caffre chiefs in presence of the officers, were as follows: The Captain, passing along the path, saw certain Caffres resting with their loads grounded, as is the custom, and as they require to do: he ordered them to proceed: they answered, that they would, after the necessary halt. Not satisfied, he struck them sundry blows, and said, " Get on, sots: this journey is the fault of your mistress, who gave so many porters; if you had run away like the rest, the Governor must have stopped." They added that the Captain had twice or thrice so treated them without my, knowledge; that they had not fled, on account of their mistress's express orders, but that they must do so if such maltreatment continued. They owned that they had come into collision with the Caffres of the indiscreet Captain because, when raising their bows to lessen the strength of his blows, his " captives," who presently fled leaving their loads, had thought that the action was done in opposition to their master.

If this be true, that Captain João da Cunha Pereira punished the men for not deserting, there is little doubt that this bad man, without compromising himself, had held out similar inducements to his own followers, especially when, despite my urgent want of hands, he proposed to send three of his Caffres from Maxinga to Tete. It is certain that the Quartermaster (o Furriel) of the little gang of porters who carried my small palanquin, persuaded his men not to desert this morning, as they had resolved to do in consequence of the Captain's maltreatment. I had heard a fair portion of his bad language, but I kept silence, judging that it might be used with some good reason, and I awaited the report upon the subject with which he ought to have supplied me.

When Lieutenant-Colonel Pedro Nolasco and the other officers who covered the rear-guard reached the place of the fray, they found all D. Francisca's Caffres, men and women, gathered together, and ready to give up their loads before returning to Tete. They declared unanimously that they could no longer endure the Captain, adding an account of his rebuke —I ought to say his advice—together with the orders given by their mistress. The officers persuaded them to take up their loads and to complain to her, who would hear their representations. Thereupon I satisfied their headmen and themselves with good words and a few gifts. A sharp rebuke was sent to the Captain who had caused the mutiny, and the affair requiring further investigation, I shall see what more is to be done. We passed a village called Murambalo, and all the soil thereabouts appeared to me auriferous.

20th.—My company was not the only one which had an affray ; that of the Chief Captain of the Bush (Mixonga), whom I met at ten o'clock, came to blows with certain Maraves who had attempted to plunder his people.

21st.—We arrived at Java.* About sunset an envoy of Mussidansáro brought a message from his master that the Maraves, having robbed a package of porcelain beads (velorio), Crown property, which had been entrusted to them for transport, his master would enter the robbers' village, seize three of them, and not release them till the plunder should be restored. He added that he would carry off as much millet as he could, but that the delay would not permit him to visit me at Java. This prince Mussidansáro is a great knave: he came from the Cazembe as a man of business to visit D. Francisca, whom, being highly respected by blacks as well as whites, they call Chiponda, that is to say, " the lady that treads all under her feet," to beg that she would send her son to the king. D. Francisca, availing herself of this opportunity, requested her lord the Cazembe to treat me as her son sent under his care, and to defend me from all dangers.

The Amazons (women porters) being now weary and footsore, I ordered Gonçalo Caetano Pereira—the scandal of the Teto people, simply because he had supplied me with Caffres—to collect Marave porters for carrying the goods as far as the Aruangôa River, and then pass them on to the Muizas. As I wanted many Maraves, we stayed in that place several days.

22nd.—To-day I have twice crossed the large Aruangôa River.† In one place the water reaches the bend of the leg, in another part, somewhat higher up, there is a bridge of canes (bamboos) tied together. I already know in this part of Africa three streams of that name: this is the first; the second ‡ is that falling into the Zambeze near Zumbo, dividing the lands of the Maraves and Muizas; and the third is in the lands of the Barôe, between Sena and Maniça.

The mines of Java, here called Bar,§ were discovered seven or eight years ago by Gonçalo Caetano Pereira ; at present they

* In Dr. Livingstone's 'Second Expedition,' we find Góa or Gova, which may be the same word (chap. xxvii.) In chap. xxxi, however, he mentions " Jáwa " (Jáoa).

† This is the Aruángoa-Piro or Jáua of Monteiro and Gamitto, who make it flow westward into the northern Aruángoa-Poaso (p. 31). " Pire," in the local dialect, means a range of hills, a Serra, and the adjunct distinguishes the stream from its northern fork, the Aruángoa-Poaso. The difference between the Aruángoa-Loangwa and the much smaller Aruangôa River has already been noted.

‡ The first (northern Aruangôa) is one of the headwaters of the second.

§ I have before explained the meaning of Bar. The proprietor's house is called " Loane."

are worked by the negresses of only one inhabitant of Tete,
and all these women fled to the bush, justly thinking that I might
require their services. These diggings might pay, but they are
despised because men ignore working them : all know that gold is
not always superficial, and that, when deep, considerable excava-
tions are necessary ; whereas the mining women of the Rios de
Sena, failing to find the metal on the surface, at once abandon the spot. They know absolutely nothing of the conducting and the levelling of water, without whose aid gold will
not pay even in the best placeros. The want of blacksmiths is
another obstacle of the many that prevent efficient working. I
saw Caffres in Maxinga baling up stagnant water with baskets as closely made as possible: in this sort of "litus
arare" business many negresses were employed. Knowing these
errors and defects, I have neither time to remedy them, nor,
if I had, would skilled officials be forthcoming. Such, however,
is the state of that Sena whose fame reaches the clouds.*

I passed the day in subsisting my people and in enduring
their importunate demands, which make this my purgatory.
Visiting in the evening the quarters of the Muizas, I thought
myself in a village of artisans. Each family or individual has
a hut of tree-boughs, and the air resounds with the blows of a
kind of club or wooden axe upon the slabs of bast, which they
convert into clothing, and with which they buy provisions from
the Maraves. The latter, on the other hand, have no manu-
factures, but occupy themselves solely in growing millet, sweet
potatoes, and large yams—the "cará" of the Brazil†—and in
plundering passengers. Here the millet-stalk attains a height of
two fathoms, proving the fertility of the soil. During the famines
of Tete, the people used to come or send for provisions, with
great cost and toil, to this place, where, the valleys being fresh
and cool, want of rain-water has very little effect. There is also
a quantity of the Nhamudoro bean, which the Brazilians call
Guandu.‡

23rd.—Until 7 P.M. the expected Marave party did not
appear, although I was informed that they were being collected.
About 150 are wanted, and if they fail us, it will be trouble-

* The traveller would have found the English Gold Coast quite as backward as
Sena. The place is a mine of wealth, and yet I doubt whether a pound of mercury
or a cradle has ever been seen there. And in London he would have met with
statesmen, even more unprogressive than the Gold Coast men, who are capable
of telling you that gold is becoming too common. Will posterity believe it ?
† The Cará (Helianthus tuberosus), a favourite Brazilian vegetable.
‡ This is the Doll-plant of India, the "Thúr" of Hindostan, the Turiyan of the
Arabs, the Mbarazi of the Waswahili, and the "Cajanus Indicus." See 'Journal
of the Royal Geographical Society' (vol. 29, p. 400). It enters largely into the
dish called Kichhrí.

some. In such a case, only the negresses can extricate me, and even then many loads must be left on the ground. The number cannot be filled up with those working at the gold-washing, as both sexes would fly to the bush.

The two Muizas, Chinimbu and Mussidansáro, took up my time, and stunned me with their disputes, already reckoning upon the honours and gifts of the king (Cazembe). They wish to decide who shall conduct me to him. The former pleaded priority of claim as bearer of the royal message; the latter that he had been sent by the King to request a visit from D. Francisca's "son," in which category I was committed to him. When made umpire, I pointed out Chinimbu and Catára as the King's envoys, they having first brought me a direct message and having accompanied me as Manibo or great man. On the other hand, I owned that Mussidansáro was carrying me as a "son" of D. Francisca—as all held me to be, either because I was inferior to her in reputation, or because I had lodged in her house. And neither having any present superiority, I told them that they must be friendly till we should reach the King, when the weighty matter could be decided. They wished to continue the dispute, but the spirit and eloquence of a flask of strong waters were more convincing than my reasons or the joint tongues of Cicero and Demosthenes would have been.

24th.—Knowing by short experience the habits of the Maraves, I was aware that one of them receiving pay would bring with him the whole village. The few, however, that came, demanded, contrary to their practice with the Portuguese paupers who have passed this way, such exorbitant wages, that I preferred to continue the journey as well as might be with the negresses. Almost all the wheaten flour was divided amongst the soldiers and the remaining escort: we resolving to rely, by way of bread, upon the Angú or country millet-dough. Cases of rum and brandy from Portugal, intended for emergencies and as presents to the kinglets, the salt, the remaining vinegar and three cases of bacon, shared the same fate. He who can eat without salt and vinegar, wants not bacon. In this there is nothing strange, except to one who says, "Deus meus venter est": it is natural in one who eats to live, and who does not live to eat. My proceeding was caused, not only by the exorbitant demands of the Maraves, but by the certainty that the Muizas, if not equally favoured, would revolt, and with good reasons, as they had often done before in lesser matters. They would have stacked their loads near the camp, and they would have gone their ways—what could I do to them? Unable to punish even my slaves, I was obliged to submit.

26th.—My sickness did not delay us. After resting for some days, the start is ever slow; the people become idle, and their loads must be redistributed, as twenty-seven have fled from Java. We crossed the ridge lying to our east and halted at the small stream Chigumunqnire, where the messenger of a kinglet ruling the lands beyond the stream came to beg from me a little cloth. As Portuguese rarely pass this way, it is a much esteemed article, to be obtained by any means, fair or foul. Few possess any, and when they do it is old. They cover their waists with tiger (leopard) skins, and having neither mines, nor ivory, nor many slaves, and consequently little cloth, they think of nothing but plundering the feeble traders, who fear their numbers. Hence their arrogance, their pilfering, and robbery, and the injury which they inflict upon themselves and others.*

27th.—Tortured with the insatiable thirst and the intense cold of the Sezão (a seasoning fever or fit of ague and fever) which attacked me at 5 A.M., I set out three hours later. Nothing more miserable than to have to do with men wanting common sense like these Caffres, who are absolutely indifferent to good and evil; who feel only when they suffer, and who cannot allow themselves to be persuaded. No reason will convince them that, when possible, we should march together to baffle enemies and robbers, and that we should start early and travel farther, lest the failure of the military chest leave us in woful want.† Until they see me en route all hide in the bush.

I pushed on, by the officers' advice, as far as they would go, to some place where I could nurse my violent fever; when about midday I halted, and was informed that the Maraves had insulted, robbed, and maltreated the party. A violent headache and abnormal prostration prevented my going back; and, thinking the quarrel settled, I sent the sergeant-major of ordnance, José Rodriguez Caleja, who pusillanimously went off with a bad will. The force having as usual been distributed amongst the party, I remained with my escort. At 4 P.M. our people arrived, excepting the chief captain of the bush, Gonçalo Caetano Pereira, who remained in the Marave village with his folk and the Muiza porters. I directed Lieut.-Colonel Pedro Nolasco, who was present, to draw up a procès verbal, which was of the following tenor:—

" On the 27th instant (July) His Excellency the Governor, according to habit, set out in the vanguard, accompanied by the

---

* " O povo Marave passa por ser o mais ladrão de toda esta parte da Africa."— See Monteiro and Gamitto, p. 25.

† I found things exactly the same when marching from the Zanzibar coast to the Tanganyika Lake.

Rev. Father Chaplain, the sergeant-major of ordnance, José
Rodriguez Caleja, and the fort-adjutant of the Fort of Sena,
José Thomaz Gomes. They were followed by Gonçalo Caetano
Pereira, the chief captain of the bush, by Captain João da
Cunha, and after them came Pedro Xavier Volasco, the chief sergeant of militia, and the Lieutenants Antonio José da Cruz,
Manoel dos Santos e Silva, and Antonio José Pereira Salema.* The last-named, arriving at a Marave village, were
stopped by three Caffres, who, coming forward, attempted to
seize their cattle. The sergeant-major advancing to inquire
why this was done, the soldiers of the train replied that the
Maraves demanded pay, as the cattle had eaten some of their
millet. At the same time other Maraves assembled, and declared
that this was not the land of the white men (Muzungos), that
the latter must pay for transit, and if not, that they would seize
the cattle which had eaten their grain. The chief sergeant
replied that the first who dared to do so should be shot dead.
They then pretended to calm down, declaring that it was a
boyish plot, but that something must be given to end the
'palaver' (Milando). They followed our people to another
village, where the sergeant and Lieutenant Antonio José da
Cruz met Captain João da Cunha Pereira and Gonçalo Caetano
Pereira. The latter, persuaded by them, offered a Chuábo,† or
twenty strings of white beads, and when they were discontented
he added a capotim or two cloths. Still, emboldened by having
bullied the poor traders, they refused, and began to set upon
him face to face. Captain João da Cunha, wishing to retreat
from the fray, ordered his bearers to bring his hammock (Man-
chila). The Maraves opposed this, and when beaten off by his
slaves they attacked the hammock of Gonçalo Caetano Pereira,
carried it away into the bush, and drove off a cow. Our
Caffres, seeing this open theft, rescued the beast with club-blows,
and used sharp weapons upon a few who must have suffered
severely. The Muizas came to our people's assistance, beat all
the Maraves they could seize, carried off their arms and put
them to flight: they then destroyed the neighbouring villages,
razing six, after looting all the millet and other things they
could find. Gonçalo Caetano Pereira came in for a few blows ;
Vasco Joaquim Peres (Pires) escaped being treacherously
killed with an assegai, and Pedro Xavier Velasco avoided an
arrow. The village-Fumo and another Marave were seized to

---

* In other places called José Vicente Pereira Salema.
† Monteiro and Gamitto mention the Chuábo (de Miamoga) p. 113, and in p. 11
tell us it is equal to twenty strings. It is in fact the equivalent of our fathom of
cotton cloth, the braça or the shukkah of Zanzibar.

account for the missing hammock and for two packages of white
beads (mutores de velorio) * robbed during the affray. Presently all the plunder was restored: I did not, however, omit
to blame the officers for supporting too patiently such annoyance on the part of the savages, and for not using their fire-
arms upon the thieves.† "

28th.—The Muizas, who had remained at the place of
plunder enjoying their spoils, came up to my quarters. I
changed my mind about their not being cannibals, as they sang
a song to the purport that " had such a thing happened in their
country, they would to-day have eaten much roast meat." My
complaint so increased that I doubted my surviving it, and I
had no other remedy but recourse to " Agua de Inglaterra "
(English water?) against the opinion of our doctors, who can
hardly read. They know but three diseases, " constipacão " (cold
closing the pores and often bringing on fever), " mordaxim "
(gripes or colic), and " fraqueza " (general weakness, especially
impotency). On the 30th it was reported to me that there was
no provision for the people, that no village was in sight, and
that many of our Caffres had fled. I ordered that on the
morrow they should put me in my palanquin, no matter how
deplorable might be my state, and set out in search of food.

31st.—Quinine had prevented the increase of my illness—the
only improvement, but no small one. I was carried to my
palanquin and took bearings to the best of my power so as not
to lose the line of our march.

August 7th.—Fever prevented my keeping the Diary till
to-day. No news except that we have crossed the little
streams " Ruy " and the " Bua,"‡ which falls into the Chire
(Shire). The country traversed is so poor that nothing can
be procured but millet, sweet potatoes, yams, ground-nuts
(Amendoim), and a few bananas: these, however, are abundant
and cheap. My only support is rice-water. Not a chicken
during my sickness! not the smallest bird to be seen, and no
sign of game: possibly the famished Caffres, after finishing their
stores, declare war even upon the butterflies, and have thus
exterminated birds and beasts. A few slaves are the only

---

* Motor or mutor is explained by Monteiro and Gamitto to mean bronze, a
bundle.

† The officers were probably right. A few deaths might have stopped the expedition, and would certainly have ensured its destruction on the down march. But
Dr. de Lacerda did not expect to return this way, and African fever soon exhausts
the traveller's patience.

‡ Monteiro and Gamitto give a River Ruui, and several called Bua, Vua, or
Mvua, which in Kiswahili would signify rain. The Shire River, draining the
Lake Nyassa, was evidently, I have said, well known to the Portuguese.

traffic, not an ivory, not a grain of gold, which, however, abounds here.

Since yesterday we have seen hares, she-goats, and black cattle. The latter would be fat and sightly, if not kept entire : still both are large, and they have not the evil savour of uncastrated animals. I have ever heard it said "this or that thing is bad as goat's meat." The adage is not true of the she-goats in this country and of Sena; without exaggeration, their flesh is better flavoured than the mutton of Lisbon, and it is used at the best tables. Ivory also begins to appear. At the narrow but deep Uzereze River,* which receiving the Bua, falls into the Chire, we met some flying Caffres, who trade with Mozambique. I could not converse with them, as they at once disappeared. We halted on the banks of the Uzereze River, near the village of the King Mocando, the most powerful in people, and dreaded Marave chief of these parts: he was in great fear because of our sickness.†

8th.—Almost all our journey has been more or less towards the N.N.W., but since yesterday we have made westing. It is this bend that places the Cazembe's country so far from the western (eastern ?) coast, and to the distance must be added the perpetual troubles caused by the carriers. Since we crossed the chain whose valleys we threaded from the Maxinga Station, we have wanted water, and that found in the villages is taken from pits (mixciras), and as white as milk.‡ I sent forward to the Cazembe the chief sergeant of militia, Pedro Xavier Velasco, who with his armed slaves volunteered in this expedition to serve the Crown, taking with him the ensign of militia, (and?) Manoel Caetano Pereira. To Velasco was committed a copy of the instructions appended to the Diary.§

The dearness or want of salt is here so great that it becomes an article of commerce, and is very rare. To-day I saw a Marave woman making it; it was a mere ley of ashes, with hardly the sharpness of the lixivia, and without any likeness to the piquancy and flavour of salt. Perhaps, however, habit makes men prefer it to ours. Amongst the Indians of the Rio Negro, in the captainship of Pará (the Brazil), I saw a salt

---

* Monteiro and Gamitto (p. 113) call this the Ruareze River: they describe it as running east (to the Shire River or to the Nyassa Lake), eight fathoms broad and three deep. They also mention the Mucanda, Mambo (chief) of the Chévas (Shevas), as the most powerful between the Zambeze and the Aruangoa rivers, and in p. 418 they call him " king of the Chévas."

† There is always much trouble if a foreigner dies in this part of Africa.

‡ I found the same in the Ugogo country, a dry land lying to the west of the Usagara Mountains, the eastern Ghats of the Zanzibar coast.

§ This document never reached head-quarters.

different from sea-salt in its outward colour, not in its taste; it was extracted from the ashes of a small wild cocoa.

9th and *10th.*—The Caffres, not contented with our halts which, as the Diary shows, were frequent, and scandalised by our marching on an average 2½ leagues a day, refused to advance, and sent back some of those who had gone on. I had no remedy but to await them in a village called Chitenga. The unreasonableness of these negroes is shown by my Diary, but the cause of disorder may be traced to certain members of the party, against whom I will proceed in due time. At present I must bear all, and dissemble my thoughts, with the sole object of forwarding and successfully finishing the expedition. To-day (10th) the said Caffres arrived, and to-morrow we advance.

11th.—It was necessary to halt at 10.15 A.M., as the Caffres are accustomed to night in this place—a poor excuse, which would be valid if water lay afar. I am in despair, thinking of the want of supplies, of the necessity for wintering in the interior, and of this delay in carrying out the orders of the Crown. My blood boils to see the likeness between the Caffres and the whites who, introduced to me as knowing the manners and customs of the natives, have adopted only their superstitions and abominations which, added to their own, render them truly detestable.[*] Lieut.-Colonel Pedro Nolasco and the chief sergeant Pedro Xavier Velasco are the only two hitherto found faithful, and with whom I can unbosom and solace myself.

From the Mocando's country to the (southern) Aruangôa River,[†] another tribe, the Mutumbuca, is mixed with the Maraves, subject to the chief of the latter, whose sons govern them.[‡] Generally speaking, both these Caffre families are well formed and robust, but the women are rendered horrible by their habit of piercing the upper lip to admit an ivory circlet, or a bit of dried gourd of more than a thumb in diameter; you may say that the upper lip serves as sun-bonnet to the lower. I saw only one of them with the lower lip similarly pierced and bunged. The men wear in their ears stars or rings of pewter, or, lastly, young bamboo shoots—canes about one palm long.[§] On their bodies they draw star-like lines and patterns, which

---

[*] I have abbreviated this and many similar passages. The traveller's unfinished journal is not a work of art, and therefore there is no fear of mutilating it.

[†] Namely the marches of July 26th, 27th, 31st, and August 7th.

[‡] Thus the Motumbukas, also called in the Diary (August 20th) "Botombanas" are clients or helots of the Maraves. I have treated the subject of double races in my work 'Zanzibar City, Island, and Coast.' Monteiro and Gamitto (p. 130) make the "Tumbuca tribe serfs of the Chevas" (Shevas or Anshevas). Mr. Cooley writes the word "Matumboka."

[§] I do not know whether this is the short palm of 4 or the long palm of 8 inches.

are not without their own peculiar beauty. They wear various head-dresses and necklaces of velorio* or of cowries: this last is of the best quality, and passes not through Sena, where an inferior sort is current as the first. Others part their hair into as many ringlets as can be made, about the size of quills; each lock is plaited with tree-fibre from the root to the point, so closely that it is hard, and projects spike-like from the head.† Some few begin to tie these pigtails round the roots, and thus they fall over the head with a graceful bend.

12th.—To-day I passed two places: one showing saltpetre on the ground-surface, and the other evident signs of gold. Both are inserted in the map.‡

13th.—At 10·30 A.M. we reached the village of the chief Caperemera,§ son of the Mocanda. The villages of the latter are very populous, but those of the former much more, since many Muizas, driven by hunger or attracted by the fertility of the Marave lands, here assemble. I propose to myself on my return to make further inquiries; these people are ever exaggerating or diminishing, without apparent reason.

My sleep is lost and my days are spent in thinking how to obviate the delays, the slow marches, and the Caffres' insolence. From my own people there is no advice, beyond a cold "We must do what your honour orders." If I propose a plan, they approve of it in my presence, and disapprove of it in their private conventicles. When I send a command to be executed, all cry out and do nothing: my hands are tied; the few soldiers are mere Caffres, like the rest. When I proposed, after the time specified, to arrest some sixty of the most mutinous porters, those who advised the measure opposed it in a cowardly manner, declaring that if the Caffres—who differ from our American negroes as the moon does from the sun—were made prisoners, the Maraves would become dangerous. As though a single shot or death would not—so at least our men often have boasted—put to flight a Marave army !‖ Presently, these half-a-dozen white men so thwarted me, that I resolved to keep my own counsel, and to manage everything myself.

---

* I have before explained velorio to mean a large opaque porcelain bead.

† The Wagogo of Eastern Africa also plait their hair with tree-fibre, and the effect of the head-dress is that of the Sphinx. Monteiro and Gamitto (p. 154) describe and sketch the spike-coiffure alluded to in the text.

‡ A foot-note informs us that this map never came to hand.

§ In August 1831 this chief ("Capriméra") was visited by the expedition under Messrs. Monteiro and Gamitto. They remark that the old man boasted much of having received Dr. de Lacerda.

‖ I think that the reader will here agree with the party, not with Dr. de Lacerda; at least I should. The account in his text is inordinately diffuse, and calls for abridgment.

Finally, on reaching Caperemera's village, I sent to inform him of my illness, and my wish to see him. The chief (Mambo) presently appeared,—a fine-looking man, full of natural grace. Summoning all the servile head-men of porters (Mocazembos) I said in their presence that I had much friendship with his father (the Mocanda), in virtue of which he had at my request sent orders to all his vassals and villagers living on or near our road, to seize and to bring before him all the Caffres taken without a pass from me, and to sell them for his own profit. I authorised him to put to death those whom he could not seize, promising on my return an ample reward. The truth is, I had failed to obtain this from his father, because the latter had feared to visit me, and moreover because I had neglected, through ignorance of their customs, to delay with him for a day, which they hold a high honour. I added that it was my wish similarly to contract with himself strict friendship, and to open commerce, by which he would be the gainer. By sending to Sena his tusks and gold, as his land contained it, he would obtain more cloth than from the slave-factors (Mossambazes or Pombeiros) of Mozambique, and on my down march he ought to despatch with me some of his "children" to Tete, where they would see the advantages of such traffic. I expressed, furthermore, a desire that he would respond to my offers of friendship by posting three of his messengers (Patamares) on the different roads, and seize as his own slaves all the fugitive Caffres who could not show my token of dismissal.

The present of a red cloth (xaile), a piece of thin Indian cotton (zuarte), a flagon of rum, and a cloth of cauril * (um panno de cauril), confirmed our friendship. The chief in person leading the Caffres who accompanied him, sent for three of his slaves, and, before all of our head-men of porters, he gave to each a bit of paper, which I had stamped with my arms, and he ordered them at once to carry my plan into execution, adding that if any runaway showed a similar token he was to be brought before me, that it might be verified. I admired the presence of mind shown by this Mambo, and the vivacity with which he replied to one, who asked what he would do with the Caffres who might now desert. He said at once that he would sell the runaways, as all fugitives had been given to him by me.

The Mocazembos, hanging down their heads, hastened with

---

* Dr. Kirk says, "It is uncertain how much this measure of cowries may be. It is probably an equivalent of the panno or pano (cloth), the unity of monetary value and worth in 1832, as we are informed by Monteiro and Gamitto (Appendix I.) 120 reis fortes = 6d.

the intelligence to their companions, and all showed, I am told, such sadness that the inference is either they intended a general desertion after the departure of the women, or they feared future chastisement, finding the door of escape shut, and compelled when avoiding Charybdis to fall upon Scylla.   The Mambo replied to me that he valued my friendship; he had not, however, sent his "sons" to Tete, as his ancestors had never so done, and that his people did not extract gold, because they knew not what it was. Hoping that by these measures my Caffres will march further, and that in case they desert, despite all these precautions, others will be forthcoming, I determined to dismiss the negresses who had accompanied me with so much good will, and who had proved themselves so useful upon the tardy journey.

14th.—Caperemera came to see me, and in sign of friendship gave me a tusk, upon which I directed the royal mark to be placed. Thus the Treasury will be indemnified for a large cloth (roupão) and other trifles which he begged. As he would give a superabundance of porterage, even though all the Caffres should desert, his wishes must be consulted. He tells us that he expected eighty Muizas, on account of the chiefs of another village, and that if forty or fifty men are wanted he will supply them. I cannot, however, move even to-morrow, as the porters must prepare provisions for the first few days. When the fort adjutant of Sena told him to thank the Manes of his ancestors (Mozimos),[*] whom these people deify, for my passing through his land, and for making him those presents, he replied that he was not a slave-boy (Caporro), and that he had a large heart.[†]

15th.—My dependence upon Caperemera made me lavish upon him the greatest signs of friendship that I have ever yet shown to man. I marvelled at myself, as I had ever detested flattery, especially of those who were powerful enough to advance me. On the other hand the Mambo, expecting all things from me after my return to Tete, showed no remissness in urging the presence of his Muizas; and moreover, he protested that he would make me a dash (Saguate) of all the slaves and ivory that he might henceforth collect. I on my part promised to send him so many things that he would be rather richer than the grand Turk; this made the Caffre dance with joy. To ascertain the value of his tusks, I directed an official to bargain with him for a tooth, as if it were a private purchase unknown to me.

---

[*] The reverence for the Manes, or rather the ghosts, of those lately departed, is the only sign of worship amongst these tribes.

[†] Meaning that he was a chief, and therefore no niggard.

The Mambo observed that he wondered at the audacity of the man, who must have known the promise made to his master. I asked him where was his market for slaves and ivory. He said they were sold to the Manguros,* living on the banks of, or near to, the Chiro (Shire) river, who trade with the Mujanos (Wahiáo), but that the greater part of the ivory exported by these Caffres comes from the Cazembe's country.

My rod skull-cap, dressing-gown, pantaloons, and baize socks of the same colour, the hut or house that rose so suddenly, the make-believe soldiers, the bales (muntores) of cloth, and other trifles, are great things so wondered at that I want words to express their veneration for me. It is well to remember that the experienced Solomon found nothing but "vanitas et afflictio spiritus," or a conceited mind might have been upset by it.† In presence of this awful confession, which must sadden and terrify all the world, what enjoyment can we find in things that are not founded upon the security of our consciences?

But as moderate enjoyment in honest things is not vicious, so I accuse myself of indifference and insensibility, because I consider and hold it to be the effect of . . . .‡ its not proceeding from the cares which keep me ever pensive, and inaccessible to all pleasures, so that I can truly say "I live not for myself an instant a day." When considering, in fact, that we have passed with such ease through the lands of these kinglets, excepting only the little robber who tried to molest us; that we have been received with such respect and affability where it was predicted that we must fight or pay our way—especially through those of the Mocanda, all the world of Sena speaking of him with outstretched necks—and that my white companions and the black-slave-factors have been my only difficulties in carrying out the commands of the Crown, I feel bursting with rage. But let us stop here. It is not right that the readers of this Diary should be made partners in my sorrows, increased as they are by the lively grief caused by the death of my beloved wife, whom God

---

* The Manguros, according to Montairo and Gamitto (p. 420), do not live near the Shire River. They are "Maraves inhabiting the banks of the Rio Nhanja" (Nyassa Lake?), and they trade with the Arabs of the Zanzibar coast. These may be the Marungu—two tribes at the south of the Tanganyika Lake, of whom I heard from the Arabs of Unyamwezi. Mr. Cooley (reviewing my book on the Lake Regions) says, "It is evident that the Arabs confound the Arungo in the north-west with the Anguro in the south-east, on the other side of the Arungos." The Anguro have been mixed up with the Wahiáo. The Mujanos or Mujáo, as has been said, are the Wahiáo.
† This repeats what I remarked of negro flattery to Europeans in my 'Mission to Dahome.'
‡ Here there is a lacuna.

G

was pleased to take to Himself in the flower of her age, on the
first of April. Even so quoth Horace—

" Ut ridentibus arrident, ita flentibus adflent
Humani vultus."

I inquired about the Caffre way of killing elephants. The
Mambo sent two iron spears, four (short) palms long, and one
inch thick. One end was flat, like a lance-head, but nowhere
was the iron broader than a man's thumb. The other extremity
was firmly inserted into a piece of iron-wood, and the whole
might weigh 8 lbs.* The sportsman climbs a tree over-
hanging the elephant's usual path, and, with this weapon,
which penetrates to the socket, wounds and kills the beasts as
they pass. The Maniça Caffres, who yearly come to hunt the
Crown estates of the Sena district, now adopt these means
which are better and more destructive. Leaving aside their
mummeries, medicines, and oilings—which are supposed to
bring good luck—when they sight a herd they separate from
it some of the animals by whooping, and then they slip at
them trained dogs, that engage their attention by barking from
some distance. Meanwhile the Caffres, watching their opportunity, hamstring them, and despatch them on the ground with
their spears.†

For the first time I saw the mops or head-thatches of the
Muizas, powdered with dust red as carmine. Supposing the
colour to be ochre, I asked for a little of it, when Caperomera
explained to me that it was not clay, but wood.‡ He gave me
a cake or loaf of the dust, which has been preserved for the
Crown; and when I wanted a log or trunk, Catára told me that
he would procure one for me in the lands of the Cazembo, where
it abounds.

We well know that the natural taste of men brought up in
the ways of simplicity rejects with loathing our highly-seasoned
food. The same is the case with the other senses. Two Caffres
of our party skilful in playing the horn performed before some
vassals of Caperomera, their compatriots, as well as to Muizas.
Hearing these sounds the younglings uttered terrible cries; the
women, the boys, and some adults fled, and the field remained
empty. After losing, however, their panic, all returned, and

* This is the elephant-spear used in Unyamwezi and the adjacent country:
the people, however, do not mount trees, but throw like the Maniça Caffres. They
have the same superstitious preparations.
† The people of Ugogo, east of Unyamwezi, do the same.
‡ Monteiro and Gamitto (p. 29) describe and sketch this " chingengue," as
the mop is called. They name the wood " páo muedra (sorte de páo Brasil). The
tribes of Fernando Po also ornament their hair with a powder of red wood, which
I mistook at first for clay.'

appeared to enjoy the instruments, perhaps more from novelty than from their melody, such as it was.

16th.—I was getting ready to move forward, but the Muizas had not returned from the villages, where they had been to collect millet for the first day's march. Besides which, Caffres never hurry themselves—African Caffres at least. When sold to America they take example from their elders, and become far more diligent. It is a fact a thousand times observed here, that a Caffre has never carried a letter with haste, even though threatened by his master with punishment for delay and bribed with cloth for despatch.

At my request Caperemera sent many couriers to summon the party, who at last arrived: some of them, however, wished to return their pay rather than carry our loads. The Mambo very angrily ordered them, under pain of expulsion and compulsion, to "clear out," and they knew the power of his bow. He was named Caperemera, meaning "the brave." Sure that our Caffres would not fly, fearing sale at Mozambique, with its consequent exile from Africa—the severest penalty to a Caffre—and resolved to show them that their reign was over, I summoned them as if to muster them, and when they were gathered together I sent soldiers to their encampment (Mussassa),* with orders to bring and break before them their bows and arrows. They were seized with consternation, it being a dishonour to travel without weapons, as only criminals and fugitives go unarmed. So when the subjects of the King of Barvé (the Darôe) in Maniça, and the people of that neighbourhood see one of our Caffres without bow and arrows they seize him till claimed, and take pay for their work and for his board and lodging. I left the village at 3.30 P.M.†

17th.—I travelled, but not as far as could be desired or could have been done, awaiting those detained since yesterday at Caperemera's village in the hope of collecting fresh Muizas: to-day my Caffres being much more humane and listening to reason, which before they did not. Those left behind arrived at night, and I gave orders to collect provisions, as for some marches ahead there are no populous villages, nor can we halt in what there are, as they are not in fit places. From the abode

---

* The " mussassa " is the " khambi " or kraal of the Zanzibar regions, a collection of little huts made of boughs and dry grass, and generally surrounded by a ring of thorns: hence the word kraal from curral.

† Dr. de Lacerda evidently owed much to his "Caffro friend," Caperemera, and the expedition which followed him was as generously and hospitably treated by the Muiza chief, Chinti Capenda (p. 394). Without these moral oases in the howling waste of barbarism, the African traveller would worry himself to death.

of my Caffre friend the land is composed of low and gentle hills, partly stony, partly of good soil. In the latter are many small hamlets, and to-day we found two streams of good water, which greatly refreshed us.

18th.—The first high ridge which we traversed divides the lands of Caperemera from those of the kinglet Massé. We are still crossing sundry valleys and ridges, auriferous but unworkable for want of iron tools, skilled labour, and high water,* except such as could be brought from afar. The streams run, more or less, from W.N.W. to E.S.E., and their watershed forms, I believe, the Aruangôa River.† I called the range Cordilheira Carlotina.‡ This was our first day of travel, if real marching be regarded.

19th.—Wishing to observe an eclipse of Jupiter's satellites, which will occur to-morrow, and wanting a place with a name, I made a forced march, so as to reach the village of Mazavamba. We halted at the River Ircugûze (Ircusuze),§ after traversing a depopulated country, full of lions.

20th—At the end of the wildest and roughest of our marches lay the village of Mazavamba, a great thief. All the resident Muizas and Botombucas ǁ who came to see me were exceedingly drunk, and Mazavamba, who continued his carouse till the 22nd, was too far gone to visit me.¶ I found the position of the village to be in time 2ʰ 45′ 46″, i. e. 41° 26′ 30″ E. of Lisbon (= 32° 18′ 18″ E. of Greenwich), and in S. lat. 12° 33′. The variation was N.W. 21° 58′ 30″.

21st.—I had an attack of ague and fever, which was increased by the news that the greater part of the Muizas had deserted. Caperemera behaved like a friend, sending back to me those who arrived at their villages, and punishing the families of those who hid themselves in the bush. The want of supplies and the small quantities of provisions brought in cause consternation to all the Caffres of our party.

---

* "Aguas altas," means waters with a fall for "hydraulicking."

† The watershed is still to the Shire River or to the Nyassa Lake. So in Monteiro and Gamitto the Bucuzi River and Rivulet shed to the east.

‡ The traveller having now reached the outliers of the great mountain-plateau known as Serra Muxinga, named them Carlotina, in memory of D. Carlota, wife of the Prince Regent of Portugal. It is the southern boundary of the northern Arangîa river-basin, and its northern slopes discharge into the Bemba or Bangweolo Lake. Monteiro and Gamitto (p. 125) term Massé "Mambo Muassé," and call this part of the highlands Serra Capira. It is alluded to by Dr. Livingstone, who, writing to the late Earl of Clarendon from Ujiji (November 1, 1871), describes it as a mountain mass, not exceeding 6000 or 7000 feet in altitude, and rising from a broad upland between S. lat. 10° and 12°, and over 700 miles in length from east to west.

§ The next expedition called it Riacho Bucuzi, the northern streamlet of that name flowing to the west when the southern sheds eastward.

ǁ See August 11th.

¶ This frequently happened to my expedition when crossing Ugogo.

22nd.—I spent all the last night and the greater part of to-day cogitating how to collect bearers that will not willingly abandon their loads. Then I issued an order containing the reasons for my resolution,* and I gave it to the chief captain of the bush, Gonçalo Caetano Pereira, and to the chief sergeant, José Rodrigues Caleja.

23rd.—From Mazavamba's village I made for the Northern Aruangôa River. The ague and fever which attacked me so violently on the 21st inst., came on to-day with increased vigour, from 9 A.M. to 9 P.M. Suffering it as I best could, we marched upon the River Remimba: only a brook at this season, it must carry a considerable volume during the rains.

I halted at a village near that stream, not so much to nurse my ague as to collect provisions for 3½ to 4 days of march upon the nearest Muiza village. The price of provisions was six times greater than through the lands of the Maraves to the Mocanda; beyond the latter point they will sell nothing except for cloth, despising our first-class beads (velorios) because, as I have said, they have larger samples. Enough to say that there a goat costs one chuábo, a cloth of any quality: here its value is not less than six, and other things are in proportion. The worst is our not being able to buy wholesale. Each Caffre brings from his yearly store a small portion, at the utmost reaching a "quarta" (fourth of a bushel).† In the same river appeared fish called Pendes,‡ small, but savoury; they are equally good and larger at Tete; during the winter (i.e., wet season §) these, perhaps, may attain the same size. There are also other species, owing to the anastomosis of this stream with the Aruangôa River; they describe the latter to me as tolerably broad, but at the present season shallow.

24th.—In order not to place my people in the wretched state of having nothing to eat, and no provisions for the three or four days of desert-march (sertão), I did not purge myself to-day, and from 1 A.M. I began to cut short the ague with quinine. We halted at the village of Capangura, the most wretched yet met with; there was absolutely nothing for sale; no rations (Maronda) were brought even when the highest prices were

---

* In a foot-note we learn that the paper has been lost.

† The traveller now approaches the waste lands that divide the basins of the Northern Aruangôa and the Chambeze rivers. The water-parting is a N.E. prolongation of the Serra Muchinga, called by Dr. Livingstone "Lobisa Plateau." This is the desert which caused such losses to the expedition that followed Dr. de Lacerda.

‡ Monteiro and Gamitto (p. 193) mention this fish, and compare it with the "dourada" of Portugal.

§ In these lands the rains begin in our autumn, reach their height in December, and end with our spring (see Sept. 7th).

offered. A little before reaching the village of Mazavamba, the mountains which begin at the other end near the settlements of Caperemera and Massó terminate ; the chain is all auriferous, but, for the reasons before stated, it will be hard to work.

25th.—This day (thirtieth) I resumed my Diary, though still suffering very severely from fever, of which I have had four attacks since the end of March. I did not expect to escape the three first. Perhaps the third would have been less trouble-some, had I not been travelling, and in want of everything. Enough to say that his Excellency the Governor of the Rios de Sena, the successor of those heroes who never left the house ex-cept in a sedan chair with two large velvet sun-tents (umbrellas), carrying big silver knobs on both sides, in order that the glances of the Lord of Day, even though setting, might not annoy them ; who lived wrapped up in silks, and in the lightest white clothing ; who often suffered from indigestions and other incon-veniences, the effect of a too splendid and profuse diet, and who finally passed their time in scattering cloth, and in gathering gold and ivory—this successor, I say, spent many an hour shirtless, and wrapped up in a baize, because his clothes were left behind, while during his sickness he had not a chicken for broth. "Deus super omnia!" The route, which I never ceased tracing even at times of my greatest weakness, serves me as a guide to work up this Diary. I cannot, however, offer very many details, as my malady often prevented my taking notice of everything.

After marching two hours we made the (Northern) Aruangôa River.[*] Its breadth is irregular, owing to the friable nature of the banks. Where I crossed it was sixteen to eighteen fathoms wide, and three and a-half palms (1 ft. 2 in. ?) deep. Seeing that it can be navigated by all manner of boats only during the rains, I did not carry out my intention of sending down one of the officers to Zumbo, the settlement at its junction with the Zambeze. As far as the Aruangôa I had not seen a single tree of which a good-sized plank could be made ; beyond it, but only on the lands adjoining the course, many fit both for boards and for canoes were found growing. A number of Muizas marched along the river, to lance hippopotami. All the Caffres of these lands and, as far as I see, of Inner Africa generally, prize the flesh, and the more tainted it is the better they like it.

---

[*] According to Monteiro and Gamitto (p. 139), when they were encamped at a place 5 leagues from the village of Mazavamba, they were 2½ leagues from this Aruangôa, which they forded on September 6, 1831. It must be remembered that the second expedition crossed the stream, June 12th, west of Dr. de Lacerda's line, whilst Dr. Livingstone marched between the two very nearly as far as the Chambeze River. (See September 6th.)

CHAPTER III.

August 26, 1798.—This day I made a long march to reach
a lake or lagoon; all the ground was marked with elephants'
trails, the first seen since we left Tete.*

27*th*.—I halted near the village of Caperampande,† and, with
the view of sending carriers to assist the second division, I
waited over the 28th instant, supposing that these people are
subject to, or at least that they fear, the Cazembe, and would
not dare to desert like those of Caperemera.

28*th*.—I could not obtain people; they were numerous
enough, but they demanded for four days as much as the
Muizas had received for the whole journey to the country of
the Cazembe: they at last confessed that, not being accustomed
to carry, they would leave their packs on the path.‡ The
millet harvest-home having just ended, here, as in the land of
Mazavumba, the people are in a constant state of drink, which
they call a festival. Since my arrival the drum has never been
silent at night, and when I asked if it was to collect a party
for me, they replied "No;" it was a sign that on the morrow
they would "raise Pombe." After inquiry, I found the phrase
to mean that, when the Fumo, or village chief, caused his
drum to sound in that way, it was an order for all his "sons,"
or subjects, to come on the next day with their pots full of
country-beer to be drunk with shouting (war cries?) and
dancing.

29*th*.—A short march to water. Passing the village of Caperampande, I found the people at their orgies with the red wood-
dust, before mentioned, covering their hair, which thus looks as
if the stuff lay upon it in swathes. The place appeared a hell—

---

* The wooded lands noticed on August 26th account for the presence of
elephants.

† We find (Diary, August 16th) that Caperemera means "the brave": this word
is also evidently a compound, to be pronounced Caperampande.

‡ Though a superior race to those of the seaboard, the inner peoples of Africa
are often less manageable by the traveller than the "coast ruffians": they are
absolutely ignorant of the value of money, and they refuse to abate whatever their
want of knowledge demands.

the Muizas its devils. On the festal days when they collect to-drink, all wear their best clothes, if they have any.

30th.—At the beginning of the march we ascended low and gentle ridges, which were followed by one that was high, great, and rough ; it trends, they tell me, to the Zambeze and the River Chire (Shire). It is called Serra Muchingua. I named it Antonina, in honour of our august Prince, whom the Lord prosper and preserve.*

31st.—At 6.30 A.M. I broke up the camp and entered a riant, spacious valley scattered with settlements; from the Aruangôa River to this place the land is too rough and stony, too arid and waste, to invite lingering. A multitude of Muizas begged me to stop and be stared at : they ran after us, men and women, more than a quarter of a league, trampling on one another. clearing the bushes, falling and rolling (arranhando-se) at our feet, but were persistent in satisfying their curiosity.† They do not carry bows and arrows, like the Maraves, and in both tribes I never remember seeing a lame or a maimed man. Finally, amongst the Muizas to-day there was not an inch of cotton-cloth, all being dressed in fibre-fabrics.

Sept. 1, 1798.—As the powerful Muiza kinglet Mucunguro—of whom they say that he is not really a subject, but an ally, of the Cazembe—was absent from the village, I marched to meet him in the place where he lives. Thus I hoped to succour the second division, which must have suffered from hardship and hunger. These difficulties arose from the Tete Caffres having deserted after hearing their proprietors exaggerating the difficulties and dangers, the terrors and horrors, of a journey before made by Manoel Caetano Pereira, and by the slaves of D. Francisca, of Curvo, and of others.

The country to-day travelled over is high and rocky; the settlements are small, wretched, and starving. It is sad to see so many well-made and robust Muizas with teeth destroyed by the loss of enamel when jagging them like saws.‡ This deformity is Fashion's work—of whom we may say, as the Latin poet said of language—

> "Si volet usus,
> Quem penes arbitrium est, et jus."

This excuses every folly and ridicule of dress, and adds arti-

---

* This is the well-known Serra Muxinga, a name which Monteiro and Gamitto (p. 171) have very properly retained. It is spelt Maxenga or Machinga, by Mr. Macqueen, and Muchingas by Mr. Cooley, who translates it the "deep defile." See note to August 18th, of Dr. de Lacerda's 'Diary.'

† This scene I have frequently witnessed in Central Africa, where the people never knew any " white " but an Albino.

‡ I never saw the enamel injured by jagging, but it is by smoking, and more so by chewing tobacco mixed with earth, lime, or saltpetre.

ficial to the natural miseries of human life.   What a profit to
a people who, contented with modesty, decorum, and cleanliness, would minister to the caprice, the vanity, and the folly of
others, that live upon such trifles and unnecessary inventions.
La Moda, I believe, would thus be the most valuable article of
traffic to a nation that refused to use her.

2nd.—About midday Mucungure visited me with a long
"tail," under two very old and broken umbrellas, preceded by
many drums, which, with the clamour of his people, made a
truly infernal music. He appeared to be in his second childhood; and when I began to talk business about his assisting my
people, two of his magnates told me not to trouble myself—that
all should be done.   He brought a pair of wives: these ladies,
like himself and his subjects, wore tree-barks with girt waists.
The Caffres and their spouses habitually appear in the poorest
attires, by this mute language appealing for cloth.   Although,
for reasons above given, I have no good opinion of, or trust in,
the Muizas, I was satisfied with this chief and his grandees,
who gave me 50 men to forward those left behind.

3rd.—To-day I was confirmed in my opinion, that all the
Muizas are not subject to the Cazembe, by seeing the respect
with which Catára, a courtier of the king, spoke to the Mambo
Mucungure.   My questions elicited the :fact that 'the latter is
an independent and powerful Caffre.   Similar falsehoods were
told to me by eye-witnesses when I was serving the Crown in
Mato-Grosso: this caused great expense to the Royal Treasury, whilst I and my companions went through many perils and
hardships, spending six months near the Lake Xaraos, hemmed
in between the Payaguá and the Equestrian (Cavalleiro) tribes,
the bravest in our America.   These things, I say, have made of
me a complete Pyrrhonist.   I remember having heard Manoel
Caetano Pereira and his Muizas asseverate that on this side of
the Aruangôa River begin vast pampas and plains:[*] hitherto
the country has changed in nothing from the bushy lands which
commence at Tete, except in the better or in the worse quality
of its soil.

4th.—To-day we had three troubles,—a long march to water
through a depopulated country (the most easily endured), a thigh-
deep marsh near a ridge; and, thirdly, the most dangerous, a
grass-fire, which surrounded us, and which gave us great trouble
to escape.   Being sure that the Caffres can no longer fly, I did
not administer at the village of Caperemera corporal punishment, that they might be able to march; yet two of those who
escorted me, believing that they could escape castigation, did

---

[*] He will presently find out that this is correct.

their best to deserve it. After sending an order for them to be flogged, one of them, being a head-man (Mocazembo), was put into the bilboes.* This example has so altered the Caffres that I no longer recognise them: they are now most obedient; they are ready without murmuring to make any march I please, nor do they require driving to work. And, remembering Hippocrates,—"Quæ applicata juvant continuata sanant,"—I shall not forget to apply to future sick men a remedy which has already worked so well. Bravery, honour, and fear keep men in the right path. The two first virtues have fled so far from Caffre-land that no human force can bring them back; to the third, however, the people are by no means insensible; only, as they care nought for good or evil to come, they require at times a present example to bring them to a sense of their duty.

5th.—In 1 hr. 45' we crossed the Serra Rodrigo, passing over a level break in the mountains, and then down a very gentle and easy declivity. The wintry rains flowing from this open country, and those of the other serra near which I halted, form a second swamp as troublesome as that of yesterday.

6th.—To-day the shrubs and bush which cover these lands were so thick that the Caffres who carried our luggage found it hard to remove them. The depopulation of the place, the famished state of our party, the marshes, our having to cut lines and paths, and the thirst which often afflicts us, the fevers caused by nightly cold and by fierce suns of day—to say nothing of my sickness—all combine to make the land appear wild and sad. Were there game to supply the want of millet, or small birds to charm us with their song, the transit would have been less tedious. For the last three days we have made much westing. I never supposed that we should have to approach so near the Equinoctial line.

7th.—As soon as I marched, the Caffres began their journey. Noteworthy are the uniformity and regularity of the ground during the last three stages. After a serra or ridge, whose end, however, is not perceptible, but whose breadth is inconsiderable, comes an open country of a league and more, then a lagoon, and finally another similar ridge.† I halted at a large streamlet,‡ near a settlement, and from this point forwards the land became more populous. In the village I saw two Muiza iron-smelting furnaces; they were too ruinous to give

---

* Na gargalheira, an Africo-Lusitanian word ; the Anglo-African phrase is " in log."

† Showing that the country rises in steps and plateaux to the north.

‡ Portuguese, especially the Brazilian dialect, is very rich in names for every description of water-course. See my ' Highlands of the Brazils.'

me an idea of their construction, but Catára assured me that in
the Cazembe's country I should view all at my ease.   The
furnaces appeared to me conical and truncated pyramids.*
An evening spent in questioning Catára convinced me that
without a knowledge of the language of, and a habit of intercourse
with, these people, their information is useless, and that nothing
they say is reliable.   To-day he contradicted the deposition
which I had taken from him and from Manoel Caetano Pereira
touching the Muropúe being the father of the Cazembe.†   In
order not to be ever saying and unsaying, I will wait for
information in the town (Zimboe)‡ of the said king, and then
set down all that I know for certain.

The Muizas count months by moons, of which they have
eight good (dry) and four bad (wet); the twelve make their
year, which begins with the first bad moon : this at present is
the rainy season, corresponding with our December.   The want
of judgment and discernment of these Caffres, the difficulty
of finding a man who understands their language, and at the
same time one instructed in chronology, and (as I perceive by
their replies) the pertinacity with which the interpreters dis-
figure my questions whilst adapting them to the limited intelligence of the hearers, make me despair of obtaining from the
Caffres much information of the kind wanted by learned men.
José Thomaz Gomes, fort adjutant of Sena, is an excellent
linguist for non-scientific purposes; he knows most of the Caffre
dialects, and he easily learns them.   He has hitherto served me
well, and I hope that in the city of the Cazembe he will serve
the Crown still better.

8th.—To stifle our hunger and collect six days' rations at the
village of Morangabambara, near the Zambeze River,§ I went
to-day a long march through champaign lands clearer than
before, and lacking high ridges and difficult swamps.   I passed

---

* Monteiro and Gamitto explain them (p. 38), and give a sketch of one,
fig. 2.
† The fact is that the traveller had misunderstood the word "father."
‡ Monteiro and Gamitto (p. 428, &c.) write the word Zimbáoé.   Mr. Cooley
rightly prefers Zimbáwe, and translates it "royal residence."   African kings
often live in quarters, or even in detached towns, inhabited solely by their wives
and families, their fetish men and their slaves.   An instance of this is Fuga in
Usambara.
§ The reader will bear in mind that this is the "River Chambeze," famed for
oysters, of MM. Monteiro and Gamitto's map, flowing to the left or south-west,
and now known to fall into the Bangweolo Basin or Bemba.   In his wonderful
'Inner Africa Laid Open,' p. 23, Mr. Cooley calls it the "New Zambeze," and to
fit his theories he makes it turn to the north-east and fall into his fabulous
"N'yassi, or the Sea."   Dr. Livingstone crossed it in S. lat. 10° 34', further east
than Lacerda, whose line again was 60 to 62 miles east of Monteiro and Gamitto.
(See note to August 21st.)

some villages—what villages!—four or five huts, so small and
low that one can hardly guess how the Muizas can lodge in
them. It is well known that a cylinder or an upright conical
pyramid forms the Caffres' houses. Amongst the Maraves
the cylinder base may have a radius of 6 (long) palms·
($6 \times 8 = 48$ inch. $= 4$ ft. diameter), and 4 to 5 of height. Upon·
this cylinder is placed the pyramidal roof, and as the radius of its
base is broader than the cylinder, the projecting eaves defend
the huts from the violent rains, increase the difficulty of entering and make the interior very dark. Those of the Muizas
are even smaller in base and height, and I wonder how
several people can subject themselves to occupy a single tene-
ment.* Still we see many animals inhabiting close and narrow
caves.

9th.—The village referred to lies but a short way off the
road; being indisposed, I did not visit it, though they tell
me it is one of the largest we have passed. The Muizas sold but
little millet-flour, because they possess little: this, too, in early
harvest time!—what will they have in three months hence,
and how do they manage in years of scarcity? The meal
offered by the Maraves was very white; amongst these negroes
it is wheat-coloured, because they do not clean it of the bran
lest the waste should leave them without food. Necessity obliges
man to all things. For this small quantity they hoe the
ground into mounds, and upon these they plant millet and some
beans. I judge that one of the bases of their support is the
sun-dried and sliced sweet potato (*Convolvulus batata*);† of that
they sold a fair portion, but they would not take up the fresh,
although it was either full-ripe or over-ripe. Sometimes they
attempted to sell the old, reserving the fresh for their own use.
Half a bushel (alqueire) of flour, a chicken, and a little basket
of sweet potatoes, was the present sent to me by the powerful
Morungabambara. We raised our hands in thanks to Heaven,
when, after abundant difficulty, we bought ten lean cockerels,
which seemed to us so many fat turkeys. We also obtained
some ground-nuts, of which we made oil as seasoning to our
rice, lest the meat and dripping might injure our stomachs and
salt produce painful thirst. The information touching salt
existing in this country, as given by Manoel Caetano Pereira
and by the Caffres, is wrong: if there be any, it is so little that
not a grain has appeared. What there is comes from the city

---

* Monteiro and Gamitto (pp. 64, 362) give a sketch of these huts. They are
not so uncomfortable as our author imagines, being cool in hot weather, warm in
the cold season, and air-tight at night—a defence against ague and fever.
† I found this food a favourite about Msene, in Western Unyamwezi; the leaf.
also makes a tolerable salad.

of the Cazembe or from its vicinity, where, they tell me, are
salt-mines as at Tete.

10th.—After 1 hour 20 minutes' march we reached the
Zambeze (Chambeze), measuring some 25 fathoms (braças) in
breadth, and at this season from 4 to 5 palms (2 feet 8 inches
to 3 feet 4 inches). Here end the starveling lands of these
high-haired and ringleted people. The number of Muizas
passing to the dominions of Caperemera was, not without
reason, agreeably to our proverb, "Where I am well, there is
my home."* As the Caffres are perfectly happy when they can
eat without labour, and as they must work hard to live poorly
in their own lands, whereas in the Marave country they have
abundance without much sweat of brow, we cannot marvel at
their emigration. I do not regard those who stay at home with
so much horror for being Anthropophagi, since "necessity,"
which, as they say, "has no law," compels them, after every
opportunity of battle, to batten upon human flesh, even if this
abominable custom does not proceed from satisfying their wrath
and revenge. On the other hand, again, I make their ignorance
an excuse for the unnatural action; for what is the African knowledge of good and evil?—they seem to me, indeed, not to know
that they have reason. If I had brought the geographical
books which I left at Tete, I should now imitate the Barber
Maese Nicolás and the Licentiate Pero Perez,† when they burned
to ashes Amadis de Gaul and all the chivalrous library of the
ingenuous knight Don Quixote. Thus would I have punished
the authors for disfiguring the face of the earth, describing
whatever their fancies (heated with rum and strong liquors im-
bibed against the cold) painted during sleep; attributing to whole
peoples and nations characters which they neither have nor
ever had; I would do the same with what they say of the
Paulistas, to whom Portugal knows not how much she is
indebted, or, if she knows, at any rate she does not recognise the
debt; and also with that which a celebrated modern Portuguese
(I know not whether as author or translator, but certainly as
impostor and defamer) said so impudently with respect to the
Americans, that he blushes not at being impeached for falsehood
or credulity, since we are not in the Iron Age; all, excepting those
who have written or spoken things which approach the truth as
declared by studious men of known veracity, not by secular
(ignorant) minds that take no interest in the progress of
science.‡ I would also burn the manuscripts in which I took

* This is the "Omne solum forti patria," a truth so distasteful to the Earl of
Chatham, and which railways and steamers realise to our minds every day.
† See Chap. VI.
‡ This fearful sentence is left as a specimen of the difficulties of translation.

down the depositions of Manoel Caetano Pereira and the
Muizas, touching the journey to the Cazembe, at least the
parts proved so far from truth, if I had but time to expurgate
them, or if there were anyone to do it for me.   But in time
justice shall be done ; meanwhile remains to me the consolation
of being a poor geographer, yet one of the six most veridiques,
since lying and geography, especially that of America, Africa,
and Asia, " sunt duo in carne unâ."

My principal desire being to obtain exact notices of the size
and the direction of all streams found between Tete and the
Cazembe's country, and from the latter to Angola, I laboured
to extract information from different Muiza Caffres, and from
Manoel Caetano Pereira, making repeated and compared
inquiries to avoid errors arising from strange languages.   All
uniformly and repeatedly assured me that the Zambeze (Chambeze) and the Ruçurue River *—15 fathoms broad and deeper
than the Zambeze at the part where I forded it to-day—ran to
the right of one travelling to the Cazembe.   Pereira confirmed
this information; from which I infer that he knows not his
right from his left hand ; and such must be the case, since he has
almost always lived amongst the Caffres, and has inherited
their intelligence, as experience is showing me.

To-day I sent to inquire about the course of the Zambeze
(Chambeze) from sundry Mussucumas, a tribe mixed in small
numbers with the Muizas on this side of the Zambeze, some of
them vassals to the Cazembe (these were my informants), and
others independent.†   All said that it trends to the river which
runs by the city of the Cazembe,‡ whatever be the truth of
their information, which at present I neither allow nor dis-
allow.

11th.—To-day nothing remarkable occurred, except that the
ridges and hillocks from Tete to the Zambeze (Chambeze)
River are now ended.

12th.—During the march we covered some leagues of open
plain, with as many of the usual ground, and we left on the
right hand a great standing water.   We halted in the large and
populous village of the Fumo Chinimba Campeze.   Here I was

The "Paulistas" I have already explained are the people of the Province of
S. Paulo, in the Brazil, who waged of old fierce wars with the Jesuit Spanish
colonies, and were abused accordingly by Charlevoix and his class.
* Mr. Cooley ('Inner Africa Laid Open,' p. 29) insists upon changing this to
Rusuro, a " Muconango word.'   In Kihiáo, or the language of the once powerful
Wabiáo tribe, " Meal " (Maji in Kisawahili) is water, and Busuro, or Lusuro, is
flowing water—a stream.
† The Musukuma seems to be an unimportant tribe.   "Usukuma," in
Unyamwezi, means the "northern country."
‡ Meaning that it joins the Luapula, and this we know to be correct.

visited by sundry Muizas returning from the city of the
Cazembe with ivory, intended for sale to the Caffres of the
Eastern Coast. From two of the slaves I attempted to extract
some information touching the River Chire (Shire). They
replied that their nation did not travel, and that it is only since
the Cazembe conquered them in war that they ever leave their
country, and even that now they never go further than the city
of that king. Some Caffres sent to buy fowls failed to procure
any. A tribute of poultry is exacted by the Cazembe, to whom
the people send as many as they breed.

13th.—We spent an hour in crossing the worst swamp yet
seen. Many Muizas passed us yesterday, coming from the king
with ivory and copper-bars for sale. I now think with reason
that the great number of tusks which once went to Mozambique, and which certainly came from these lands, goes at present to Zanzibar, or the neighbourhood, not only because they
get more for their ivory, but also because Zanzibar is nearer
than our possessions.*

14th.—A short march placed me at the village of Fumo
Chipaco, the largest and the most populous of all. I judge that
this must be one of the grandees, as Catára spoke of him with
respect. He at once sent him to call upon me, with a civil
message that, as a friend of his master, I was in my own
country, and that he, as a slave of the Cazembe, was also mine;
moreover, that all things in his village, and in those under his
command, were at my disposal. I was pleased by such attention, and by a message which I never expected to hear from a
Caffre who had never seen any but Caffres.†

As I cannot think of anything but my present undertaking,
I begged from him people to assist the 2nd Division, of which
he had already heard from Catára. The latter lay sick at a
village near the River Zambeze (Chambeze). He answered
that he would give me as many as I wanted, and that he would
presently order his drums to sound the assembly and to collect
all, when I could take what number I pleased. His answer
about our provisions is also worthy of being recorded literally.
" Tell the Mambo that he is in the village of Chipaco." O vanity

---

* This was the case two-thirds of a century ago, and of late years the Zanzibar
market has greatly increased. I stated, in 1859, that the north of the Nyassa
or Kilwa Lake had been visited by hundreds of caravans (' Journal of the Royal
Geographical Society,' vol. xxix. p. 272). Mr. Cooley, who quotes largely from
Doctor de Lacerda, but who apparently has read him partially (' Review,' p.
15), calls this a "monstrous assertion," simply because they would then march
over his purely imaginary "sea." Dr. Livingstone has performed this feat
during his last expedition, and apparently was not aware of the impossibility. ·

† The contrary is the case; the African borrowing from the European as much
rudeness as he dares to affect. Witness " S'a Leone."

and *amour propre!* Is it possible that, even in the depths of
the jungle, thou canst not leave free from thy poison these wild,
half-naked men? But vices are born with us.

We will see if his works belie these good signs. I hope not,
as yesterday and to-day we have seen many human skulls and
corpses cast out upon the road. These frequent examples must
make men respect and fear this king; as the latter, they knew,
sought our friendship, they will not fail to assist us.* Some of
those wretches had lost their lives for witchcraft, there being a
belief in all this part of Africa, even amongst many whites (as I
saw in Mozambique), that no man ever dies except by sorcery.†
Whenever a Caffre accused of this crime denies his guilt—some
coarsely confess their guilt—he undergoes the Mavo ordeal.‡
It consists in administering a tincture of some bark (the tree
being called Muána), which is a violent purgative, and, as the
dose is copious, the wretch generally dies in horrible pains.
When I lay very sick on this side of Java (Jáua), the Muizas
said that, had the Cazembo been in my case, many would have
been slain. How blind, how heavy, and how afflicting, is this
thraldom of Sathanas! How gentle, how peaceful, is the yoke
of Jesus Christ! If the supposed wizard is lucky enough to
vomit, his innocence is fêted with great joy, and his accuser is
fined. The Maraves burn their sorcerers.§

15th.—Since crossing the Aruangôa River my illness kept me
between palanquin and bed. Wishing to receive at my ease the
visit of Chipaco, and to return the visit which he paid me to-day,
so as to despatch sixty men to-morrow, I entered my palanquin.
His settlement is large, though it does not appear so. According
to country custom the huts are so close, and without order, that my
vehicle could hardly thread its way between them, and so small are
the tenements, it was often carried over the lower part of the roofs.
Chipaco alone supplied us with sweet potatoes and meal, besides
that which we were obliged to buy from his subjects. He also
offered to lead in person sixty Caffres for the assistance of our
lag-behinds, and thus he hoped to avoid the chastisement of the
Cazembo for idleness on the part of his "sons." His second in
command, however, undertook this commission—such is the fear
and respect with which they regard their king.

---

* It is always a pleasure, after travelling through the semi-republican tribes
of Africa, to arrive at the head-quarters of a strong and sanguinary despotism.

† This is the universal negro belief.

‡ Monteiro and Gamitto (p. 89) describe and sketch the "Muáve Ordeal."
This poisoning the "Sassy (Saucy) Water," the "red water," the "Calabar
(or ordeal) bean" of the Western Coast, and the Tanjîna of Madagascar, is
almost universal in Africa.

§ I found this custom of burning magicians fearfully prevalent in the Lake
Regions, especially among the Wakhutu.

This Fumo, when visiting me, rose up brusquely, and retired, as if cutting short the conversation: I wondered at the proceeding, and thought that perhaps he had been offended by me unintentionally. But two Caffres, who had thrice made this journey, informed me, in reply to my question if any cause of scandal had been given, that such is the custom of the grandees, and that I must not be astonished to see it in the king's city.*

This gives me an opening to describe Caffre greeting ceremonies between slaves and freedmen, and between Maraves, Munhaes,† Muizas, and other natives known to us. With scanty difference it is almost the same. When Caffres meet and wish to salute one another they mutually clap palms in measured time and in silence, after which they enter into conversation. When visiting they do the same: but if the master of the house be unwell, he does not beat hands, and his visitor, seeing the state of things, does it softly. It is not a fixed rule to clap palms, each one slaps the part of the body which, according to position, he deems most suitable. Amongst some nations subjects, in the presence of their chiefs, lie on their sides—a sign of inferiority: our Caffres, and the labourers of the Crown lands, when not in revolt, do the same. The Maraves, and others who are not subject to us, never prostrate themselves, except when visiting our lands. In their own country it is a token of friendship for, or an acknowledgment of benefit, gift, or praise from, a white man. The Muizas on these occasions also rub dust on the breast and arms, and lastly, on the breast: the males beat palms with the hands upraised, as we do in prayer, whilst the women hold them horizontally.

16th.—With a mind somewhat at ease I continued my march, and, after crossing some rivulets, at the end of the day's work we forded sundry large streamlets; besides others, the Ricena and Mocanda. The Caffres never pronounce this initial "R" as if it were double.‡ Before arriving at these waters, whether great or small, the land slopes gently down, and, after passing

---

* The great 'Times' Correspondent, Dr. William H. Russell, complained, we may remember, of the same abruptness in the citizens of the United States. It is generally the case in Africa, where it contrasts strongly with the elaborate nature of the greeting when men meet.

† According to Monteiro and Gamitto (p. 47, &c.) the Munhaes, neighbours of the Maraves, live on the west of the Great Zambeze, and are governed by the Mambo as Chedima, whom the Portuguese call the Monomotapa. They are evidently the Banyai of Dr. Livingstone.

‡ According to Monteiro and Gamitto (p. 205) the "R" is not pronounced, and the "L" often takes its place, as Luena and Levago for Ruena and Revago. This is general amongst the Maraves. I have elsewhere spoken of other tribes.

over the bed, it rises similarly; so that the drains flow either
between ribs or waves of ground, or through low hills."

17th.—To-day's march was of moderate length. Some Caffres
brought us a few chickens, which, having no large porcelain beads
(velorio), greatly to our sorrow, we were unable to purchase. I
think to have heard that the best quality of beads comes to
Mozambique, and that the Banyans, the true traders of that
place, sell them to the Moors or Arabs of Zanzibar, or dispose
of them by means of the Mujão† throughout the interior. In this
journey I do not remember seeing any Caffre ornaments of
small beads (Missanga), between the Mocanda and our present
camp: all are made of the said large velorio, and few are of the
so-called first quality which comes to Rios de Sena.

18th.—Our only novelty to-day was the slow and patience-
trying work of clearing the path in many places; happily
the bush was not strong. We crossed the little River Ru-
cure.

13th.—However good the water may appear, it cannot be
healthy from where the swamps begin. It always runs through
stagnant formations, and is tainted more or less by the vegeta-
tion that rots in it. We are often obliged to use dammed-up
and standing water.

20th.—The village of the Fumo Mouro-Atchinto‡ ends the
district of Fumo Chipaco, which began at the River Zambeze
(Chambeze). Here I halted for three reasons. Firstly, to rest
the party and prepare for a forced march of seven to eight days
through the waste and desert country before us. Secondly, to
collect supplies on this day and the 21st. Thirdly, to observe the
immersions of Jupiter's satellites, if my illness permit, and the
bush burnings which begin at 9 to 10 A.M., leave the air clear. Of
late the atmosphere has been thick, and only about dawn it thins
with the fall of dew (cucimba), which is cold and heavy. This
chill is followed by an intense heat, the effect of sun and grass-
smoke, and at 11 A.M. it is at its height. To-day we suffered
from the smoke which was all round us, and, fortunately for
us, the dried herbage was not very high. We crossed a River
Ruanzeze.

21st.—The Caffres say that on both sides of and near the
high road are small villages. They also assured me that to

---

* This exactly describes the region traversed when approaching the Tanganyika Lake.
† The Wahiáo of whom I have spoken in 'Zanzibar: City, Island, and Coast.'
(see Diary, August 15th).
‡ Evidently the proper name of the Mfumo. The country is called "Chaum,"
and when the next expedition went there, they found it under the Mfumo Mulza
Mcasiro-Chirumba.

northward lies the Uemba nation,* between the Muizas and the
Mussucuma, who reach the banks of the Chire (Shire) or
Nhanja.† Also they assure us that the Uemba and the Mussucuma are mortal enemies to, never sparing, the Cazembe's
people; but they are equally so with the Muizas, whom they
know by their combed heads. On the south are the Arambas
and the Ambos, peaceful friends of the Cazembe, who trade,
they declare, with the Caffres near Zumbo.

Despite my serious weakness, I observed the immersions of
Jupiter's first satellite, which gave me for the position of
Mouro-Atchinto, 2 hours 36 minutes 40 seconds east of Lisbon
(or 39° 10′ 0″=30° 1′ 58″ long. E. Green.) The latitude was
S. 10° 20′ 35″.‡

22nd, 23rd, 24th.—Many elephant-tracks in these lands; the
trees increase in height and thickness.

25th.—I halted at a village of a few huts, inhabited by some
Muizas, who are obliged every three days to collect the Sura,
wine extracted from a wild palm called Uchinda. I preferred
it to that supplied by the Palmeira mansa, or cocoa-nut-tree.§
Here I received news of the chief sergeant, Pedro Xavier
Velasco, who was sent forward from the Mocanda; possibly
sickness has, contrary to my instructions, detained him so long.

26th.—This day's country is hilly and stony, chiefly in the
ascents and descents, but there is a kind of plain or plateau
which forms the highest levels,‖ and which apparently con-
tinues, seeing that nothing is in view but low hills.

27th.—Feverish and weak, I marched over the desert and
crossed some swamps. A Caffre guide assured me that in the

---

* The Anembas, Muembas, or Moluanes, are mentioned by Monteiro and Gamitto (p. 408, &c.) as a nomad tribe from the W.N.W. of the Cazembe's country,
which has seized part of the lands of the Muizas. Their chief is entitled the
Chiti-Muculo. In the 'Mittheilungen' we read that the Awembe and Mluana
are mixed or half-bred Milua (the Sowahíli Warúa), congeners of the Alunda,
the subjects of the Muáti yá Nvo.

† The Nyassa Lake. This passage shows how well the Nyassa Lake, and its
drain the Shire, were known, even in 1798.

‡ This was the lamented traveller's last observation. According to Dr. Livingstone ('writing from Lake Bangweolo, July 1868), "one of them (the four brooks),
the Chungu, possesses a somewhat melancholy interest, as that on which poor
Dr. Lacerda died; . . . . his latitude of Cazembe's town on the Chungu being
50 miles wrong, probably reveals that his head was clouded with fever when he
last observed." But at the tenth parallel of south latitude, Dr. Livingstone was
close to Lacerda's path, and he also places the Chungu rivulet about south
latitude 10°. The fact is, that Dr. Livingstone's map misled him.

§ I have always, on the contrary, found the toddy supplied by the cocoa-tree
(Cocos nucifera) the best flavoured of all palm-wines.

‖ A common formation in the African and Brazilian interiors is an upland
plateau of earth, bounded by descents, from which wind and rain have swept
away the humus, leaving the shoulders bare and stony. These places are always
the worst riding.

highlands to the left hand (westward) is the Great Lake which he and his master Manoel Caetano Pereira—who, however, made it larger—had crossed on their last journey.* It must be a continuation of that near which I nighted, perhaps anastomosing with the other water which we have passed, since the owners of certain miserable huts where we are now, there catch, it is said, large fish. I wonder at the scarcity of game in this bush; whatever may be to come, I expected in this desert-march (Travessia) to see some animals at a distance.† But if we fare badly in this part, we are recompensed by the absence of the mosquitos with their burning sting and their infernal song.

28th.—At 1 P.M. I reached a village governed by the Fumo Mouro, of the same grade of vassalhood, but nearer related (mais conjuncto) to the Cazembe. About half a league before our arrival a vast crowd of both sexes and all ages awaited me with festive instruments: so anxious were they to see me that some were perched on tree-tops, and after I had passed they descended and accompanied me, singing, playing instruments, dancing, and at the same time clearing the road. Those who were on the ground ceremoniously rubbed themselves with dust, and showed their wonder of all they saw, not only by the expression of their countenances, but by holding the forefinger in the mouth ‡ and by biting the hand. I did not see one Muiza here. In the afternoon Mouro sent me his present of Pombe, four large chickens, and a gazelle almost decomposed, with a message that he did not visit me in person, as he was preparing subsistence for my people. To-day's march was clear of trees; but all suffered from want of water, which was not found till wo reached the Daro or halting-place (pousada).

20th.—As the Fumo did not keep his word touching supplies, I sent my people to buy what was offered, namely manioc flour, as good as any I have seen in Mozambique, millet still in spike, but very black from the smoke with which they drive away the insects.

All the manioc meal (farinha), even in the Zimboé or Cazembe's city, is made in the same way. They soak the roots,

---

* This is evidently the Bemba or Bangweolo Lake lately visited by Dr. Livingstone. It was foreshadowed in our map by the Shuia Lake, which I had named " Ghama."—(' Memoir on the Lake Regions of Central Africa,' ' Journal of the Royal Geographical Society,' vol. xxix.). I must observe that there is a Lake "Suai," or " Zwai," near Gurague in Abyssinia; and so there is a Karagwah or Karagwo, north of Unyamwezi.

† The deep African forest is everywhere unfit to support animal life, unless it is broken by large clear spaces, where wild beasts can enjoy sun and air.

‡ This is also a popular way of expressing extreme astonishment amongst many Asiatic peoples. Biting the hand is mostly a mark of regret or disappointment.

peel and sun-dry them whole: they pound and grind them on a stone when wanted for use, and then they make the so-called massa, dough, or unleavened bread. Whilst travelling they carry the roots entire, and expend them as they are required. They also eat, but not often, the sweet manioc* roasted: I tried this plan, not liking the dough. In the afternoon a visit was paid to me by the Fumo; he exaggerated the honour by assuring me—so infatuated is he with his dignity—that he will explain the extreme measure of leaving his village by considering us to be the Cazembe, the only person who can claim such devoirs.

30th.—Leaving a road formerly well trodden and populous, I followed another shorter and clearer path which was opened, they say, when the Cazembe changed the site of his settlement (Zimboé) for one more easily fortified. This line is at once shorter and clearer. To-day I had news of the chief sergeant Pedro Xavier Velasco reaching the Zimboé, where the Cazembe had immediately ordered one of his grandees to prepare subsistence and to meet me. They say that the king expects me with transports of delight.† May it be true! But I doubt it, having observed that a Caffre's mouth never opens without a lie slipping out. It is a people wholly regardless of duty in matters of truth.

October 1st.—Approaching the halting-place I travelled between two high rough ridges stretching out of sight. I passed some villages lately deserted and founded on good sites, the soil being good and the forests like that of the Brazil, the trees being tall and large. It was said that the people had fled after suffering much from lions.‡

2nd.—When beginning the march I met two brothers of the Cazembe and a son of the Fumo Anceva,§ his relation, escorting a goodly store of manioc, sun-dried "bush-beef," and two she-goats for our Caffres: the soldiers had their portion of the same separately.‖

My intention was to-day to travel as near as possible to the Zimboé, but these messengers told me that being a Mambo, or chief, like the Cazembe, I could not advance until their

---

* This is the Macaxeira or Aipim (J. utilissima) of the Brazil; it contains no poisonous principle, and therefore it does not require to be soaked and pressed.

† As the first European who ever visited the country, Dr. de Lacerda might expect a most ceremonious reception.

‡ Monteiro and Gamitto also here found lions dangerous.

§ According to Monteiro and Gamitto (p. 236), the Fumo Anceva is a functionary who watches over and is answerable for strangers at the city of the Cazembe, and through him they must seek their audiences with the king. There is such an officer at all the African Courts, and a mighty post, as a rule, he is.

‖ This exactly describes the preparatory reception of a visitor by the Kings of Dahomey, Benin, and others.

father, the king, had first rendered to his ancestral Manes
(Mozimos) due thanks for my arrival in his country. Also that
I should advance a little nearer the place, town, or house
(Massanza *), where the Cazembe's father is buried, and there
express proper gratitude for the said benefit. Withal they
would not agree for me to enter the place to-day, nor could I
do otherwise than conform to their wishes. They begged me to
pitch the camp outside, as they had to give me the message of
their king. They said that the Cazembe was so much satisfied
with my coming that he soon would plaster his body with
chalk,[†] in sign of thankfulness to his "spirits," and would
send to fetch me.

I was also directed to leave at the burial-place of the royal
ancestors a blue cotton (Ardian), 4 fathoms of cotton-cloth, and
a small quantity of white and coloured stoneware beads. The
king did the same with Manoel Caetano Pereira. As far as I
can see, travellers pay up the vows and offerings with which the
king supplies the spirits for benefits received. At the same
moment the two officers sent a messenger to the king.

Whilst they were preparing the hut and bed, between which
I am now compelled to live, I called up these officers, but they
would not answer a word to my questions. When, wondering
at this profound silence, I was told by the interpreter that,
though they could listen to all I had to say, they could not
speak till after delivering the royal Muromo.[‡] Finally, when
they brought me the message, I ordered, in token of respect, a
mat to be spread for them, but they always seated themselves
upon the ground, saying that I was a second Cazembe, and that
such was their only place in my presence.

At 6½ A.M. returned the messenger, who was sent forward
yesterday by the brothers of the Cazembe. These two officers
said that the king asked me not to move to-day as it was unnecessary for me to visit his father's burial-place (Massanza),
that it would be enough for me to forward the cloth yesterday
mentioned, and that to-morrow, after the ceremonies, I could
continue my march. He presented to me two tusks in token of
friendship.

It is clear that I must agree to what the Cazembe asks,
despite the injury which the delay will cause in my present
state of health. But seeing that these exceedingly superstitious
Caffres hold their dead to be gods, and reflecting that the faith

---

* This burial-place of the Muáta, or Cazembean kings, is called by Monteiro
and Gamitto (p. 229) "Máximo."
[†] It was a white powder, called "Impemba."—"Uma sorte de gis (gypsum)."
[‡] In Portuguese Boca, or "mouth," signifying that it allowed free intercourse.

which the Demon engraves upon the human breast must lie deep, I resolved, by a stately ceremonial, to obtain their good will for myself, and thereby to forward the views of the Crown. Wishing to give an idea of their rites, I sent Lieut.-Colonel Pedro Nolasco and Lieutenant José Vicente Pereira Salema with soldiers to the grave, and ordered them to fire three salutes with the usual interval, exaggerating as much as possible the obsequies in token of friendship, and carefully noting everything they saw.

This had an excellent effect upon the crowd, and upon the guardian-priest (Muine-Máximo),[*] who, externally, was not distinguished from other Caffres. The latter, after consulting his oracle, the ghost of the Cazembe's father, exclaimed that I who had bewailed with them the death of their king was a god who had come to them; that I should go wherever it pleased me, all the country being mine, and so forth. His good will was confirmed by a present and by a message from me begging him to take particular care of the respectable house, where lay my friend the Cazembe's father, whose ashes I so much respected.[†]

*   *   *   *   *

End of Dr. de Lacerda's Journal.[‡]

REMARKS BY THE TRANSLATOR.

According to Monteiro and Gamitto (p. 370), the history of the Cazembe's people is wholly traditional.[§]   It is said that the

---

[*] Monteiro and Gamitto (p. 230) were received by the priest sitting cross-legged on a lion's skin, and all whitened with Impemba. And they had to pay for this African apparatus.

[†] According to Monteiro and Gamitto, the stages from Tete to Lunda (the capital of the Cazembe) are as follows:—

			Days.	Leagues.
1st.	From Tete to the Aruángra River	..	.. 25	.. 120½
2nd.	„ Aruángra River to the Chambeze River..	22	.. 80½
3rd.	„ Chambeze River (a desert) to Lunda city	29	.. 90
		Total	76	291½

[‡] Mr. Cooley, 'Geography of N'yassi' (p. 34), says, "the expedition arrived at Locanda (the Cazembe's city) on the 2nd of October, and Lacerda, worn out with fever, died on the 18th." For 2nd read 3rd. According to Monteiro and Gamitto (p. 337), the traveller was buried a day's march from the then capital, and there is still in the place a Muine-Máximo, or Lord of the Tomb. When the expedition returned, the bones of the unfortunate explorer were, as will be seen, exhumed for the removal to Tete, but the Muizas attacked the carriers, and thus they were dispersed in the bush.

[§] Mr. Cooley in 1845 ('Journal of the Royal Geographical Society') borrowed the history of the Cazembe from Pedro the Pombeiro ('Annaes Maritimos,' No. 7, p. 290). In 1851 appeared 'O Muata Cazembe,' the work of MM. Monteiro and Gamitto; it is a far more reliable account than the former. Mr. Cooley had

"great potentate Muropúe, or Mwáté yá Nvo," hearing of white men living towards the east, sent a Quilolo, or captain, named Canhembo,* to open intercourse with them. Under this captain's charge was placed one of the potentate's sons, for whom cruelty and insubordination rendered exile advisable. The Quilolo, with an army of Alondas (speaking the Campocólo language), subdued the Wasira (Messira),† lords of the soil. At last, discovering a plot laid against him by the turbulent prince, he resolved to return with him to the Muropúe and to report his success. This he did; but when again sent eastward with "Chambançua," the big drum of terrible notes, this Captain, Canhembo, was treacherously drowned in the Lualáo River by the prince, who was, in his turn, put to death by his father.

The Muropúe then sent his Fumo Anceva, Canhembo, the son of the murdered man, who, when the Wasira (Messira) rebelled, finally defeated them. In memory of their founder all the other kings took the name of Canhembo. At first they were mere vassals of the Mwáté yá Nvo; presently they sought independence, and established a royal court. Canhembo IV., surnamed Lequéza,‡ was the next; and he received Dr. de Lacerda. Of his valour, humanity, and generosity, many tales are still current. He was succeeded early in the present century by Canhembo V., who is described by the second Portuguese expedition as a barbarian and a coward; in fact, a facsimile of the first Canhembo's assassin.

In these Diaries we find neither the name of the city nor the ruler. This is truly African, arising from the superstitious fear of either being known. The expedition seems to have left the country persuaded that the name of the old capital was "Chungo," or Chungu ('Diary,' July 24, 1799). According to Mr. Cooley, it is 10 miles south of the modern capital, and 20 miles north of the River Luo. Ladislaus Magyar declares that the true name of the Cazembe's capital is Tamba-la-meba, but I do not know how he heard it. The Arabs of Zanzibar spoke to me of it as "Usenda," possibly a corruption of Lucenda, Luenda, Lunda, or Londa. It is now assumed, I do not know why, that Lucenda is a pure error for Lunda.§

---

unfortunately published his 'Inner Africa Laid Open' in 1852, and, therefore, we detect in it all his old errors.

* This may explain the King "Kiyombo of Ururwea," whom the Kazeh Arabs spoke of ('Journal of the Royal Geographical Society,' vol. xxix. p. 253).

† The 'Vacira' of the Chaplain (Feb. 18-21), and of 'Inner Africa Laid Open,' p. 89.

‡ Pedro the Pombeiro called him Hunga Amurongu, but this is probably some title.

§ 'Bulletin,' Series V., tom. iii. p. 337.

DIARY OF DR. DE LACERDA'S JOURNEY.

Station.		Date.	Remarks.
1	July	3, 1798	From Nhaufa Fatiola Estate, north of Zambese River, to Mitondo; short day's march.—N.B. The average is stated to be 2½ Portuguese leagues, per diem.
2	„	4, „	To Inhacenguira (Nhassengeira?) the last of the Crown properties, distant one league from Mitondo: here the land of the Maraves begins.
3	„	0, „	To a nameless plain or prairie in the Marave country; short march.
4	„	7, „	To a similar halting-place; short day.
5	„	8, „	To the Mashinga estate, a gold-digging; march ending 2·30 P.M.
6	„	14, „	To a Marave village.
7	„	15, „	To a large village not named; march of two leagues.
8	„	16, „	To near the Lupata (or gorge), the end of "King" Bive's land; short march.
9	„	18, „	Marched with the Cordilheira Mariana to the east, and on the west the Cordilheira Joanina; short stage.
10	„	19, „	Entered the Cordilheira Mariana; halted at the Caruziasira stream; short march.
*11	„	21, „	To the Lupata Jaua, full march.
12	„	22, „	Twice crossed (crossed two branches of?) the Aruangôa.
13	„	26, „	Crossed the eastern ridge and halted at the streamlet Chigumumquiro; short march.
14	„	27, „	To a Marave village: marched from 8 A.M. till noon.
15	„	31, „	To place not named.
†16	August	7, „	Crossed the Ruy and Dua Rivers; halted on the banks of the Uzeruze River in the country of the King Mukando.
17	„	8, „	March with more of westing.
18 19	„	9–10, „	To the Chitenga village.
20	„	11, „	Very short march.
21	„	12, „	Passed gold-field and salipetro; also short march.
22	„	13, „	To the village of the Chief Caperemeru at 10·30 A.M.
23	„	17, „	A short march.
24	„	18, „	Over the Cordilheira Carlotina; *the first long march*.
25	„	19, „	To the Ircumzu River; forced march.
26	„	20, „	To the village of Mazavamba—the wildest and roughest of all the marches.
27	„	23, „	To a village near the Rio Remimba.
28	„	24, „	To the village of Capangura.
29	„	25, „	To the (northern) Aruangûa River; march of two hours.
30	„	26, „	To a lagoon; long march.

* Bowdich (p. 58) makes Jaua 5 days' journey from Tete.
† Bowdich (loc. cit.) makes "Boca" three marches from Jaua.

DIARY OF DR. DE LACERDA'S JOURNEY—*continued*.

Station.	Date.			Remarks.
31	August	27,	1798	To near the village of Kapera Mpande.
32	„	29,	„	A short march to water.
33	„	30,	„	To the Serra Mushinga.
34	„	31,	„	In a spacious fertile valley.
35	September	1,	„	Over high and rocky ground; settlements small, and starving, under the Mambo Macungure.
36	„	4,	„	A long march; crossing a desert and a marsh; much wasting.
37	„	5,	„	Crossed the Serra Rodrigo in 1h. 45m.; another marsh; much wasting.
38	„	6,	„	Bush very thick, had to be cut away; heat and cold excessive; much wasting.
39	„	7,	„	March like the three last, first over a ridge, then open country, then another ridge; halted at large stream near settlement; land waxes richer.
40	„	8,	„	A long march to the village of Morungabambara, near the Chambeze River.
41	„	10,	„	After 1h. 20m. to the Chambeze River.
42	„	11,	„	The ridges and hills extending from Tete to the Chambeze are not found on this march.
43	„	12,	„	Plain country; then usual style, large lagoon on right; to the village of Mfumo Chinimba Campeze.
44	„	13,	„	Took one hour to wade worst swamp yet seen.
45	„	14,	„	Short march to the large village of Mfumo Chipako.
46	„	16,	„	A gentle descent to the Hroena and Mokanda streams; after that an ascent.
47	„	17,	„	A moderate march.
48	„	18,	„	Had to cut a path through the shrubbery; crossed the streamlet Rukure.
49	„	19,	„	The water bed.
50	„	20,	„	Crossed a Hoanzeze River; reached the village of Mfumo Mouro Achinto, where last observation was made; N. lat. 10° 20' 83". Time, 2h. 86 m. 40 sec. east of Lisbon.
51	„	22,	„	}
52	„	23,	„	} Many elephant-tracks; forest of tall trees.
53	„	24,	„	}
54	„	25,	„	To a small village; some of the people Muizas.
55	„	26,	„	To a plateau.
56	„	27,	„	Land still desert; a great lake in the highlands to the west (Demba or Bangwoolo).
57	„	28,	„	To the village of Mfumo Mouro; no water on road, which was clear of forest.
58	„	30,	„	A shorter and clearer road, lately opened to the Cazembe's new city.
59	October	1,	„	Between two high rough ridges; people driven from villages by lions.
*60	„	2,	„	A short march towards the Mazanza, or burial-place of the defunct Cazembe. Death of Dr. de Lacerda, near the capital of the Cazembe, on October 18, 1798.

* Bowdich reduces the journey (Pereira being his authority) to 42 days from Maonempanda to Tete. The Diary (July 13, 1799) makes the march from the city to Tete 270 leagues.

CHAPTER IV.

DIARY OF THE EXPEDITION SENT BY HER MOST FAITHFUL MAJESTY TO EXPLORE THE AFRICAN INTERIOR, AND TO THE COURT OF THE CAZEMBE, DISTANT 270 LEAGUES FROM TETE, KEPT BY THE CHAPLAIN AND COMMANDER FR. FRANCISCO JOÃO PINTO, IN CONTINUATION OF THE DIARY OF DR. FRANCISCO JOSÉ DE LACERDA E ALMEIDA, TO BE PRESENTED TO THE MOST ILLUSTRIOUS AND EXCELLENT SENHOR FRANCISCO GUIDES DE CARVALHO E MENEZES DA COSTA, GOVERNOR AND CAPTAIN-GENERAL OF MOZAMBIQUE AND THE COAST OF EAST AFRICA.*

SECTION I.—*From date of Arrival at the City till December* 31, 1798.

November 6, 1798.—At 2 P.M., as the Second Division was on the line of march, arrived two soldiers, with official letters for the commandant of the first division, Lieut.-Colonel Pedro Nolasco Vieira de Araujo, stating that His Excellency the Governor of the Rios de Sena, Dr. Francisco José Maria de Lacerda e Almeida, had expired at the court (capital) of the King Cazembe, on October 18, 1798, and had appointed me to the charge of the expedition, with instructions to carry out all that he had begun by order of the Crown. At 4 o'clock P.M., the principal individuals and members of the second division being present at the halting-place (Daro), I directed the lieutenant of that division, Antonio José da Cruz, to read out my nomination as commandant; and by virtue of it I installed myself in lieu of Lieutenant Manoel dos Santos e Silva, who, from October 22nd, had commanded the second division, succeeding, by wish of the deceased governor, Gonçalo Caetano Pereira and José Rodriguez Caloja.

At 8 P.M. came to my straw hut (moçassa) the above-mentioned Lieutenant Manoel, to inform me that his late colleagues, together with Captain João da Cunha Pereira, desired to deprive me of the commandantship, although it had been

---

* This title will show the varied errors of Mr. Cooley ('Geography of N'yassi,' p. 40), that on the unfortunate Governor's death, "his followers, panic-struck, fled precipitately, and the whole property, including a good sum in gold, remained in the Cazembe's hands." In another place he asserts that Dr. de Lacerda "died immediately on his arrival, and never entered the place,"—what manner of "bull" is this? While in a third place we are told ('Geography of N'yassi,' p. 86), that the Cazembe refused Lacerda permission to proceed westward.

transferred to me in the name of the Crown; and to take it themselves—the captain as senior commissioned officer, and the other as being experienced in the country.

I recommended Lieutenant Manoel to allay, as well as he could, the rising mutiny, and to inform the mutineers that, if necessary to prevent disturbances, I would resign the command, but that they must understand the case to be the same as the rebellion at Cape Corrientes.*

These and other reasons, principally their incapacity to undertake so important a business, and to report of it to Lisbon and to Angola when the opening of the road shall have been effected, persuaded them to desist from their project.

7th.—The second division set out for a more populous country, to collect supplies which were much wanted. From this place, within two days' journey of the Cazembe's city, I sent a bearer with a "mouth"† of 200 cloths (each 2 fathoms) and 200 strings of beads (mutaia‡), to report our arrival, and to obtain the king's beneplacet for our entrance.

8th to 10th.—The permission arrived, but the hour being late, it was resolved to wait till the next day.

11th.—At 8 A.M. the second division marched in the usual order to enter the city. After thirty minutes on the road we met the Fumo Anceva, secretary, treasurer, and "landlord"§ of foreigners, who, being considered merchants, give him his name—Nanceva, being corrupted to Anceva. He was seated, a little off the road, in his chair, which resembled a plain taboret, and dressed in his mucanzo (mucônzo), the finest cloth amongst them. We at once sent to compliment him, and he told us that we might advance. We proceeded, and he followed us on foot, making use of Caffres when he had to be carried over mud and streams.

When we reached the place where the Muzungos of our party—they so call white men and all who are not Caffres—were halted, the Fumo Anceva appeared in his great houses, which the commandant of the first division had hired for me for a piece of Indian cotton, until others could be built. There he complimented me on the part of his master, and delivered to me a present of two ivories and two Caporretes, or Caffre lads,

---

* There is no other allusion to this mutiny.
† This has been explained before. The usual opening present to the King of Dahome is rum.
‡ This word will be found afterwards, written "Mutava."
§ Meaning Mehmandar, or host of stranger visitors. So at Dahome there is an English landlord, a French landlord, and so forth, and all strangers are officially looked upon as buyers and sellers, who must pay for the privilege of buying and selling.

16 years old. This offering is called "mouth" (boca), because all Caffres, except familiar friends who often see one another, never receive nor send messages, nor even speak, without a gift. The gifts were committed to the lieutenant-receiver, Manoel dos Santos e Silva, who carried them to the account of the Royal treasury. In the afternoon, by the advice of the more experienced who had preceded me, I forwarded unasked a "mouth" of 36 cloths, informing the king that we had arrived at his court.

12th.—The Cazembe sent a big sow for the Muzungos (white men) to see, saying that she came from Angola, by which they understand their trading-places near our establishment. When we asked if she had ever farrowed, they replied "no," and that the hog had died at once.

The Cazembe presented his new guests with a skinned and divided racaja*, and he recognized me as commandant, which was necessary before I could be so considered in his country.

13th.—The Cazembe having sent for our inspection various lots of woollen cloths, such as calamanhas,† lastings (durantes), fine serges (sarafinas), shaloons (saetas), opaque stone-ware beads (pedras de côr), and coloured ditto (pintadas), inquired if such articles were found in our country. He also made us a present of some blue drinking-glasses. Notwithstanding all this kindness, all those who from 3 P.M. came to our camp with wood, flour, legumes, and comestibles for sale, were seized and maltreated by the Fumo Anceva, and from that time natives were prohibited from selling anything to the strangers.‡

14th.—With the aid of the first guide of the bush (pratico dos mattos), Gonçalo Caetano Pereira, I began to prepare on the part of the Crown a present (mirambo) for the Cazembe, and persuaded by him that such an offering should be quite satisfactory, I invited the Fumo Anceva to be present. Our landlord did not fail us. Dr. de Lacerda had told him that the Second Division would bring up fine things, which the King of Manga § —so they call all the lands of the Muzungos—was sending to the Cazembe. The Fumo therefore pretended discontent with everything, and declared that the whole, being sent by the

---

* I cannot explain the meaning of "Racaja, esfolada e partida."
† Calamanhas, also spelt Callomanhas.
‡ This is a general proceeding in Central Africa, where the King wishes to be the only customer.
§ In this part of Africa "Manga" means the region of Whites. Monteiro and Gamitto (p. 165) translate it "Reino de Portugal." In 'Zanzibar' (vol. i. p. 20) I have explained it to mean literally rock, rocky ground—hence the Arabs are locally called Wamanga.

Crown of Portugal as a present, belonged to his master the
Cazembe.* It was therefore necessary to haggle about
the quality of each item composing the Mirambo; as for the
quantity, he wanted everything, even our private luggage.

15th to 17th.—The Cazembe, impatient at the delay of his
present, and loth to believe that impertinences of his officer
were the cause of obstruction, ordered the latter to give me two
tusks, by way of "mouth," begging me not to make him wait
any longer. The Fumo, however, kept the tusks and forgot the
message; and until the battle of the gift was decided, we had to
suffer not a little from the grossness and brutality of the Minister. On the same day, accompanied by some who better knew
the country custom, I gave the Secretary his private present of
36 plain cloths (pannos de fato), 1 fine coloured cloth (getim),
4 little ingots (pendes) of calaim (East India tin, mentioned by
Do Couto and others), 200 strings of glass beads assorted,
5 cloths, 20 strings of white opaque beads, also assorted, and
4 "porcelanas" of small cowries. Although he had been
promised a gift after my presentation at Court, he feared the
contrary, and now he was out of his misery: his return gift was
an ivory. But though afterwards he became more placable, he
did not cease persisting in attempts to swell the present of his
king by asking for everything he saw.

18th to 20th.—The Fumo Anceva broke his promise about
bearing away the "dash" made to his king.

21st.—With much trouble the Fumo was persuaded to carry
off our offering to the Cazembe, who was satisfied with it. The
conciseness of a Diary prevents my enumerating the multitude
of things of which it consisted, and, moreover, all appear in the
Receiver's account. It was to be supposed that the Cazembe,
according to country custom, having received such a gift, would
acknowledge the receipt by a "mouth," or counter gift of ivory
and slaves—he did not return even a message. To the Muenempanda, commander-in-chief and especial favourite of the Cazembe, I gave 30 plain cloths (de fato), 1 looking-glass, 1 piece
of fine "getim," † 4 zinc bars, 200 strings of beads, 5 pannos de
velorio, also assorted, 10 douros sortidos, 4 porcelanas of cowries.
He was pleased with his gift, and returned a copper bar and a

---

* The same was done to the second expedition. At Dahome it is a legal fiction
that everything belonging to strangers is the property of the King as long as it is
in his city. Also there is a considerable tendency to look upon all foreigners as
slaves.

† In Monteiro and Gamitto (p. 153) "getim" is explained as "pintado de
côres mas depreciada por mi." Pannos of velorio are the equivalents in beads to
fine cloths. Douros may be an error for Dorira, explained by the same explorers
(p. 189) to be synonymous with Canutilho.

small ivory (dente de marfim miudo),* a name given to all between 7½ to 14 lbs.

22nd to 23rd.—A similar present was made to the King's nephew, the Sana Muropúe,† who, more generous than the Muonempanda, returned an ivory weighing upwards of 64 lbs.

24th.—My position compels me to make the greater presents, because the Cazembe's friendship is in every sense necessary to me. The haste with which I left Quilimani to join, as chaplain, the expedition at Tete, having allowed me no time for preparations, I indented upon Lieutenant Manoel dos Santos e Silva, the Receiver of the Crown property, for some articles to be repaid in money, after our return. For this both he and I were severely censured and criticised by José Rodrigues Caleja and his acolytes.

25th.—The first guide (pratico dos mattos), Gonçalo Caetano Pereira, with the Receiver, Lieutenant Manoel dos Santos e Silva; the notary Antonio José da Cruz, and Captain João da Cunha Pereira, came to inform me that the Cazembe was so dissatisfied with his presents that the Royal stores and the Receiver's office were in danger of being plundered. I at once gave orders secretly to make up 400 ball-cartridges, in case of need.‡ By the Receiver's advice, I resolved to advance pay to all on the list, that, should the report prove true, the Crown stores might not suffer so much: all the soldiers were allowed to draw three months' advance pay; the officers had already received more. On this occasion I drew my salary as chaplain for six months, no other falling due, and a prepayment of ten, amounting to 395 plain cloths (pannos de fato) = 197·500 dols. of this country, or 98.750 of Portugal.

A great Chiraro (officer) complained before the Cazembe that the Captain João da Cunha Pereira had dishonoured him through his wife, and demanded satisfaction: the King, in reply, bade him chastise the woman for troubling the whites, and thus the injured husband lost his damages.§ The reason of the Cazembe's reply was that before the arrival of the expedition, which was known to march without women, he had recommended his officers to look after their wives, and had told them that if any went astray, either with a white or with the Caffre of a white, there would be no "palaver."

* The Portuguese divide their ivory into two kinds, grosso, meio (middle), miudo, and acra, the latter being "Scrivellos," from 1 lb. to 2 lbs. in weight.
† He is one of the great officers at the Court.
‡ In these cases it is generally the civilian—say missionary, doctor, or chaplain—who first shows fight.
§ These palavers (Milandos) are of almost daily occurrence in the countries of the Cazembe and of the Mwata yá Nvo. And the "panel-dodgo" is perfectly well known in Eastern and Western Africa, especially at Abeokuta.

28th.—To-day the Cazembe gave his first official reception to the whites of the Second Division. He was sitting on his Hytanda,* a low, plain, country-fashioned taboret, lined with red cotton (Xaile), a stuff brought from the north. The reception place was the principal entrance of his palace, under two large and roughly-made umbrellas of Tucorim,† the common Balagate. The open space, which is large, was filled with an immense crowd, and in front of the people were seated his grandees, his son, and his brother—all upon the bare ground. Those whom the king addressed or looked at, acknowledged it by clapping their hands, with cries and shouts of joy, which others accompanied with short bursts of the marimba ‡ and other instruments. Those not so honoured remained silent. The grandees, moreover, rubbed earth upon their arms and breasts, in token of humility and vassalage. When we arrived, the king was sitting, as I have described, outside his palace, with a little brazier before him, surrounded by various horns containing charms against witchcraft. For us a certain post had been appointed, thirty paces from the presence; there we were conducted by our guide, the Fumo Anceva, and we were soon surrounded by a mighty crowd of gazers. The Fumo then retired and knelt down four paces behind his master, to receive orders.

At once, out came Calira, the Micrunda Caffre who had met us at Tete, and began to "pemberar," that is to say, to dance, in token of joy, as is the custom, pausing in his steps when near the king, who was some eight steps distant. With his knife he pointed to the directions where Angola and Tete are supposed to be, signifying that the Cazembe was very happy in being visited by whites from both countries. Our soldiers who were of the party went through some evolutions, and fired, to the great pleasure of the king. I sent to compliment him, but the Caffre interpreters of Gonçalo Caetano Pereira, when giving my message, presented as a "mouth" seventy cloths and a mutava (200 strings) of velorio beads. The Cazembe only replied that it was well, and with signs of satisfaction ordered the offering to be taken up. He returned three tusks, each weighing more than 32 lbs, and two slaves, after which he soon disappeared.

Thus ended our first audience, if it can be so called. Before the

---

* In the Sawáhil country the Kitanda is a cot, a "lit de sangle."
† Tocorim, in Monteiro and Gamitto (Appendix B), is a stuff like Dollam, but much inferior, striped whitish and white.
‡ The Marimba is a well-known negro instrument, a rude piano. Dr. Livingstone has given a sketch of one ('First Expedition,' p. 293).

soldiers had set out for this ceremony there had been some dispute touching command between Captain João da Cunha Pereira and the Lieutenant Manoel dos Santos. The latter pleaded seniority, and as he resolved to precede the former, whose nomination as Captain had not been confirmed by His Excellency the Captain-General of Mozambique, and whose commission had not arrived, the dispute rose to such a height that the two officers abused each other violently in presence of the troops waiting to march. The Lieutenant went so far as to call the Captain "cullion," and the latter showed so little proper spirit that he at once put up with the disgrace, and next day he became a friend of his insulter. Such was the character of most of the members of the expedition.

November 29th to December 2nd.—Since our arrival here Lieutenant Manoel dos Santos suspended the issue of velorio beads, with which, from the beginning of the journey, the people bought their provisions: at their request, I ordered the said beads to be issued.

3rd.—The Receiver, who had been directed on the march by the late Governor to have his accounts drawn out and ready to be presented on our arrival at the Court, forgot all about it, judging that his superior having died, nothing would be required. When I called for the balance, after time enough he gave me a list of the remaining effects in the Royal treasury. But having heard of certain lâches, I directed him in eight days to produce his detailed accounts, as the list of existing articles did not content me.*

4th.—I was informed that Gonçalo Caetano Pereira had, by means of his Caffres, reported to the Fumo Anceva, intending the Cazembe to hear of it, that I had appropriated the presents sent to the king. He thus alluded to my having transferred to the public account the king's gift on the 11th ultimo, which was in return for the present of the 7th November, and the three tusks and two slaves sent to myself on the 28th ultimo in return for my private gift of the same date. Having ascertained that this bad man had been guilty of such an unworthy proceeding, in order to stop his calumnies, I sent the private presents alluded to, that of the Fumo Anceva (17th ultimo), that of the Muenempanda (21st), and that of the Sana Muropáo (22nd), to the Receiver, with orders to place them in the Royal treasury, and I took from him an equivalent of the effects which I had expended.

5th.—The Cazembe summoned the Expedition, and the

---

* Here begin the ignoble money-disputes, which are enough to ruin any expedition.

I

soldiers to assist at a triumphal entry which he was giving to one of his Cabocecrs who was returning from war.* Sickness prevented my obeying the summons. The king appeared seated under his principal gateway, as when he gave us audience. All being assembled, the chief in whose honour the fête was given appeared with a few beads of those whom he had killed in battle and some captives. When the latter had been paraded, he began the usual dance of gladness, and as he approached the king's feet the monarch, in token of having been well served, lowered the knife which he was holding. As the chief continued to dance, he was interrupted by a sign made by the Casembe to our soldiers, whose firing at the end of the ceremony caused him the liveliest pleasure.

6th to 8th.—A violent quarrel arose in our camp (mussassa) between the slaves of Gonçalo Caetano Pereira and those of the chief sergeant, Pedro Xavier Velasco: the former would insist on following up the latter, who, persuaded by their masters, were retiring. I ordered Captain João de Cunha Pereira to end the tumult by sending the negroes to their quarters (intembas),† and, when nothing was done, I gave directions to fire with ball, so that a death or two might terminate the fray. There were no bullets, but some small shot, with which the soldiers fired a few times, and some of them retired wounded with arrows.

At that moment appeared a Xiraro‡ Caffre of the Cazembe, who, being very drunk and mixed up with the Caffres of Gonçalo Caetano Pereira, received one or two grains in his ribs, and fell apparently dead by reason of his intoxication. Upon this the original quarrel ended, and a second trouble began. The negroes, parents and acquaintances of the fallen man, raised him in their arms, and, weeping, brought him to me, saying that we had killed him. The Caffre vassals of the Cazembe, our fellow-travellers to this place, who had received at Tete the greatest civility, were the loudest in their threats. But they were Muizas, who for that supposed death promised us real destruction in order to get our heads. Things looking ill, I sent the chief sergeant, Pedro Xavier Velasco, who then was most in favour, to take or to forward an account of the accident. The king heard it all calmly, saying that he would pronounce judgment on the next day, before all the whites, who were directed to be present.§

* The second expedition was treated to a similar spectacle, and I witnessed it at Dahome. It is probably a part of the official programme.
† In Unyamwezi, "tembe" is a large house.
‡ Shiraro, an officer.
§ There is sure to be some dispute of this kind: the same happened to me in

9th.—All the whites who were able—I was still sick—went to the court. The Cazembe, after hearing the case and approving of Pedro Xavier Velasco's conduct, said that the strangers were in his country, and must live in peace, leaving their quarrels to be fought out when they return home: moreover, that, if they turned a deaf ear to this salutary advice, he would act otherwise another time. Gonçalo Caetano Pereira had the indiscretion to say that on his side the dispute had not ended, but the Cazembe, pretending not to hear him, dismissed the assembly, telling the Caffres who had threatened us that they were running the risk of a miserable death.

On the same day and occasion Gonçalo Caetano Pereira, José Rodrigues Caleja, and Antonio José da Cruz spoke privily to the Cazembe about opening the Angola road, though, knowing their imprudence and their wish to do everything in a hurry, I had long before forbidden the subject. It was clear to me that they found the Cazembe irresolute. At first he gave leave; then, warned by the Fumo Anceva, he withdrew his words, under pretext of the difficulties of the road; so that he neither granted nor promised anything. I arrested Vasco Joaquim Pires, ensign of militia, for his intrigues on the occasion of yesterday's quarrel; but he so managed that the Fumo Anceva hastened to beg his release in the name of the Cazembe, whom they thus drew into all our affairs. I at once ordered him to be set at liberty.

10th to 19th.—The Receiver of the Royal Treasures, Manoel dos Santos, handed me in a badly drawn up account.

20th and 21st.—After examining the account, I transferred the Receivership from Manoel dos Santos to José Rodrigues Caleja, who was ordered to take charge of the effects belonging to the Royal Treasury. The Fumo Anceva failed not quickly to come and tell me that his master the Cazembe wished Manoel dos Santos to remain in office; and when I would not consent, seeing that the Royal Treasury had suffered enough, he replied if the lieutenant stole it was no matter, he would be answerable for the theft. Suspecting the message to be fictitious, I promised to go at once with my reply to the Cazembe: it was too late, however, to see the king, and the business remained for the next day.

22nd.—According to promise, I went to the palace accompanied by Lieut.-Colonel Pedro Nolasco Vieira de Araujo; the chief sergeant Pedro Xavier Velasco; the guide, Gonçalo Caetano Pereira, and the serjeant of ordnance, José Rodrigues

---

Dahome, and the people attempted to make a "po'aver" because I stopped it with a stick.

Caloja. We were at once admitted into a circular house, a
form affected by all the Caffres of the interior; here the Cazembe
was seated, with many courtiers outside. All was disposed that
we might be alone; nevertheless, his brother, the Sana Muropúe,
his son, Muenebuto,* and some imprudent domestics remained
to gratify their curiosity.

All this ceremony was because the king had heard that we
had brought a camp-bedstead of Macao-work, and he wanted
to see it set up. Whilst we were satisfying him, he never
ceased eyeing the curtains, which were of very light and transparent silk.

When the bed was ready, the Cazembe wished to dismiss us.
I told him that a representation had to be made, and that I
ought not to leave his presence without making it. As he bade
me speak, I began by telling him that I came to answer the
"palaver" (milando) of the day before. Then the Fumo
Anceva, who was near, took up the thread of my discourse, and
made known to the king what he had delivered to me yesterday
as a message in the Royal name. I took the opportunity of
showing the enormity of the offence, and the unworthiness
of the offender to be protected by his master, adding, that till
now the Cazembe had not known what had happened, and that
the message in his name was the result of an understanding
between the Receiver and his minister; thus the latter exposed
himself to be disbelieved when bringing even a true message.†
The Fumo replied that I had done well regarding the interests
of my Sovereign, and that I might punish the criminal and
secure the Royal Treasury as I best pleased.

23rd to 27th.—Since the guide Gonçalo Caetano Pereira and
José Rodrigues da Cunha had treated directly with the Cazembe
about the transit to Angola, all my endeavours through the
Sana Muropúe did not progress; I therefore begged the
Cazembe to give me an audience on the next day—a request
at once granted.‡

28th.—I went, accompanied by the two guides, to the Cazembe,
and seeing him surrounded by his court, I attempted to speak
with him alone, but found it impossible. This was an occasion
not to be lost: the members of the Expedition were criticising
my inaction, as if a superior were bound to satisfy the curiosity

* The heir-apparent of the Cazembe takes the title of "Muenebuto" for
"Muroneputo;" in the original misspelt "Muembuto."
† This is the usual African trick: the king and the minister play into each
others hands—the latter does the dirty work and the former profits by it, whilst
both are too cunning for the white man.
‡ It is very clear that the Cazembe never intended to allow transit to Angola:
such a permission would have been quite contrary to all African policy.

of those under him. I therefore opened the subject of the
Angola journey, when the king at once objected wars, famine,
and the death of Governor de Lacerda: he did not wish all the
whites to perish on the road to Angola, and to be accused of not
having warned them of their danger, and of having permitted
them to incur it. Finally, he declared that we had better return
and report his views to our Sovereign, and that if, despite these
difficulties, we were sent another time, he would "give pass." *

I insisted that there was neither famine nor war, and the
carriers of the Muropúe, lately arrived, had brought no such
intelligence; that our deaths would not lie at his door, even as
we blame no one for the Governor's decease, well knowing that
all must die, without the intervention of anything extraordinary.† Finally, I said that, in our desire to open the road,
two whites would remain after the departure of the Expedition,
with the view of passing to Angola when the carriers sent to
ascertain about the way might return.

29th to 31st.—The Cazembe began to feel sick, with acute pains
in the head, which presently extended over the body.

SECTION 2.—*Continuation of the Diary from the beginning of the Year 1799,
to February 17, 1799.*

January 1st to 3rd, 1799.—José Rodrigues Caloja presented to
me a general requisition, begging that the comestibles might be
divided amongst the members of the Expedition; and that, provisions being damageable goods, each one wished to take care of
his own portion. I ordered this to be done.

4th and *5th.*—The Cazembe's sickness so increased that his
recovery was doubted, and knowing his dangerous state, he
repeatedly recommended, should he die, his son, his brother,
and his chiefs, in no way to molest the whites (Muzungus), who
being traders are privileged people.‡ His physicians were un-
wearied in sacrificing as many human victims as possible to
their fancies or barbarous politics. They went forth at morning,
at noon, and at 10 P.M., beating their tambourines on the road,
and all those at whom they pointed were seized as wizards and
unsparingly slain.§ With the king's malady our fears increased;

---

* Another very transparent "dodge," apparent to every experienced African.
Gelele, King of Dahome, acted precisely in the same way when I wished to cross
his northern frontier.

† On the other hand, as has been remarked, these Africans, like all savages and
barbarians, believe that no man dies except by witchcraft or other cause.

‡ Had the Cazembe died, probably the whole expedition would have been
molested.

§ Compare with this Dr. Livingstone's statement ('Second Expedition,' chap. xxv.):
" In one remote and small corner of the country, called Dahomey, the African

we knew that in case of his death, despite his good word, we could not avoid the robbery general throughout the kingdom— it being a Caffre practice to celebrate the deaths of great men by theft, and the higher is the deceased's rank, the greater is the disorder. I therefore ordered a sufficiency of ball-cartridges to be prepared.*

6th to 8th.—For the purpose of promoting good fellowship, I had kept up a general mess: at the end of a month no one attended. My party at once demanded cloth to buy rations. I referred to the Receiver, who being the author of the requisition, at once replied that it was only reasonable. Thereupon I sent to settle the quantity required for each person.

9th.—This point determined, I ordered the Receiver to supply each person with ten cloths per mensem.

10th to 13th.—The Cazembe had thrown off his malady, but had not appeared in public. Caetano Fabião, chief of squadron, when ordered to proceed with despatches for the Government of Tete, went to take leave of the king in hope of a present. The Cazembe, after ascertaining that the object of his journey was to report the Governor's death, gave him an ivory weighing more than 80 lbs. He added, that, being ignorant of writing, this was his letter reporting to the actual Governor the unhappy news of the death of the Geral (General)†—so governors are called by Caffres. The tusk was taken by the Receiver, José Rodrigues Caleja.

14th to 18th.—The Sana Muropúe, the king's brother (nephew?) came to my quarters as invited, to discuss a project of free-trade. After showing him all its benefits to the king and the country,. I begged his interest with the Cazembe, before whom the affair must come at last. He promised me his assistance.

19th and 20th.—Amongst the dried fish brought by the Caffres for sale, appeared garôpas,‡ bagre, and rock fish, all peculiar to salt water. After inquiry, I found that at the place where the

religion has degenerated into a bloody superstition." Has the writer never heard of Ashanto and of Benin, of Uganda or of Unyoro? Again we read, " this reckless disregard of human life mentioned by Speke and Grant is quite exceptional." Exceptional! If Dr. Livingstone had taken the trouble to read my book on the 'Lake Regions,' he would have found how exceptional is the "mildness" of the African religion.

* This anarchy and tumult after the sovereign's death are not without a cause. The savage Solons have instituted it in order to accelerate the choice of a successor, and to read a practical lesson touching the benefits of the twin forms of tyranny, despotism, and democracy.

† The next expedition, in 1831-32, found Dr. de Lacerda remembered as the "Geral."

‡ The Garoupa of Madeira is a small fish much prized. The "Bagre" in the dictionaries is a long fish with a forked tail, and Rock fish is too vague to ascertain species.

Xibuiri (Shibniri) or son-in-law of the Cazembe lived, and where he had fled after killing four Caffre head-traders sent by the Angola merchants, there is a salt-water river, called Nhanza-Mpote,* which ebbs and flows. The distance from the Cazembe's court to the Chumbo is, according to the Caffres, one month's travel, which we may reckon to be 15 days, as they walk only three hours per diem. Thence to the Muropúe are eight short or four long stages, and the same to Mueneputo,† the king nearest Angola.

Perhaps that river may be the Coanza, and we have left behind us the Conenis for want of astronomical observations. This, however, and other interesting points, must remain unsettled; such were the hurry and impetuosity of the Governor do Lacerda, and so wild and disorderly is the present party.

21st to 26th.—The Caffres of Lieutenant Antonio José da Cruz pursued the country negresses who came to sell flour, maize, and millet, and stole sundry cobs of Indian corn. This they have done before, and not without their master's knowledge: hearing of it, I asked him to chastise them for conduct which might bring us into great trouble.

27th.—The Fumo Anceva appeared with a message from the Cazembe, complaining that certain Caffres of our party, not content with running over all the plantations (mundas) and crops (searas), had carried their insolence so far as to plunder the property of his wives, which the latter would not suffer. He had therefore determined to divide a plot of manioc amongst the whites and their slaves (checundas),‡ the captives and half-civilized property of those dwelling at the Rios de Sena. Thus on the next day all the slaves were summoned for muster, in order that each might carry away his master's share. I satisfied the complaint to the best of my ability, and I accepted the offer, admiring the king's generosity.

January 28th to February 4th.—On the latter day the Cazembe showed himself convalescent to his people, who received him with palm-clappings, with shouts of joy, and with concerts of marimbas and other instruments. Vasco Joaquim Pires showed his libertinism by saying that he wanted no mass, and from that day forth he never attended divine service. To-day I heard

---

* Which we should write Nyanza-Mpúta. The " water of Portugal " usually means the Sea of Angola. The Shibuiri is clearly the " Quibari," then brother-iu-law of the Cazembe, and described by the Pombeiros.

† The ' Second Expedition ' also mentions a king called Muenemputo, near the Muropúe; whilst the traveller J. Rodrigues Graça says that the Muenemputo das Pralas obeys the Matlamvo (Mwätä yt Nvo).

‡ Properly meaning Caffre slaves speaking Portuguese. Dr. Kirk informs me that only the chief of a trading expedition is so named. But Monteiro and Gamitto (p. 14) say, " Aos escravos chamam Checunda."

that all the Caffres were freely selling their stores of ivory and
slaves (merendas).

5th to 9th.—Jose Rodrigues Caleja informed me that Pedro
Xavier Velasco was still intriguing with the Cazembe to prevent our passing on to Angola. His reason was, that by
the Governor's death he had lost the chance of certain advantages promised to him in case of success. As José Rodrigues
Caleja said he could prove the charge, and offered to swear to it,
I ordered the members of the expedition to send in their attes-
tations on oath, with a view of documenting so extraordinary a
proceeding.

10th to 11th.—The same José Rodrigues Caleja, despising
my prohibition and taking up, with the greatest imprudence,
the subject of our advance to Angola, asked me to go with him
about the matter to the Muenempanda, the influential war-chief
of the Cazembe. When I asked him his ground for expecting success from such proceedings, he simply replied that
they were necessary. Not wishing to involve myself in his
imprudence, I refused to go; but, as he had proceeded so far,
I authorized him, accompanied by Gonçalo Caetano Pereira
and by Lieutenant Antonio José da Cruz, to take a piece of
cloth as an unasked "mouth" to the Caboceer. They carried
with them the Fumo Anceva: the latter, and the Muenempanda,
after long debate touching the difficulties, promised that day to
speak with the Cazembe, and informed the whites that they
must appear on the morrow before the king, with a certainty of
their request being granted.[*]

12th.—Sickness having hitherto prevented my personally
congratulating the Cazembe on his recovery, I begged audience
of him, and he replied that he would receive me on the evening
of that day. Accordingly, at 2 P.M., I went to the palace, but,
as the king. together with his grandees, was in the assembly
of Pombe,[†] the porters would not allow me to pass the first
gate, and quickly shut it. I spent an hour and a-half at the
entrance, to prove that I had not missed my appointment,
when certain grandees came out and showed themselves concerned by my waiting, without, however, being able to remedy
it. At last appeared the Prince Muenebuto sufficiently disguised in beer. As he wished to carry me before his father,
his uncle (cousin ?), the Sana Muropúe, whose head was cooler,

---

[*] It need hardly be remarked that the idea never once entered either black
head.

[†] "Sitting on Pombe" is the Kisawahili phrase, meaning that he was
"drinking for drunk" native beer: most African chiefs in the interior do this
regularly every day after noon. Monteiro and Gamitto (p. 291) say, "eatar no
Pombe."

prevented this proceeding and took me to his own house. He apologised for the porters, assured me that his brother (uncle ?) had not heard of my coming, and, finally, he declared to me that the king, being in his Pombe, could not have spoken with me.*

13*th.*—José Rodrigues Caleja told me that the Cazembe had summoned the whites for the next day, intending to concede transit through his country to Angola; and that he wished to see those chosen for the journey. As it appeared that some difficulty might be caused by sending Pedro Xavier Velasco, who was personally distasteful to the Cazembe, I nominated in his stead Lieutenant José Vicente Pereira Salema.

14*th.*—I went with all the whites to the palace, and we were at once conducted to the place where the king was giving audience to his Caboceers and people. He was, they told me, admonishing them to abandon and abominate the crime of sorcery, to which he attributed all his illness. Having waited half-an-hour till this levée ended we followed the king, who passed into another place. There he inquired for the envoys, Lieutenant-Colonel Pedro Nolasco Vieira de Araujo, chosen by Governor de Lacerda and Lieutenant José Vicente Pereira Salema. Having seen and recognized them, he entered into the former difficulties, beginning with the Governor's death and ending with the scarcity on the road. José Rodrigues Caleja at once assured the king that, being ordered by Her Most Faithful Majesty to execute the journey at every risk, the envoys would go, if it cost all their lives. The Cazembe turned in wonder to his people: exclaimed "Truly these messengers greatly fear and respect their Sovereign, not even objecting to incur death." Then, continuing the address to us, he granted the wished-for leave to the two envoys; and promised guides to the Muropúe, cautioning us, however, not to delay, as his messengers were ready to depart.† I acknowledged the kindness, and we retired to make preparations, whilst the others, on their side, showed no less activity.‡

15*th.*—At 9 A.M. came the Fumo Anceva and his party, requesting me to assemble the whites, as he had a matter to lay before them. When this was done, he declared that the Cazembe had revoked his permission of yesterday: it was not right for us, on our first visit to his country, to carry out this project; we must return to Tete and report to our Sovereign the troubles and dangers of such an undertaking; and then, if

---

* At last, the truth !
† The form "lie circumstantial" is instinctively a prime favourite with Africans.
‡ A mere pretence, as will presently appear.

we were again sent, we should have his leave and assistance.
He concluded with saying that the ardour with which I, Gonçalo
Caetano Pereira, and José Rodrigues Caleja, had entered into
the affair had estranged the king's heart, and that we had
shown but little judgment.

Such a message was not from the Cazembe. The Fumo
Anceva made me come to the ball, as they say, either because
he thought that I, as Commandant, had egged on the other two,
or because, having taken an aversion to me, he wanted the
chance of snubbing me, or because he feared that I might
report his evil doings to the Cazembe. After consulting those
present, I replied to the Fumo Anceva that we had not looked
for the Sovereign breaking his word, such never being the
custom of the kings (Mambos), but that, after mature delibe-
ration in a case so new to us, we would send a reply. I said no
more, hoping that the Cazembe would hesitate to tarnish his
name by a breach of faith and would withdraw the prohibition.
José Rodrigues Caleja announced to me that Pedro Xavier
Velasco, having gone yesterday at noon to visit the Cazembe,
the porters had shut the door in his face.

16th.—At 10 A.M., the Sana Muropúe took his seat outside
my door, and requested that I would muster the whites to hear
his message. This was done when José Rodrigues Caleja, assum-
ing a prophetic strain, declared that he knew the business to be
a demand for the presents (mirambos) destined for the Muropúe, the Mueneputo, and the minor chiefs on the way to
Angola. His conjecture, however, proved to be untrue. The
Sana Muropúe told us all at once that the Cazembe had sent
him to verify the message yesterday delivered to the Fumo
Anceva in his own presence, and that, seeing our readiness to
rush into danger, he would not allow us passage to Angola till
our second visit. Moreover, the king found it hard that he who,
opening the roads which had been closed by Chibuy, Governing
Fumo of the Muizas, had sent his vassals to buy cloth, and to
bring whites with much treasure to his kingdom, should see
such valuables pass out of it.[*]

When the message was over, José Rodrigues Caleja caused
it to be explained to the Sana Muropúe that the whites
also did not wish to expose their lives for the purpose of
death, and that they returned thanks to the Cazembe. I at
once stopped the message, asking José Rodrigues Caleja
how it agreed with what he had spoken on the 14th instant,
in presence of the Cazembe and his chiefs. Ashamed of his

---

[*] This again is the truth coming out at last. José Rodrigues Caleja had
doubtless been intriguing to bring it about.

rashness and cowardice, he changed colour and held his peace. Having taken all the votes, they were unanimous for our acting according to the Cazembe's wishes. This did not quite please me, but, to gain time, I assented. The mild address of the Sana Muropúe giving me an opportunity to publish the insufferable arrogance with which the Fumo Anceva had spoken yesterday, I asked him, before replying, if the Cazembe really held me to be a man of as little judgment as his officer had declared; also, if it was true, as the same person had asserted, to a Caffre linguist of Gonçalo Caetano Pereira, that, had the whites (Muzungos) been Muizas, the king would have cut off their heads.

Here all my party present showed their timidity and their habits of murmuring; even unto openly asking me whether I wanted satisfaction from the Cazembe or from the Fumo Anceva. Not heeding their criticisms, I ordered my question to be put to the Fumo Anceva, who denied the whole, declaring it an imposture. After this reply, which showed to all the confusion of the proud Caffre, I sent to say to the Sana Muropúe, that I had never expected the king to break his word, a thing impossible even amongst the Caffre chiefs near his country; but that, as the king desired it, we would speak no more about Angola. He left us, and on the evening of that day I proceeded to a judicial inquiry upon the subject of Pedro Xavier Velasco's offences.

CHAPTER V.

February 17, 1799.—At 8 A.M. the Sana Muropúe returned
to my house, and, in presence of all the whites, delivered a
message from the Cazombe, that, as there was no more talk of
Angola, he wanted the now superfluous presents intended for
the Muropúe and the Muenepúto.* I put it to the vote of
all: they were in a panic lest I should refuse: knowing the
demand would be made, they augured the worst; some, for fear
of being plundered and stripped, could not sleep at night.
Lieut.-Colonel Pedro Velasco (sic pro Nolasco) Vieira d'Araujo,
the chief sergeant Pedro Xavier Velasco, and Antonio José da
Cruz, were the only officers who did not show fear.

All being of one opinion, namely, that refusal would be
dangerous, I was obliged to consent; but before doing so, I
inquired of the Sana Muropúe what the Cazembe meant by
such a claim; he replied it was all done in good friendship. I
added that the presents should be put into his hands, not into
those of the Fumo Anceva, as the latter had received a considerable gift in the name of our sovereign, and we did not
know whether it had reached its destination. Moreover, that
besides plundering what was given to his master, he robbed
what the Cazembe sent to his friends and relatives (buenozes).
But I insisted that in presence of the king the first present should
be referred to. The Fumo Anceva changed colour, now deny-
ing that he had received the gift, then affirming that he had
given up all to his master. The Sana Muropúe confirmed this
last assertion, and relieved the Caffre whose guilt was evident;
either to please the Cazembe who much affected his minister,
or to draw him from a confusion which also fell upon all the
nation (Murundas).† Yet I persisted that the present gift
should be reported before delivery, and to that purpose I sent

---

* This was one of the strongest reasons for the transit not being allowed. The
message was delivered by the apparent friend of the party, the Sana Muropúe,
after the bully Fumo Anceva had been allowed to frighten them. All was
perfectly *en règle.*

† Monteiro and Gamitto (p. 243) call the people generally Lundas, Murundas,
or Arundas.

the lieutenant, Antonio José da Cruz, who could not, however,
find the Cazembe at home. The poor king has the naiveté to
believe that over-zeal for his interests makes the Fumo Anceva,
who is the greatest thief in his dominions, suffer from our false
charges. I was therefore obliged to deliver the present without further ado, and without verifying the delivery of the
former gift, a fact committed to paper and signed by all the
party.* In the evening I began to inquire into the misdemeanour
of Pedro Xavier Velasco.

18th–21st.—There was drumming and dancing (tombocaçao),
which other Caffres of these parts call "Pemberaçao,"† between
Prince Muenebuto and his brother-in-law Chibuery, already
alluded to on January 20th. The Cazembe was present with his
usual dignity, but guarded by armed Caffres, as the prince
danced with his large knife drawn in order to touch with it
that of his father, a sign of honour and respect. The Cazembe,
however, thus favoured only his son. The ceremony took place
in the open space before the principal gate of the palace, a
great crowd of people having instruments collected, and there
also were our troops, for whom the Cazembe sent, and whose
discharge of musketry he himself directed. It was said that
this fête was to celebrate his having closed once for all the
Angola road, so as to increase his connection with Tete, whence
their best things came. This was not confirmed, as they do not
wish to break off with Angola.

I will now describe Muenebuto the prince, and his Murundas.
Muenebuto is tall, good-looking, and well proportioned; his expression is pleasing, nay, almost always cheerful and smiling; he
cares only for amusement, and his age—twenty years—permits
nothing else. On the contrary, the Cazembe shows gravity
and inspires respect; he also is tall, and well built, and his age
may be about fifty. As he has many wives—the greatest sign
of Caffre dignity—he becomes every year the father of two,
three, or four children. He is very generous at times in giving
slaves and pieces of cloth to his vassals, as well as to strangers
and whites, when he is not set against them; and every day
he sent the Muzungos money and different presents of provisions, captives, ivory or copper bars, in proportion to their
offerings of cloth and beads, and according to his regard for them.

He is severe; death, or at least amputation of the hand, being

---

* Those who have not travelled in Africa often wonder at all the importance
attached to these trifling presents. But the fact is that without supplies the
journey is brought to a dead stop, not taking into account the hardships and
sufferings of return. The explorer, therefore, must fight for every cubit of cloth,
and this is, perhaps, the severest part of his task.
† Native festivities, including drinking and dances.

the usual punishment. He is barbarous; every new moon he causes a Caffre to be killed by his medicine-man, and with the victim's blood, heart, and part of the entrails, they make up his medicine, always mixing it with oil. When these charms are prepared, they are inserted into the horns of various animals, and even into scrivellos, which are closed with stoppers of wood or cloth. These fetishes are distributed about his palace and courts; they are hung to the doors, and for fear of sorcery the king never speaks to any one without some of these horns lying at his feet.[*]

He holds assemblies of his chiefs, who are invited to drink pombe, or millet-beer, which is mixed with other pulse or not, as each man's taste is. These drinkings begin with the full moon, and continue to the end; they commence daily at or before 1 P.M., and they last two hours. All those present drink as much as they please, but should any one vomit in the assembly, the wretch is instantly put to death. Though superstition-ridden, like all these people, the Cazembe is not so much so as are others. He visits no one in person, and never leaves his palace to walk; he has the name of being proud, but his people make him inconsistent.

The subjects (Murundas), who say that sixty years ago they came from the Western regions and established themselves in the lands of the conquered Vaciras (Mcasiras), are of the same nation as the Cazembe, whose rites and customs they follow.

Usually the men are tall, dark, well made, and good-looking; they tattoo (incise), but do not paint their bodies, nor do they jog their teeth. Their dress is a cloth extending from the waist to the knees, which are exposed by the garment being raised in front; it is girt by a leathern belt, 4 to 10 fingers broad. Their gala-dress is called "Muconzo;"[†] it is of woollen or cotton, but it must be black. To make it they cut a piece 5½ fathoms, or a little less in length, and if it be too short they add a bit of the same quality; the breadth is 2½ hands, and if wider it is reduced to that size. It must be finished with a full edging, which increases it in all parts; this border is made of three strips of a different cloth, each 4 fingers broad. When the colour is red, for instance, the middle is white; it is yellow if the middle be red or white. Finally, they diversify these strips as they please, always taking care that the colour differs from the body or the principal part of the cloth. When putting on the "Muconzo," they cover the waist

---

* Small horns of goats and antelopes are thus used in Unyamwezi, stuffed with thin iron wire; in Congo with strips of cloth.

† Monteiro and Gamitto (p. 238) call it Mucônzo and Mocônzo.

and legs, finishing at the front of the person with a great band of artificial pleats; and the larger it is, the grander is the garb. For arm-ornaments they use strings of fine beads like bracelets; their feet are covered with strung cowries, large opaque stoneware beads (pedras de côres), and white or red porcelains (velorios). Over their combed head-dresses, which are of many braids, large and small, they wear a cap (carapuça), covered with exquisite birds'-plumes; the locks are also striped (barradellas) with a certain clay, which, when dry, resembles the levigated sandal-wood used by the Moors and Gentoos (Hindus); the stripes, however, are only on the crown and temples (molleira). Others rub their bodies upon the waist and upwards to the hair with a certain vermilion (vermelhão),* here common.

Such is the gala dress. Their every-day clothing is a little cloth, 1½ to 2 fathoms long, with or without a border of a single strip; others wear bark cloth, like the Muizas, or edgeless cotton; and finally, coarse native cotton (maxilas de Gondo),† as each one has or can afford.

As usual the women dress better than the men, as to the kind of cloth, which is of wool (collomanha) or similar stuff. They also use, like the males, strings of many sorts of beads, to cover their ankles, but they are not so fond of cowries or porcelain (velorio). Their coiffure is unlike that of the men; they cut off all the hair, leaving a little lock in the middle, which in time, growing long, serves to support a kind of diadem; the rest of the hair, when it grows, forming sundry lines of short braid. Their ordinary dress is extremely poor, consisting of one very small cloth. These women, who also can be sold by their husbands, lead the lives of slaves, doing all the labour of domestic slavery.

The Murundas,‡ like other peoples of this country, have no (practical) religion. They recognize the existence of a sovereign creator of the world, and call him "Reza," but they consider him a tyrant that permits his creatures' death. They have great veneration for their Azimos (murimos), or dead, whom they consult on all occasions of war or good fortune. The Caffre servants of any Moçazu,§ or place in which a king is buried, have many privileges. The Azimos require offerings of

---

* It has previously been described as being wood-powder.
† The expression is fully explained in the diary of June 20-23. Dr. Kirk says that a "Maxila de garda" is a hammock of native cloth. "Maxila de Gondo" is a stuff so coarse that hammocks can be made of it. Hence Monteiro and Gamitto (p. 70) call the coarse cotton cloth made by the Marave, "Manxila." See June 20-23, 1799, where the Chaplain explains the words.
‡ In the original misprinted "Morundas."
§ Mussassa is a camp: here it must be the burial-place before called Máximo.

provisions, as dough (massa), a food made of manioc flour, to stew with the porridge, which in the Brazil is called Angú; of quiriaça (any mess of meat, fish, or herbs), and of pombe, the millet-beer before described. They greatly respect what the oracle says to them. Their sons are circumcised between the ages of fourteen and eighteen,* and they affect polygamy, which they regard as their greatness, much wondering at the one-wife marriage of the whites.

Their unions are effected without ceremony: the would-be husband goes to the father or guardian of the girl, who may be quite a child, and with him arranges the dowry in cloths, which, if great, may reach a dozen. After this arrangement, called betrothal (roboraçilo), the payment being left to the bridegroom's convenience, they arrange a day for leading home the bride, who, until of nubile years, remains with her parents. Consummation is done thus: carried by the horse of some Caffre, and accompanied by her female relations and friends, beating drums, the bride is escorted to near the bridegroom's house, and when close to it they send him word that they bring his wife. This done, they drum and dance till some velorio beads are sent to them, after which they advance two paces or so, and stop till they get more. Thus, on his marriage-day, the poor Caffre must not only strip himself, but also go out borrowing, to show that he has given all his own. Seeing nothing more come, they inspect the sum offered them, then they advance nearer, and at length they hand over the bride to the chief wife and her companions, and retire to their homes, leaving her in tears. As the Caffres may buy an unlimited number of spouses, even their slaves being wives to them, they choose one, and call her the great woman, and she is the most respected. Her peculiar duties are to preserve the husband's wardrobe and medicines, and to apply the latter when required; without using them no one goes to war, to hunt, or to travel, or, indeed, on any important business.

The funerals of these people are proportioned to the means of the deceased. Their pomp consists in the great cortége by which the body is borne to the grave, and in the quantity of food and drink expended upon the crowd of people, who sing and dance to the sound of drums. If the deceased be a king, he must carry with him all that he possesses, with slaves to serve him and women for his pleasures.† Throughout his

---

* In Dahomey this rite is deferred often till the twentieth year, and then it becomes dangerous. I have repeatedly recorded my opinion that it is of African origin, borrowed by the Jews from the negroid race.

† This, says Dr. Livingstone, is still the general practice of Negroland, but it

dominions robberies and disorder (cleirero) are allowed for ten or fifteen days, or even more. Their deadliest crimes are witch-craft, adultery, and theft. The first, and the most enormous, is always punished capitally; the second sometimes, but more often by mutilation of the hands, the ears, and the offending member. They are less severe with the women, as a rule, but some plaintiffs are not satisfied except by death. Although they cut off the thief's hands and ears, many wretches have exposed themselves to such mutilation.

The soil of this land is fertile, and would produce all that the people want; there are many kinds of food, but the principal is manioc. They eat it in dough, toasted and boiled and even raw; and they drink it in pombe with a little mixture of millet. Manioc flour for dough is easily made in the following way: after gathering the root, they peel it, and soak it in a stream for three days; on the fourth, when it is almost rotten, they dry it in the summer sun, or in winter over a fire which they light under the cots used for this purpose; and, finally, they pound it in a tree-trunk mortar. We may say that they are collecting and sowing this root all the year round, but the harvest is when provision is wholly wanting. At such times they dig up a small quantity to last for a few days, and in its stead they bury a few bits of stalk which act as seed. The rains are abundant and regular. Fruits are few, except bananas of many kinds: of live stock, poultry is the most plentiful and goats are rare. Game and fish suffice, but they cannot salt their provision, so to keep it they dry it with fire and smoke, making it unfit for us to eat. The black cattle is well flavoured, but only the king keeps them in certain places, to show his greatness: he does not eat their flesh, saying that they are Fumos, like himself; also he does not milk them, not knowing how, so the cows are almost wild. Here we find traces of the Metempsychosis theory.[*] With this idea the king sends his cattle as gifts to his guests, and when they die or are killed for injuring millet fields—these animals pasture by night and sleep by day—he divides the meat amongst his people, who, not considering them, like their king, great Fumos, eat them unscrupulously. Cow leather makes their girdles, that of other horned cattle their dress, and cows' blood enters into their medicines. Therefore they sent us only dead and skinned animals.

There may be many articles of trade, but it is now confined

---

is not confined to that part of the world. Perhaps we may better define it, "the general concomitant of a particular phase of society."

[*] Superficial observers often confound the highly philosophical and complicated theory of metempsychosis with the vulgar metamorphosis of the savage African.

to two—ivory and slaves. A tusk of 32 lbs. to 48 lbs. costs 2 to 3 pieces of cloth, the piece being 1½ to 2 fathoms long, and ten couros.* The tusk of 80 lbs. to 96 lbs. is worth 5 to 6 pieces, with a little couro or velorio. There are copper bars sold for four common cloths, or pagnes (pannos de fato), or 40 to 50 couros ; the small bars cost as a rule one cloth's worth of missanga. Uncut greenstone (malachite †) of different sizes is sold cheap, but the two latter articles are not indigenous.

22nd.—The Sanu Muropúe took away, in presence of all the whites, the gifts destined for the Muropúe and the Mueneputo, as was promised at our assembly on the 17th instant.

23rd.—Having ordered Lieutenant Antonio José da Cruz, commandant of the troops, to chastise a soldier with forty blows, he not only disobeyed me, but he also falsely reported having carried out my orders.

February 24th to March 1st.—The men, instigated by their officers, demanded an advance of three months' pay, which I sent to them without receiving any reply.

2nd–4th.—I gave Pedro Xavier Velasco leave to go back to Tete, not only at his request, but because I wished to avoid the disgust shown by all the Expedition to the Cazembe, with whom, it is said, this arrangement of return had been made in anticipation of my desires. José Rodrigues Caleja, hearing this, wished to interfere and exceeding his duties as guide and Receiver of the Treasury, he addressed me a note in which, after a fashion, he made himself accessory to the command. As I took no notice of his false reasonings, he began to show me aversion and to seek his revenge.

5th.—The manioc grown in the land which the Cazembe had offered to the whites (muzungos) on the 27th January was divided, but their carelessness prevented them sending their slaves (checundas) to receive the portion appertaining to them.

6th–9th.—Loud murmurs arose about the Expedition arriving at the Cazembe's city—which it could not at once leave—during the early month of January, when the evils caused by the wet season and the country rendered a long rest necessary. As José Rodrigues Caleja, by declaring me to be the cause of the delay and of their consequent sufferings, showed signs of stirring up against me even the most indifferent, I assembled all the whites. They knew what were my reasons for wintering here, so I resolved that each should separately declare his opinion touching our inaction, whether it could have been avoided or not and

---

* From the context it would appear that these couros are some kind of bead.

† Monteiro and Gamitto (p. 283) mention malachite "malaquitea," which the Cazembes call "chifurla." I have seen fine copper from the Cazembe's country.

how. I told the writer, or notary, to take the paper in which all had recorded their opinions, to draw it up in legal form, and to get their signatures. It was late when we separated, and the scribe was not skilled enough to draft the deed without the aid of others. He went to José Rodrigues Caleja, being of that party, and with him falsified not only Caleja's vote but also that of Vasco Joaquim Pires, as is proved in the forged paper. I was disregarded by Captain João da Cunha Pereira, and when I wished to punish him there and then he would not be arrested, nay, with threats he declared that His Excellency, the Captain-General of Mozambique, should not deprive him of his receivership, as had been done to Lieut. Manoel dos Santos Silva.

As I had little power, nothing was effected. I asked Gonçalo Caetano Pereira, the first guide, how to ascertain from Chinbimba and Mossindassaro the deficiency of the loads entrusted to them for carriage to the Cazembe's court. He replied, in the presence of many, that this must be done with the beneplacet of the king, whose vassals they were. Finding the answer reasonable, I entrusted to him the business, which he undertook promptly and with good will.

10th.—Lieutenant Antonio José da Cruz, when ordered to attest in writing the refusal of Captain João da Cunha Pereira to submit to arrest yesterday, gave in his attestation which denied all that had happened.

11th-14th.—Gonçalo Caetano Pereira, whom I had resolved to send on the 8th instant to the Cazembe in the matter of Mossindassaro and Chinbimba, when asked by José Rodrigues Caleja not to delay, excused himself by means of his Caffre Inharugue, saying that the latter did not wish to bear any message to the Cazembe. The most embarrassing thing is, that they try to lay the blame upon me, when at the same time they bar my road to the king, and they prevent the two Caffres obeying all my summons. At last I tried every effort to send some other person on this errand to the king, who deferred it till the morrow.

15th.—Sending back to the Cazembe the messenger who had returned yesterday, I heard to-day that the king was pleased with my calling up and examining the two Caffres before mentioned. When they declined to obey my summons I reported the fact to the king, begging that his messenger would conduct them into my presence. He promised but he never performed, which I attributed to the intrigues of Caleja. This man, under colour of benefiting D. Francisca Josefa of Tete, whose niece he had married, declared that the late Governor de Lacerda, who had taken charge of that lady's venture, and whose death had caused the goods to be confused, had concealed by means of the Mossindasáro, six bales (motcros *) of cloth, and had changed the mark or mixed the articles, removing 150 pannos and two bags (guissapos)† of velorio beads. These he had wished to make over to D. Francisca's slave, Candeone, in order to exchange for ivory. And this was done with the knowledge of the governor's managing man, whose duty it was to take charge of those articles, pretexting the report spread by José Rodrigues Caleja that the manager had wished to appropriate the said spoils. This trick of José Rodrigues Caleja's was very ingenious, for not only was that Caffre encouraged to conceal 912 more cloths (pagnes) of royal property, but Chinhimba, the other Caffre messenger, also took heart successfully to embezzle from the Crown 456 cloths, three bags (guissapos) of velorio, two ditto of (red) beads, and one of cowries.

16th–28th.—José Rodrigues Caleja was always imposing upon them the necessity of giving the Cazembe time to prepare for our departure. The others being sick, I directed him to go with a "mouth" or parcel of cloth and to make preparations, at the same time reviving the matter of the two Caffres. The Cazembe received him well, and said that he knew—the winter now being over—that the Expedition would wish to return to Tete. As regards the defaulting Caffre, he said that the whites had allowed a long time to pass in silence, and had finally received everything. The first part of this reply could not have come from a Caffre, who all hold that the palaver (milando) never dies, nor wastes, but is kept up till "settled" from generation to generation. So I resolved either that the king had not said it, or had been taught to say it by José Rodrigues Caleja. The affair was not pushed further, because it was not advisable to call Chinimba to account until the appearance of Mossindasaro, who would hear of it from the Cazembe and conceal himself.

29th–30th.—I gave the said Caffres some small quantity of clothing for which they asked, thus hoping to assemble them and to elicit something about the hidden goods.

31st.—The Cazembe sent me the chair enclosed in his present (mirambo), begging me to have it lined with "cherves,"‡ which was done at once.

April 1st–7th.—By an accidental fire eight of my slaves were burned in their own huts; many of the Expedition rejoiced thereat, and a certain José Thomaz Gomes da Silveira, openly

---

* This is afterwards explained to be one-third of 450 cloths, that is to say, each 152 cloths.

† The word "guissapo" means a bag of bamboo rind or grass cloth. Monteiro and Gamitto (p. 195) speak of "um Quissipo, sacco feito de palma."

‡ Dr. Kirk could not inform me what kind of cloth "cherves" is.

wished that the accident had taken place in my house. I report this and other things, which do not exactly relate to the service of the Crown, both to carry out my instructions and to show the character of my subordinates.

8th–9th.—The Cazembo forbade the whites, who had begun their cabals greatly to his disgust, all intercourse with him, thus avoiding their impertinences, and he wondered at our disunion.

10th.—José Rodrigues Caleja, an old enemy of Lieutenant Manoel dos Santos e Silva, with whom he appeared friendly only when wishing to insult me, after visiting him in his sickness, declared to me that he wished for death, and that if he knew of anything to end his life he would take it.

11th–12th.—I had some inklings that the crime charged upon Pedro Xavier Velasco was a mere imputation, and Lieutenant José Vicente Pereira Salema confessed that he had been intimidated to give false witness by José Rodrigues Caleja. I also learned that Captain João da Cunha Pereira, after his deposition, went to Pedro Xavier Velasco's quarters, and told him that I wanted to drink his blood, which was my reason for drawing up papers against him, but that no depositions made by himself or his colleagues would do him any injury.

13th.—José Rodrigues Caleja convoked, in the house of Gonçalo Caetano Pereira, to debate over the affair of the 9th of March, all those of his party, viz., Captain João da Cunha Pereira, Lieutenant Manoel dos Santos e Silva, Captain José da Cruz, José Thomaz Gomes da Silva, Lieutenant José Vicente Pereira Salema, and Ensign José Joaquim Pires; they agreed to outrage me in that business, first by word and then by deed. The Lieut.-Colonel Pedro Nolasco Vieira de Araujo and the chief sergeant Pedro Xavier Velasco were sick, and not of the league. I had no testimony whereby to convict them, thus they could insult me with impunity. The former of these two, however, came unexpectedly upon them, and the project fell to the ground. All this was told to me by Lieutenant José Vicente Pereira Salema, whom as the most timorous they sent to me with a paper of their requisitions.

14th–15th.—José Rodrigues Caleja, who was in the habit of troubling me morning and evening, came early to report that messengers were expected from Tete to recall the troops, as there was great alarm of the French.

16th.—José Rodrigues Caleja required me to assemble the members in order to determine how to sell the Crown stores remaining in the receiver's hands. My reply was that I had reasons for not convening any more of such assemblies. He went at once and wrote me a letter representing the loss that would result from taking the goods back to Tete. In view of all this trouble I at once ordered the stores to be valued.

17th.—The effects were valued by the arbitrators at only double their cost-price at Tete, and the receiver, with sundry impertinences, demanded permission to sell them. I ordered them to be sold for the sums offered, finding that nothing more advantageous could be obtained.

18th–19th.—I sent to compliment the Cazembe, who was then a great friend of mine; he sent back that he wanted to see me.

20th.—I returned an answer to the Cazembe's message, declaring that I would call upon him personally.

21st.—José Rodrigues Caleja, angry because, without consulting him, I had allowed Pedro Xavier Velasco to return to Tete, and because I would not be made the tool of his private enmities, did all he could to annoy me. He teazed me with requests to smuggle out the cloth required for our return march, as the Cazembe would never allow it, after once entering, to leave the country. Fearing his malice, I appointed him and the guide, Gonçalo Caetano Pereira, to fix upon the quantity and the place. The former was settled, the latter they refused to tell me, pleading that, as we had travelled together, I —a chaplain—must know as much as they (the guides) did.

22nd–23rd.—I again ordered the two aforesaid guides to tell me the "cache," and they refused.

24th.—The Cazembe consented to receive me on the morrow, and to send a household officer to conduct me, as the Fumo Anceva wished all the whites to be purely dependent upon himself. José Rodrigues Caleja happened to be present, and, dissimulating his jealousy of my getting an audience when he had failed, begged me to forward the departure of the Expedition, which, depending upon the Cazembe, would easily be forgotten unless often brought to mind.

25th.—After a short delay I was admitted to the Cazembe, who received my compliments kindly, responding briefly after the country fashion. This over, I earnestly prayed him to forward the time of our return; to which he also replied favourably. I then submitted to him that on reaching Tete there would be a difficulty in explaining to my superiors the prohibition of passing over to Angola; he bade me leave two members of the party to proceed there after our departure. The Fumo Anceva wrested this into a demand that each of the whites should leave behind one or two Cheundas.* Knowing that the slaves would be pawns for our future communication, and that the Caffres being scarce, and many of them sickly, the

---

* This, I presume, is "cheeunda"—a slave.

whites would not consent to the measure. I replied that when Catára and Chinimba had come with friendly messages to Tete, we had at once set out without hostages. Hearing me speak to the soldier-linguist in the Sena dialect, the Cazembe at once explained that he did not want hostages, but two persons to go to Angola. I could not reply to so sudden and unexpected a permission, so I told the king that the presents destined for the Muropúe and the Muanebuto having been given away, and the treasury being exhausted, my confusion prevented my returning an answer. The Cazembe at once said that he would manage about the presents, and that all I had to do was to look after the subsistence and the means of travel. I finally answered that the matter should be thought over. He then spoke of the opaque stoneware beads (pedras do côres) which he wanted from the whites, who still, he knew, had good things. I contented him as well as possible, and left deeply preoccupied about Angola. After my return, José Rodrigues Caleja, on hearing the affair, malignantly remarked, that if I had proposed Pedro Xavier Velasco as envoy to the Cazembe, he would soon close the road with a new prohibition; and much of the same kind to throw obstacles in my way.[*]

26th.—José Rodrigues Caleja came, and insultingly showed me a paper in which the lieutenant-colonel Pedro Nolasco Vieira de Aranjo and Pedro Xavier Velasco had complained of him, and charged him with being their informant. As if a secret between nine persons could be kept, especially when of the many councillors are Captain João da Cunha Pereira and Lieutenant José Vicente Pereira Salema, who do nothing but tittle-tattle. I tried to avoid a scandalous rupture, but from that day forward he did nothing but oppose me, wishing to commit all the goods to the Cazembe, and thus to frustrate the transit to Angola.

27th.—The Fumo Anceva came from the Cazembe, refusing passage to Tete for Lieut.-Colonel Pedro Nolasco Vieira de Araujo, who wished to leave these bad men. I answered that he was not going, because I had not given him leave. This reply closed the Caffre's mouth. He doubtless had been taught to oppose this departure, though not by his friendship for the departer. It was José Rodrigues Caleja's plan, in opposing the going of

---

[*] This permission for two of the party to proceed to Angola was a sham, to see if any presents had been withheld, and to try the perseverance of the whites. The Cazembe must have thought unfavourably of the leader when he hesitated at once to reply—a thing ever to be avoided in Africa. The two soldiers were eventually left behind as was proposed, but they never, it need hardly be said, reached Angola. In 1806 the Angolan Pombeiros found one man still waiting for permission.

the two Pedros, Nolasco and Velasco, to forewarn all those who
might be useful to him at Tete, adding as many lies as possible,
and well knowing that the thing first heard, though false, is
generally credited in preference to truth.

Not satisfied by this mischief, that perverse man went with
Lieutenant Antonio José da Cruz to the Cazembe, designing
to traduce me and Pedro Nolasco, but the Cazembe, who hated his
mutinous disposition, refused him access. He must indeed be
a bad white man who is hated by Caffres. He reported to the
Fumo Anceva that the Lieut.-Colonel Pedro Nolasco and the
other whites had so well hidden many fine cloths and coloured
stoneware beads (pedras pintadas), that these could be discovered only by opening their boxes. The Cazembe, despite
his generosity, was persuaded to give this order, or the Fumo
Anceva fabricated it. I sent for the lieutenant-colonel, Pedro
Nolasco, to hear the message: he excused himself, but he
could not prevent the search. I positively refused to sanction
it in the case of other whites, knowing that the Fumo Anceva
wanted only to enter the receiver's house and to carry off everything for his king.[*]

28th–30th.—José Thomaz Gomes da Silveira a man at once
proud of his birth and ready for any vileness, brought, on the
part of the partisans, who knew what to expect in return, a
petition for pardon, and for the papers to be burned. Thinking
some severity necessary, I refused to destroy what concerned
Pedro Xavier Velasco, as by so doing I might expose myself to
their accusations of having made away with public documents.
The Commissary replied that he would return, in hopes of a more
favourable answer. To get rid of José Rodrignes Caleja, I
ordered the cloth necessary for the return march to be brought
to my quarters, deducting 100 cloths (pannos) according to the
valuation. I also named all those to whom cloth, fine beads,
and tin (calaim[†]) had fallen due for some months. Thus the
receiver was lightened, and the goods were safely placed in the
hands of individuals. When the corporal (cabo), Paulo da Silva,
went to take the cloth for the expedition, José Rodrignes
Caleja uttered threats, saying that, as I had not consulted him,
I should see how it would end.

---

[*] There is a Fumo Anceva at every African court, who thinks only of recom-
mending himself to the king by giving any amount of trouble to strangers. Of
course it is a shallow, short-sighted policy, but nothing better can come from the
negro's brain. It is, however, dangerous, and must be carefully watched, as it is
calculated to cause disagreeables between the members of an expedition, and
then everything goes to ruin.

[†] Monteiro and Gamitto (p. 113) speak of " um pão de calaim," a loaf or lump
of calaim (Indian tin).

May 1st-2nd.[*]—At mass-time I had just arrived at the Introit, when Lieutenant Antonio José da Cruz and Vasco Joaquim Pires set up, in the former's lodgings, a song so profane and so loud, that I could not proceed with the sacrifice, and sent to beg them to be silent. From that day they ceased attending at mass, nor did they observe Lent and other Christian duties. Moreover, José Vicente Pereira Salema, whom I, when Prior of Sena, had taught to read, write, and cipher, impudently asked me if I was a father or a priest, that he should confess to me.

Lieut.-Colonel Pedro Nolasco Vieira consented to the search, and delivered certain large "canutilhos" and other things demanded by the Fumo Anceva for his master. Catúra, seeing me assist in the search, at the request of the lieutenant-colonel, Pedro Nolasco Vieira, who, for his own justification, wished it to be public, as all those effects belonged to the late Governor, required my house also to be visited. Upon this I sent a message to the Cazembe, saying that all my cloth and beads were kept for him, that I made him small presents every fifteen days, and that I hoped he would not support Catúra's demand. He replied that Catúra had received no such power from him. Thus fell to the ground the attempt to divide the 200 cloths kept by me for the expenses of the Expedition.

At 11 A.M. Lieutenant Antonio José da Cruz brought the subsistence-roll for my signature. I notified to him in writing that one of José Rodrigues Caleja's ten Caffres having died, the name must be removed. The pair agreed to write to me in a feigned hand an insulting note, accusing me of having caused troubles in the Expedition, and of having prevented the journey to Angola, also including the calumny of my being intimidated ; so that the note might not be produced.

3rd.—I held the first general meeting of officers (cabo d'ordens), and proved the outrage of José Rodrigues Caleja, who sent his slave Maxima into my courtyard to quarrel with, and ill-treat, my barber-slave.

4th.—I addressed an official note to Manoel Caetano Pereira, the guide, naming him for the journey to Angola, with 400 cloths and porcelains (velorio) for route expenses, he being able to live almost as a Caffre, and having his own slaves who would not leave him. He returned me the document, saying he would have nothing to do with writings. I sent it back as on Her Most Faithful Majesty's service, and he tried to excuse himself by the persuasion of José Rodrigues Caleja.[†]

* In the original diary "March" is an error.
† Here the leader was decidedly wrong : he offered a sum utterly inadequate to the expenses of such a march.

5th.—As Manoel Caetano Pereira would not set out, I demanded back the order granting him 400 cloths ; he offered to return it with his reply to my official. I left it with him, thinking to annul the order by acquainting the receiver with what had happened. I then directed Lieutenant Antonio José da Cruz, who commanded the troops, to muster at my quarters two picked men for the journey to Angola. He sent me a pair of invalids, who, as he expected, were rejected, and I chose a good man, well known to me, and bade him look out for a second. At last he sent me the soldier Caetano da Costa, whom I detached for the duty together with another, giving them beads and 200 cloths. Pedro Xavier Velasco set out from the Mussana (Mussassa ?) on return to Tete, and José Rodrigues Caleja collected some of the Caffre slaves furnished to the Expedition by D. Francisca, and provoked them to leave the Mussana and to go for slaves and ivory to the Muiza country. This was to make the others desert and to hinder Pedro Xavier Velasco's journey.

At daybreak they left in my court a defamatory note, so indecent as to be here unproduceable ; it was clearly dictated by Captain João da Cunha Pereira, and it was written in a disguised hand by Lieutenant Antonio José da Cruz, who has not only this talent, but also that of forging documents, signed and certified.

9th–10th.—I issued to the soldiers going to Angola—Paulo da Silva and Caetano da Costa—200 cloths and advance pay for three months. The members of the Expedition who suffered from hunger, partly because food was not to be bought and partly from their own improvidence and waste, requested me to supply to them some powder and lead that they might remedy the the evil by hunting.

11th–13th.—I issued a keg of powder and 2 bags of lead. The Cazembe sent us a message that after a few days he would change his quarters, and that he wished all the whites to accompany him. I at once informed the members of the Expedition. José Rodrigues Caleja simply replied that if he left his present quarters it would be to go to Tete.

15th–27th.—The Cazembe asked for a tent, or as they call it, a "cloth house" of Travatam stuff ; it was the largest in the Expedition, but I gratified him with it.

28th–31st.—At 8 A.M. the Cazembe sent to say that on the next day the whites must remove to his new quarters, where he would shortly follow them. José Rodrigues Caleja persisted in not moving, and the king told him to go to Tete whenever he pleased, leaving in the hands of his Caffre Candione the business of D. Francisca, whose son he called himself.

June 1st.—At 8 A.M. the Expedition, accompanied by the

Fumo Anceva, set out for Móro (Mofo[*]), its appointed place, Captain José da Cunha and Vasco Joaquim Pires remaining behind at the old Mussana without leave. A message came after my departure from the Cazembe, requesting an escort of our troops, which could not be granted, as there were no officers to attend to it. José Thomaz Gomes da Silva, wanting carriers for his hammocks—all of them having been taken by José Rodrigues Caleja and Lieutenant Antonio José da Cruz—impudently sent to say that, as he required people, who were all carrying my ivory, he must take the same road as my Caffres, who were burnt to death on April 7th.

2nd.—José Thomaz Gomes da Silva came to obtain satisfaction for the event of yesterday : I showed him that the ivory, so far from being mine, was in the hands of the executor or attorney of the late governor, and I threatened him with particular punishment in future if the thing recurred.

3rd.—Blows were exchanged between the soldiers and the Muiza Caffres on account of a black woman belonging to one of the former having something to do with the Muiza slaves of the Cazembe's Muiza subjects. The Caffres of D. Francisca were drawn into the fray, which reached such a point that some blows were given to the highly respectable Muiza, Chinhimba. In haste I sent for an officer, but the Commandant was away, the two subalterns would not come, and José Rodrigues Caleja impudently sent to say that I might do it myself.

4th.—The Fumo Anceva applied for an escort for his king, who would arrive to-morrow. Knowing the Cazembe's fondness for firing, especially on such occasions, I ordered the receiver to issue a flask of powder. I told the Fumo Anceva that the troops should be ready when the king arrived within convenient distance. I also informed the Commandant what honours were to be paid to the king.

5th.—The Commandant applied for another flask of powder, with which and that before given he went to meet the Cazembe at his old residence, thus exceeding his orders.

6th–9th.—The Cazembe, at the advice of his medicine man, left his old court, which was considered unhealthy, for a place newly founded upon the Rio Moro.[†] He was accompanied and preceded at a short interval by his wives, and he reached his new

---

* See June 6–9th.

† The Mofo, Moira, Mofwe, Mofuo or Mofu Lakelet, on whose eastern shore is now the Gaada, Mossumba, or Chipango (palace) of the Mwáta Cazembe. According to the 'Second Expedition' (p. 310) the old place here alluded to was called l'embúe, and lay one and a half leagues (six miles) to the east. In the latest maps the lagoon has no watershed, and is probably drained by the Loapula (Roapula or Guapula) river into the Moero Lake.

palace at noon. I sent at once my compliments and a request
to see him; he politely received my present and message, but
he did not appoint a day for my visit.

10*th*–11*th*.—Lieutenant Antonio José da Cruz saluted with
firing a present of pombe sent by the Cazembe's wife.

12*th*—At 3 P.M. the Lieutenants Antonio José da Cruz and
José Vicente Pereira Salema went to the Cazembe's house,
opened the compound-fence and passed in review the king's
wives, saying to each other which was good, which each would
choose, and so on. This coming to the Cazembe's ears, he was
greatly offended at the insult, and moreover he referred to the
Lieutenant having formerly paid court to one of his women
when, being in the old palace, he had gone to fly a kite. He would
have let the officer know the extent of his wrath, but he was
prevented by his mother.[*]

13*th*.—The Cazembe sent to me, as Commandant, many com-
plaints and threats, which were received by Gonçalo Caetano
Pereira. My people deputed José Thomaz Gomes with a
forged message that the Cazembe complained of the soldiers
and the slaves (Cheundas) taking whatever they wanted on the
roads, and that Gonçalo Caetano Pereira, being too ill to bring
the message, had sent him (J. Thomaz) to request me that such
actions might be forbidden by beat of drum. I at that time
ignored the Cazembe's true message, which was, "Great had
been the audacity of the whites (Muzungos) in casting their
eyes and desires upon his wives, when there were many
women—of whom they had had the best—in his lands. They
must know him to be a tiger that carried ruin and devas-
tation in his train, and that it would cost him little to prove
to them the truth of his words." I sent to José Thomaz Gomes,
ordering each officer and white man rigorously to prohibit his
soldiers and slaves (Cheundas) from all such thieving, and
showing them the danger of insulting the Cazembe, who
deserved all our attentions, not only for his favours, but also
because he was a powerful king, upon whom our well-being
depended.

14*th*–16*th*.—The Cazembe sending a messenger to me, I
asked why the master did not permit me to see him : he replied
that the king was waiting for the porters to bring some presents
for me. I answered that from a friend this proceeding was not

---

[*] This might be the real or the official mother of the king. So when I visited
Dahomo, Mr. Hilton, a drunken "chattel" attached to the missionaries, and,
I need hardly say, a Mulatto, attempted to break into the king's seraglio. Gelele
behaved very well in the matter, merely sending to inform me that if the man had
not been of my party he would have taken off his head.

wanted: he rejoined that it was necessary, and that the king could not dismiss me empty-handed.*

17th–19th.—I reminded the Cazembe of his promise, and he said that he would summon me on the morrow.

20th–23rd.—I was kindly and pleasantly received by the Cazembe, who on this day had hardly one of his servants present as interpreter.† After compliments he anticipated me on the subject of my departure. I presented to him the soldiers who would remain behind us to proceed to Angola. He saw and approved of them, promising to forward them. This day he appointed one of his young domestics to accompany me to Mozambique, and to learn "Mainato," or washing. They ignore this art, and during our stay they had learned to wash coarse cottons ("Maxilas de Gondo"), very roughly made with wooden looms by the Caffres of Sena, and a few at Tete; to bathe themselves often with water and to anoint the head and body with a little oil in sign of spruceness. Finally, after impressing upon me that he ardently desired communication with us, and that he had taken much trouble to facilitate it, he dismissed me with great signs of satisfaction.

24th–28th.—From a slave of Catára I ascertained that the two ivories presented in the name of the Cazembe when his mission visited Tete in 1798, had been intended by him to buy stone-ware, beads (pedras), and other things required. The chiefs of the troops, malignantly encouraged by their officers, came to demand pay, though the receiver's department had only 100 cloths in stuff and 50 in porcelain beads (velorio)‡ to ration the slaves whom the Cazembe might send by way of crown-presents (Mirambo). I replied that the subject should be considered.

29th–30th.—The party against me sent José Thomaz Gomes da Silva to inform me that they intended shortly to leave for Tete, and that José Rodrigues Caleja desired to know my intentions touching the five scores (corjas)§ of cloth remaining in the Receiver's department. The deputy, when asked if he came to require congé, replying in the negative, I told him that the matter should be referred to the Cazembe. Caleja's

---

* This is the usual manœuvre of African kings before they "give pass" or dismiss their visitors. Having no return presents, or not wishing to offer anything, they waste the patience of their guest with a hundred delays, till, however greedy, he departs in despair.

† The lower people present, the more friendly, of course, is the interview.

‡ As has been said, the pano ("panno," pagne, tobe), or unity of two fathoms of cotton cloth, in 1832 worth 6d., is used to express other values, even of beads.

§ I presume this to be the Hindostani word—a score, from "kori." It is used in Zanzibar ('Journal of the Royal Geographical Society,' vol. xxix., p. 448).

question I treated as a joke. The Cazembe, to whom the white
men's project was immediately reported, declared that he would
at once give us the road.

July 1st–10th.—The party came in a mob, declaring their
intention to depart, as the Cazembe was causing delay. I replied
that everything possible had been done, and that the king had
sent Xiréros (Shire men) to collect their fellow country-folk, whom
he had long ago despatched for the purpose of recovering the
annual taxes of his lands. They insisted on setting out, having
heard, probably from their untrustworthy slaves, that the
Cazembe intended to keep us for another year. I know not
how they persuaded themselves so; they ought to have known
that their actions had made them a trouble to the Cazembe's
subjects and an object of distrust to himself. Possibly the king
may have delayed us to see if our means were exhausted, but
this was their fault for having charged Lieutenant-Colonel
Pedro Nolasco and myself with keeping back goods. I promised
to report the matter to the Cazembe, and when they retired I
prepared to do so by means of one of my servants. I had hardly
instructed the latter when Captain João da Cunha Pereira
and Lieutenant José Vicente Pereira Salema, retracing their
steps, informed me that on the morrow they would set out for
Tete. I told them to act as they thought proper, my authority
as Commandant having long ago been set aside by them. My
messenger went to the Cazembe, who said that the whites
might go when they pleased, and that his object in keeping
them was to dismiss them satisfied, and not ill-disposed towards
him, so as to prevent others visiting him.

The whites were somewhat appeased by the royal reply,
which was duly communicated to them. Some resolved not to
go without me, but Captain João da Cunha Pereira, in his
pride, determined to start, inducing the troops to escort him.
As they would not move, he committed to them all their
rations; whereas I, seeing the negligence of the men, had kept
back the stores for distribution on the day of departure, intending
to explain to the poor fellows the sufferings which would
result from the wilful waste of their only subsistence for the
journey.

11th.—Effectually Captain João da Cunha Pereira set out,
leaving his soldiers and quarters, and thus constituting himself
a deserter. When the Cazembe heard of the departure, he sent
me the present (mirambo) for Her Most Faithful Majesty, adding
that it was a token of gratitude for the favours conferred upon
him, and that his devoir being now done, he gave his pass; he
added, however, that the opening of the Angola road must be
reserved for our return.

I assembled the whites, who were surprised at the sight of the present, much expected on account of the promises and the spirit of the Cazembe. It would have been more considerable, but for the indiscretion of the Captain João da Cunha Pereira, who had left without even an adieu to the king. I received it in trouble of mind, and, whilst thinking what to say, the party told the Fumo Anceva, who escorted it, that there was no return gift for the presents which had been intended for the Muropúe and the Muenobuto, but which the Cazembe had appropriated.

José Rodrigues Caleja was directed to buy hides, and to make handcuffs for the thirty slaves of the royal gift (mirambo), and for the four others received by Lieutenant Manoel dos Santos, and committed to him. Moreover, I directed that this gang should be placed under sentinels. He hastened to say that he had resolved to distribute the slaves amongst the soldiers, and that for every head lost three-score cloths would be charged. I asked how in this way the men could guard the Crown slaves, when they did not even prevent their own property from escaping in numbers. To this objection he made no reply. I allowed him to take his own way, because it was clear that he would not obey me, or that, if compelled, he would cause desertion, to render me responsible.

The Fumo Anceva departed with his message, and José Rodrigues Caleja collected the several items of the present. I directed an account of it to be drawn up, and when he refused to sign, I caused it to be attested by all the others present.

12th.—At 8 A.M. the Fumo Anceva appeared with the return gifts to the presents intended for the Muropúe and the Muenobuto. Whilst I ordered them to be received, every one gave his opinion touching their smallness, and the worthlessness of the former largesse. I represented to them that these words would not only fail to increase the presents, but might prevent the soldiers going to Angola. José Rodrigues Caleja hastened to say that the mission could not take place, as these men intended to follow the steps of the Expedition as soon as ever it turned towards Tete. I asked him why he had not reported this, knowing that, in our impossibility to carry out the other projects of the late Governor, this mission was the only duty of which we could acquit ourselves. He was silenced by the shame of finding himself either an impostor or the person determined to frustrate our principal object. Convinced that the soldier Paulo da Silva was not capable of the intention attributed to him, I proposed to inquire concerning the second man to be sent, namely, Caetano da Costa. Finally, José

Rodrigues Caleja received the present, refusing to attest the account, and the Fumo Anceva retired, complaining that he had not received his "urné." *

13th.—Caetano da Costa, the soldier, when summoned before me, and asked concerning José Rodrigues Caleja's assertion, declared that it was false, and challenged the strictest inquiry. I knew, however, that no one would assist in it. From passages in this Diary it may be judged whether Caleja had or had not opposed the mission to Angola. As the slaves of the two royal gifts were not enough to carry the Crown loads, I directed Lieutenant Antonio José da Cruz, who had the distribution of the slave personnel of the Expedition, to set apart for my hammock twenty Caffres, and to supply those necessary to Lieutenant Manoel dos Santos and to José Thomaz Gomes. The two latter, like myself, had been carried by the slaves of the Expedition, not by their own.

I had ordered the gang of D. Francisca, who at her own discomfort supplied many hands, to carry the loads of their mistress and the property of the late Governor. This was a cause of spite to the Receiver, José Rodrigues Caleja, because it prevented his revenging himself upon the Lieutenant-Colonel Pedro Nolasco, in whose charge these properties were, by taking away his porters. The Caffres were duly supplied to Lieutenant Manoel dos Santos and to José Thomaz Gomes. By José Rodrigues Caleja's authority I remained without one, being sentenced either to walk 270 leagues, or to take from the Lieutenant-Colonel Pedro Nolasco ten Caffres whom he had brought from Tete expressly for his own conveyance.

15th–16th.—The Cazembe applied to us for powder, sending a slave as "dash." I despatched a keg, intended by the late Governor as a present to the king, who returned, by way of "mouth," another slave. Thereupon the Fumo Anceva declared that his master wished two soldiers to remain, and to escort the remittances, which, after the winter (rainy season), would be sent to Tete. The minister did not fail to show that he had been egged on to make such a requisition.

17th.—José Rodrigues Caleja and his followers called at my quarters, wishing us to go for our "pass" to the Cazembe. My reply was, that I had not been summoned. He rejoined, that the Fumo Anceva had specified me. I objected, that the Fumo might have given me the news, if true, and that they could go without me. He persisted that my presence was indispensable, to settle about the Angola mission and the Cazembe's escort.

---

* This word, from its context, means the "vails" usually given to those who carry presents.

When I asked him if that was his affair, he protested against
the evil which delay might inflict upon the Royal treasury.   I
declined to accept his protest, and reminded him that I was his
superior.   He refused to recognise me as such, and added assertions which convinced me that the Fumo Anceva's requisition
for two soldiers had arisen from an intrigue of José Rodrigues
Caleja. He had intended, if I consented, to accuse me of having
left the men for my own interest in the Cazembe's remittances;
or, if I refused, to frustrate thereby the mission to Angola, by
annoying the king with such rejection of his last request.   In
this appeared the white hand; the Caffres never remember to
alter, or to change the resolutions of those engaged in business
with them.

Resolving to make an example of José Rodrigues Caleja, I
prepared to issue, as authorized by my position of commander
of a royal expedition, part of whose duty it was to punish rebels
for the good of the Crown service, an order to the following
purport: That José Rodrigues Caleja, who had committed a
similar offence at Maniça in 1788, should, as chief mutineer
and rebel of the party, be arrested by Lieutenant Manoel dos
Santos, and held until the charge be laid before the Royal presence.   I did not, however, publish it at once, hoping by threats
to gain my object.

18th and 19th.—As my efforts were in vain, I issued the above
order against José Rodrigues Caleja, as was certified by Lieutenant Manoel dos Santos.   His obstinacy was such that he
would not yield himself to arrest, unless I could prove the
faults of which he was accused.   He thought easily to get
over this disobedience, adding the words, that the Commandant
had incurred criminality for having in that same order origi-
nated the said intrigues; and he compelled me not to publish
either the order or the signature of the executive officer to whom
it had been submitted.   Nothing remaining for me but to yield,
I left the man to himself.   On the same day, Lieutenant
Antonio José da Cruz, commanding the troops, issued an order
that no one should obey my commands unless sent through him.
This was because I had summoned in a hurry two soldiers to
stay at my huts, whilst he, the officer, was away, assisting at the
resignation of the Receiver's department, which he expected to
result from my orders for the arrest of José Rodrigues Caleja.
What, then, could I do, in any case like what happened on the
3rd of June,* when there was no regular service in the bush;
and he, the officer, was always sick when wanted for duty, and
never in health, except for his pleasures?   From that day I

---

* The occasion of a fight between the soldiers and Muizas.

never passed an easy night: the excitement in the camp (musassa) compelled me to be ever ready and to sleep with loaded weapons by my side.

20*th.*—To weaken José Rodrigues Caleja's party, I allowed Lieutenant Manoel dos Santos and José Thomaz Gomes to go forward, and to await us in the lands of the Maraves. Each received for rations a quantity of blue cottons with 200 cloths, on condition of returning into store all that exceeded their wants.

21*st.*—The troops went to take leave of the Cazembe, who delivered to the lieutenant commanding a tabaret or low stool (hytanda) covered with leopard skin, as a gift to the Crown. All having been received with apparent kindness, they fired their salutes and retired.

CHAPTER VI

July 22nd.—The troops went off this day with my leave. They
were charged with the Crown slaves, chained in twos, threes, or
fours, to each soldier, and I had no responsible party to answer
for the slaves and their loads. The cloth and porcelain beads
(velorio) for the rations being in the hands of José Rodrigues
Caleja, who was preparing to set out without my permission, as
he frequently did, I could not refuse to dismiss men and officers
under pain of risking the robbery of the ivory and other royal
effects, which that person was to convey to Tete. After his
departure, I conceived great hopes of succeeding in the mission to Angola, which had been stopped by the message of the
Fumo Anceva on the 11th instant. I went for my pass to
the Cazembe, who had appointed me to come on that day; and,
being well received, I introduced the subject. He undertook
to forward the two soldiers, after pretending not to understand
me—a difficulty easily overcome as his brother (nephew?)
the Sana Muropúe, served me as linguist in the absence of
Fumo Anceva. The latter had not come, and the opposer of
all my projects—José Rodrigues Caleja—had departed. He
reminded me of my promise to send him from Mozambique
sundry " good (pretty) things," and I hastened to repeat it. On
his part he undertook to open a communication with me
through his lands to the Mozambique, appointing for this service his merchant, Chinbimba, whom he would take from
Gonçalo Caetano Pereira.

Seeing that he wished to retire, I thanked him in the name
of Her Most Faithful Majesty for the manner in which he had
entertained the Expedition. I added that, as his friend, I was
grateful to him for his good offices. He received my compliments with kindness; his courtiers joined in the applause
probably on account of the parting-gift, which was presented
to me, and the visit ended with mutual protestations of friendship. The King, after receiving my return present, gave to
his grandees a feast of Pombe, which had been interrupted for
some days, and ordered drums and marimbas to be played, as a
sign of joy, that he was delivered of Messrs. José Rodrigues
Caleja and Co. I at once gave leave to Gonçalo Caetano

Pereira and Vasco Joaquim Pires, who, with Manoel Caetano
Pereira, set out for Tete on the next day

23rd.—The three persons above mentioned left for Tete.

24th–26th.—I started with the Lieut.-Colonel Pedro Nolasco
en route for "Chungu," the old court, to exhume the bones of
the late Governor, which the Cazembe, contrary to Caffre
custom, allowed him to do.* Thence we were to march upon
Tete. The Caffres of the Expedition having refused to carry
me, I begged Lieut.-Colonel Pedro Nolasco to lend me nine
of the slaves of D. Francisca, settling that their loads should be
committed to my wild Caffres,† who walked in neck chains. As
the acme of toil and trouble my Caffres were obliged to convoy
the ration-cloth for the expedition. I kept it by me in order
that the troops might assist me on the road. We reached
Chungu at 2 P.M., disinterred the bones, and halted there with
the intention of marching the next day.‡

27th.—We marched from Chungu to a new village of the
Sana Muropúe, there to await the Fumo Anceva, our escort to
the frontier of the Cazembe's kingdom.

28th.—The Fumo Anceva joined me, but several Caffres of
the party being wanting, we could not advance.

29th.—We left the village of the Sana Muropúe, and presently
reached, at 3 P.M., the hillock station (o lugar dos outeirinhos), accompanied by the Fumo Anceva, who thought it the best place
for halting. This day we passed by the village of a Muranda
Caffre, when our soldiers began to rob poultry: the people,
though they took up arms and wished to revenge themselves,
suffered this outrage in cold blood, remembering that the
Cazembe had ever treated white men well.

July 30th *to August* 3rd.—The Caffres not arriving, we marched
from the hillocks to the village of the Muenempanda, there to
await them.

Aug. 4th–6th.—We arrived at the place of the Muenempanda,
where he was (mussassado), and butted (abarracado) in the bush,
hunting after the country-fashion; that is to say, digging narrow
pitfalls, and covering them with dry grass, for catching careless
game. They have running hunts as well, killing wild beasts of
pasture with arrows, javelins, and spears. We also made our
camp (mussassa) in the jungle, at some distance from that of the
Muenempanda.

---

* In Monteiro and Gamitto's days they still showed the cenotaph of the
"Gend," as the unfortunate traveller was called at Lunda.

† "Caffre burras," a misprint for "burros."

‡ I need hardly say that the Commandant, thus marching last, occupied the
place of danger, especially in a caravan leaving the country. Moreover, he reck-
lessly exposed himself to the intrigues of his enemies, the whites who had proceeded him; and thus he rendered himself responsible for all their actions.

7th.—The Muenempanda sent to congratulate us with his compliments upon our arriving at his estate; he had received an order from his king and lord, the Cazembe, to supply us with refreshments and provisions; he purposed punctually so to do, and if we passed by another road, he must forward them by carriers.

8th and 9th.—We received a present of fresh and dried meat, sweet potatoes, and pombe-beer, and we were invited to the camp (mussassa), for which we returned thanks.

10th.—As I had no extra cloth for "months," the Lieut.-Colonel Pedro Nolasco went alone to the Camado (house?), bearing my excuses.

11th and 12th.—There were still wanting sundry Caffres who intended to make Tete with us, some carrying ivories, others to receive the returns of their masters' presents. Yet, to avoid the three forest marches between us and the populated part, where we could buy provisions, we took leave of the Muenempanda by messengers, and we set out, leaving the Fumo Anceva to follow us.

13th–15th.—At 9 A.M. we met a Caffre of Gonçalo Cartano Pereira journeying solus. This man told us that José Rodrigues Caleja, having caused a disturbance in the village of "Muilachiutu," had been robbed with his companions, whom he had lost when flying from the Muizas. The villagers had wounded one of the party, and had attempted to slay him, the informant.

16th–18th.—After five days of good marching, we reached, at 9 A.M., the village of Muilachiutu; here we heard of the excesses of José Rodrigues Caleja, and the run which the Caffres had given him. We halted a day and a-half to buy food.

19th.—Arrived the Muizas, whom the Fumo Anceva had hurried on with a message that we must await him in the village of Chipoco. There he had ordered rations to be prepared, since in our present place we should not be able to collect a sufficient quantity, which indeed we had ascertained.

20th.—We reached at noon the village of Chirandu, seeking rations, which were now wanted.

21st–23rd.—After spending two days in collecting a sufficiency of provisions, which were very dear, we set out for Chiliamono.

24th.—We arrived at the village of Chiliamono, whom we met on the road as he was going to meet the Fumo Anceva. Here we bought some food, of which we had but little. Hunger now began to force its way into camp.

25th and 26th.—We marched to a large village, Chiliapoco, at which the Fumo Anceva told us to await him; and there we found the senior guide, Gonçalo Caetano Pereira, who had halted his party to join us. I sent to the Fumo Anceva a small present, which did not satisfy him, but my means now forbade my being a great man. Gonçalo Caetano Pereira also recounted to me how he had been obliged to run in consequence of José Rodrigues Caleja's affair.

27th and *28th*.—To lighten my load, I sent to Gonçalo Caetano Pereira two hundred cloths for the necessary expenses, and also for the support of the soldiers, who, deserted by their officers, were straggling in the bush. He returned me a receipt.

29th.—From Gonçalo Caetano Pereira and Vasco Joaquim Pires I heard that José Rodrigues Caleja was marching so fast, that he would not trouble himself with the sick slaves of the Crown, and that whenever one could not walk his head was cut off.[*]

The Muizas are always drunk, and none more so than the Fumo, who sent to ask me why, having stayed there long enough, I did not leave his village. I replied that we were in my friend the Cazembe's country, buying provisions, and that we should await the Fumo Anceva, who was directed by his king to escort us to the Zambeze (Chambeze) River. I sent this reply because these Muizas are insolent, treacherous, and timid, and when haughtily treated they become at once disheartened. In fact they are such that a few days ago they strangled their Fumo.

August 30th to *September* 1st.—Hearing that the Fumo Anceva had reached the village of Chirando, where the rebel Muizas would not receive him nor allow him to pass, I sent bearers to urge him on, saying, that on account of his long delay we wanted to take leave of him, to march on without his escort. I bade him not to fear the Muizas, as we could defend him when he joined our party, and afterwards that he could travel through the bush, avoiding villages.

September 2nd-5th.—After four days, our party returned with the reply of the Fumo Anceva, who held himself dismissed, as he could not move forwards, and who, having reported all to his muster, must there await the royal orders.[†] I did not want to advance without informing the Fumo Anceva, for fear of offending him and his king, as the success of the Angolan mission might depend upon this.[‡]

---

[*] This is a vile African practice, done simply on the dog-in-the-manger principle.

[†] It is hardly necessary to say that the Mfumo had never intended to go an inch further.

[‡] A very simple-minded ecclesiastic!

6th–7th.—Leaving Chipaco, we halted at the first village, Lieutenant-Colonel Pedro Nolasco's illness having increased.

8th–9th.—Gonçalo Caetano Pereira, not wishing to delay any longer, departed with his party, intending to await us at the Zambeze (Chambeze) River.

10th–16th.—Lieutenant-Colonel Pedro Nolasco being a little better, we marched upon Munglué, intending to remain there a few days, taking rest and collecting rations.

17th.—When about to leave our nighting place, the Muiza villagers opposed our going, wishing us to halt for a day, and to buy their provisions, which were at double the price for which they sold them to us on the up-march. As we did not assent, they threatened us with attack. I resolutely replied that we were ready for war or for peace, that if they wanted to fight, they must look sharp, as we could lose no time in their lands. Hearing this, they gave up their plans of intimidation, and we continued our march.

18th.—At 11 A.M. we reached the banks of the Luenna River, which was full and unfordable. When canoes were found, the Caffres asked large sums for ferrying us across, and though we tried to persuade them that we had no other cloths but what we offered, they declared that I and my companion were the only ones who possessed a large quantity, and that Gonçalo Caetano Pereira had been allowed passage with many ivories, because they held him to be a mere trader, and the agent of the late governor—and so induced José Rodrigues Caleja and the rest of the whites had assured them. Seeing that the Caffres had made up their minds, and fearing the machinations of that bad man, I had no remedy but to satisfy them; after which they did not neglect to beg from time to time.

19th.—At 10 A.M. we reached the Zambeze (Chambeze) River, which was not fordable, as before. We were, therefore, obliged to bargain for canoes, and the Caffres kept us till 3 P.M. We were obliged to give up to them all our remaining cloth, copper, and "calaim," our beads, copper bracelets (manilhas),[*] and ivory. Even then, they at times objected to work, demanding new pay for persons and loads. This insolence lasted for some time, so that part of the Expedition was on this side and part on that side of the river, which involuntary division greatly aided their extortioning.[†]   In the dead of the night, those on

---

[*] These are the "Manillas" of the West African Coast, especially of the Oil Rivers, where they took the form of small horseshoes. Such "bangles" appear to have been known to all primitive peoples.

[†] I well remember the same happening to me on the Malagarazi River, when returning from the Tanganyika Lake.

the right bank were attacked by kidnappers, but they fled when discovered by our people, who pursued them.

20th.—A little more velorio-beads brought over the rest of the loads, and we at once set out for the place where Gonçalo Caetano Pereira and his party were halted.

21st.—Wishing to ration in this place, we found the Muizas so insufferable with their " palavers " (milandos), and other impertinences, that some voted to leave them : but it was agreed to night here.

22nd.—We advanced, and I resolved to halt at the foot of a little village. Here died Vasco Joaquim Pires, who, as I recounted on February 4th, always missed his masa. Although sick, his death was not expected, and he was, therefore, not sacramented; without affecting the miraculous, I may term it a palpable judgment of God, for despising those mysterica. To avoid "palavers" with the natives, his body was secretly buried in the bush.

23rd and *24th.*—We arrived at the Munglué village, which we had been earnestly making since the 16th instant.

25th–28th.—We allowed two days to rest our footsore people, to ration, and to refresh ourselves with cows' milk, which was plentiful ; we drank it now soured (cortado), now fire-warmed, but ever without sugar, which had long run out. The provisions were dear; apparently the Muizas had passed on the word to starve us. They were envious of our ivory and slaves, and they looked upon us as their rivals in the trade. Here begins a regular system of blackmail * (chipatas), and Gonçalo Caetano Pereira, having finished his cloth, gave a small slave-girl.

29th.—From Munglué we repaired to the Masungure village, seeking rations.

Sept. 30th to Oct. 1st.—We reached a Muiza village, which we were obliged to pass. The savages began to snatch from our Caffres' hands what they could take quickly and could readily carry off: they also seized two hoes (enchadas) and a large knife, the work of the Cazembe's people (Murundas), and, being drunk, refused to return the plunder. As it was already late, we went to pass the night at a village hard by, where, provisions being scarce, we were obliged to treat for them with our insulters.

October 2nd.—But little food appeared, and that little extremely dear. As we sighed for the next day's march came Condun, the brother of Chinbimba, who, finding the day too far gone, promised to procure us restitution on the morrow.

3rd.—In want of provisions we advanced, whilst Gonçalo

---

* Monteiro and Gamitto (p. 38) say "Chipáta ou Salvo-conducto."

Caetano Pereira, who remained behind, recovered the two hoes, but not the knife. After a short distance we reached a village, where they robbed us of two other hoes and a tusk. They also wounded a Caffre with a poisoned arrow: the Muiza poison is so virulent that it spreads over the body, and after a few days causes death, if the arrow be not carefully removed, and if a counter-poison, which prudent Caffres always carry on such journeys, be not applied. At the sight of our slave's blood there was great confusion; some desired a prompt vengeance, others, terrified, wanted to escape dangers exaggerated by imagination. I hastened to see what was the matter, and at once the Muizas collecting, pointed their arrows at us for intimidation. When asked why we were insulted, they replied hardily that they had done so because they liked to do it, as we were passing through their lands, and that if we wanted war we had only to begin it—they were ready. Our men replied that they were travelling peaceably, but that if attacked they would defend themselves. The Muizas at once began to throw hard clods instead of stones, ours replied, and all the women fled the village.

The carriers, standing in a body fifty paces off, grounded their loads to see the end of the affair, which began to be vigorous. Whilst I was trying to stop this stone-play, waiting for Gonçalo Caetano Pereira, who had remained behind, a Muiza, with great assiduity and diligence, threw at me a succession of clods. Seeing no hope, I discharged a gun at him, but missed. Lieutenant-Colonel Pedro Nolasco, who was near, also fired with the same consequence. Hearing the sound of shots, and the confused noise of combat, Gonçalo Caetano Pereira, whom we were waiting for—he would assuredly have been lost if cut off from us—hastened up. Meeting in his path a crowd of the enemy, he pointed his gun, which somewhat frightened them. As, however, they continued their war dance, and he would not fire, one of his Caffres discharged a blunderbuss which was ready, and mortally wounded in the side a Muiza, whom he afterwards found to be the son of the village Fumo.[*]

The terrified savages opened the road to Gonçalo Caetano Pereira, who at once joined us. We held a council, knowing that we could no longer travel in quiet through the tribe, who are a united people.

At the time appeared two of the enemy, making signs that they came to speak with us, and praying not to be maltreated. On our promise they approached, and begged a medicine to

---

[*] How remarkably this adventure resembles the accident which stopped Paul du Chaillu in 1864.

extract the slugs (zagalotes) with which the Fumo's son had been wounded. We asked why they had molested peaceful travellers; they put the blame upon their drink.* This excuse did not satisfy us. We said that if their Fumo's son was wounded, the same had happened to two of our slaves, who were brought forward, and we refused the medicine required to withdraw what had entered into the body, as they expressed themselves.

They retired discontented, and their companions, seeing this, threatened us from afar. Our slaves, and the six soldiers of the party, chased them to their houses, where a third Checunda was wounded. This brought on another skirmish, and our men sacked the now well-nigh deserted village. I and Lieutenant-Colonel Pedro Nolasco, wished to go in person, collect provisions, and burn down the place, hoping thus to terrify the Muizas, and to recover the respect for the name of white man (Muzungu) which José Rodrigues Caleja had lost. Gonçalo Caetano Pereira, however, would by no means consent to such a proceeding.

We marched to a neighbouring place where there was water, intending to rest the people, and to continue our journey in the afternoon. Gonçalo Caetano Pereira found a Muiza of the village of Mucunjure, the lord of these lands, and sent him to inform his master of what had happened, forwarding a small tusk, by way of " mouth." Having dined, we advanced in our usual order, but with the precaution of being preceded by a few musketeers. After a short march we heard a disturbance ahead. All stopped, and I, going forward, found that Manoel Caetano Pereira, who was with the soldiers in the van, had been treacherously wounded by an ambushed Muiza.† The soldiers hastened forwards; unhappily their muskets missed fire, and thus the savages retired safely. The wound proved not dangerous, and was easily cured; the arrow-head had struck against a bone, and thus the poison was not diffused.

The Caffre of Gonçalo Caetano Pereira, who, in firing the blunderbuss, had rendered his right hand useless, being braver and more judicious than the rest, proposed returning to raze the offending villages to the ground. I also approved of this, but Gonçalo Caetano Pereira, who, reasonably enough, counted upon having to see the (Fumo's) wounded son, and thus to

---

* This may be true: Africans, like the American indigenes, are almost always dangerous during a carouse. But the "Commandant" did wrong, I mean unwisely, in refusing the medicine.

† Had the medicine been given, perhaps this would not have happened. Of course the friends of the wounded savage rushed on ahead, and, knowing the country better than the caravan, succeeded in revenging themselves.

pacify Mucunjure, would not agree to this. He was the better
obeyed on account of his having many slaves; we, therefore,
necessarily following his advice, continued the march, and
arrived without accident at the halting-place (Daro). Here we
at once received a reply from Mucunjure, who sent to Gonçalo
Caetano Pereira that the latter, although the people of the
village maltreated us without right, had done badly in wounding
the Fumo's son.* Gonçalo Caetano Pereira replied that the
Muizas having attacked us without a cause, we at last fired
upon them. With this new message we despatched an ivory,
by way of blackmail. Mucunjure thought it too little; nevertheless, he sent to say that on the morrow he would hear the
whites, and if they were in the right he would punish the
Muizas. Another tusk was sent to him, but as it did not
come up to his wishes, he received a copper bar, which proved
satisfactory. He sent to say that on the next day he would
supply us with a guide to a certain place, where we would be
able to buy provisions at will. Meanwhile midnight had
passed.

Another Caffre of Gonçalo Caetano Pereira, who had been
sent to the Fumo, shrewdly suspecting from certain expressions,
and from the preparations which he saw, that the people
intended to attack us, reported it to his master. The latter,
being under the idea that all the Caffres respected him as the
Head White Man, and convinced by the Fumo's words, not only
disbelieved his Caffres, but also the more to ridicule and vilify
his informant, did not communicate to me the man's suspicions,
which I should have examined with all circumspection.†

4th.—Preparing early for the march, we awaited the promised guide till 7 A.M. As he did not appear, and the sun
waxed warm, we set out for the place where we expected to buy
food, not having any for that day. Suspecting no evil from the
Fumo, we looked forward to meeting his guide upon the road,
in which, indeed, he failed us, the better to carry out the
treachery meditated by him. Presently appeared four Caffres,
saying that they were sent by the Fumo to conduct us; whilst
giving this pretended message, crowds of Muizas issued from
their ambush, attacked us when they saw no guns, and seizing
a chain-gang (gargalheira) of negroes, pursued them into the
bush, without allowing them to drop their loads.

---

* Africans, like the Bedawin of Arabia, make a great difference between com-
paratively harmless and mortal weapons. The Muizas were throwing only clods
or stones, but the slave fired a gun, and this in the savage mind justifies a serious
affray.

† So it is that the oldest African travellers are sometimes taken unawares by the
inconsequence of the child-like natives.

Our slaves, terrified by the war-drum, fell into confusion, but soon recovered themselves enough to rob all our stuffs, which they carried in their "quituudos." * These are baskets in bandbox shape, made of scraped and thinned wood. I thus lost all my clean clothing (aceio), and what remained of my provisions: the only thing that could be saved was a box containing some shirts, which the plunderers had either forgotten, or had not yet touched, seeing me walk towards it. Withal, caring little for the loss thus inflicted upon me, I hurried up in the hope of saving my papers. Finding them scattered over the ground, my grief and disgust were such, that, forgetting danger and death, I busied myself in recovering them. Amongst these last were the order for José Rodrigues Caleja's arrest, with the countersignature of Manoel dos Santos at the foot.

When I had collected what I could, my Caffres, who hitherto had not been seen, come up and reported that the Muizas had carried off three of the gang, cutting their neck ropes, which were of leather. I requested them carefully to look after my papers, and the bandboxes containing them.

At this moment appeared Gonçalo Caetano Pereira, who told me that he was going off into the bushes to find a path to the Aruangôa River, as he now considered the road throughout the Muiza country closed; and that to march the men freely he would leave behind 600 arrobas ($\times$ 32 $=$ 19,200 lbs.) of ivory, carrying away only the little wanted for the journey.†

To raise his courage, I asked him if he intended to abandon his capital without a blow. He said, " Yes," that he was now doing so ; that on all sides nothing could be seen but Muizas collecting to surround us ; that if this were once effected we could not escape, but must necessarily perish ; finally, that I also should make ready at once to retire if I would avoid destruction. I communicated Gonçalo Caetano Pereira's determination to Lieutenant-Colonel Pedro Nolasco Vieira de Araujo, and told him to prepare to abandon the property and retreat. Pedro Nolasco, wishing to save his charge, could not make up his mind. Hurrying about the field, I missed Gonçalo Caetano Pereira and his son, who had departed: this I told to Pedro Nolasco, bidding him to push his work quickly, as we were alone in that place.

He did what he could, and he retired, leaving much ivory

---

* These boxes are used throughout Unyamwezi and Africa west of Zanzibar, where they are generally made of tree-bark. The Kisawahili name is Killndo, in the plural Villndo.

† G. C. Pereira was the only man that " knew the bush," and this action of his may be looked upon as a signal for a general *sauve qui peut*. Of course nothing could be more prudent, that is to say, more cowardly.

to the Muizas, and the trunks and boxes to the sacking of
our slaves, who did not dislike an operation that ended in
relieving them of their loads. After marching some fifty paces,
I remembered the Archives of the Secretariat, committed by
Pedro Nolasco to the slaves of D. Francisca: not hearing what
had become of them, I retraced my steps to the place where all
remained, armed only with my gun and pistol. I at once
found the document-trunk, half broken open by the Caffres, who,
finding nothing but papers and books, had abandoned it, taking
only a little volume bound with red silk. I ordered the soldier,
Antonio Francisco Delgado, who was still in the neighbourhood, to finish opening it, and I committed to his care a large
book, to be brought to me with all the other papers.

I then joined Lieutenant-Colonel Pedro Nolasco, who awaited
me where I left him. We followed the path taken by Gonçalo
Caetano Pereira and his son. After ten paces or so we heard it
said that the Muizas were on our traces, which obliged us to
hurry. Coming to a rivulet, with water to the waist, I had the
sorrow to see myself abandoned, not a Caffre of all who crossed
being willing to carry me over. At last, after many entreaties,
two men raised me, but fell with me in the water, wetting my
gun, which never left my hand.*

Whilst we were in the middle of the stream the Muizas shot
their arrows at us, and would have wounded or killed me had
not Canhac, a Caffre of Pedro Nolasco, who, being sick, could
not keep up with his master, put them to flight by a well-
directed shot, wounding one of them. In the first affray and in
this second none of our party was hurt, whereas of the Muizas
some sixteen suffered from our guns and bows.

Although the enemy had retired, we made a forced march.
As we were passing a little village, the inhabitants, who knew
our misfortunes, set fire to the grass, thinking to stop us, but,
at all risks, we forced our way through it. Till 4 P.M. this kind
of warfare continued: it was renewed successively by all the
villages near which we travelled, although we had left the road
and had buried ourselves in the bush and the grasses.

Seeing, a little ahead, a village which appeared deserted, and
being in urgent want of food, we halted opposite it, and sent a
soldier, with some Caffres, to find if it contained provisions,
and, if so, to let us know, that we might advance in a body, help
ourselves, and then burn the place.† The soldier, however,

* Dr. Krapf used his gun-barrels and the leather case of his telescope for carrying water to drink. ('Travels,' p. 324).

† Of course this buccaneer proceeding was only making matters worse. It re-
minds me of the good missionary who asked the "combustion" of Tajurrah on the
Red Sea, because the chief had taken toll out of his dollars.

finding pombe beer, proceeded to get drunk, whilst the Caffres packed up a store of provisions in their "enhabudoa." * When their "sitting upon pombe" (funcção de pombo) was finished, they burned the remainder of the provision, which was ample, and the village, too—such was their terror—merely to avoid the delay which would be required to collect rations, and in order at once to continue their march. The Caffre owner of the place, seeing this destruction from afar, threatened us with a night attack.† We marched till sunset, the Caffres thinking only of escaping as quickly as possible from the lands of the Muizas, where they considered themselves unsafe.

Gonçalo Caetano Pereira, comfortable in his hammock, did nothing but advance, halting only to rest his bearers. The moment he saw us he ordered them on, without regard to myself and to Pedro Nolasco, who were on foot, our Caffres having purposely left our hammock-poles on the field of insult. When we could no longer endure such a march, we cleared with fire a sleeping place, and issued the necessary orders for the Caffres to keep watch. This day was dinnerless, because the cook, in order to lighten himself, had thrown away all that he had prepared. At length, unable to bear my hunger, I ordered for supper a few beans, intended for seed, which had escaped plunder in a little bundle of napkin stuff.

All fell into a deep sleep, and thus the Muiza of the burnt village had an opportunity of shooting during the night as many arrows as he pleased; six persons were wounded.‡ All then awoke, full of fear and confusion; the Muizas retired before our gunshots, which did not take effect, owing to the darkness. They contented themselves with saying that they would close all the roads and kill every man.

5th.—We made a forced march. The Caffres, terrified by the events of the last night, and wishing to push us on, pretended at each step that the Muizas were coming; thus we had neither halt nor dinner.§ This disorder was caused chiefly by Gonçalo Caetano Pereira being entirely ruled by his men. As the Caffres would not carry me, I had to walk the greater part of the way; when Lieutenant-Colonel Pedro Nolasco, to whom

---

* Leather bags made of the skins of small animals, as goats and game.

† This kind of threat is almost always carried out: at any rate, one should ever be in readiness for a night attack under such circumstances.

‡ In this case the travellers had no one to blame but themselves. They might have bought the provisions, or they should at least have left the value upon the ground. And burning the village was an act of wanton mischief.

§ The forced retreat may be compared with that of Paul du Chaillu at the end of his second expedition. Happily for him he was young, whilst the poor priest was not. Such marches in a tropical climate soon kill all but thoroughly sound and seasoned men.

the hammock-men belonged, ordered them to take me up, they dropped me after a few paces, and went on, saying that they were tired, and leaving behind my conveyance, which more than once I vainly ordered them to bring up. Such are the tame slaves (Checundas), who at times threatened to abandon us, and to take to the bush.

6th.—Food being much wanted, we resolved to send some Caffres to spy out a village where we could buy it; this was for the general good, but they were too frightened to go. Seeing ourselves compelled to do as they pleased, we went on, not knowing how to support ourselves and the wild slaves (escravos burros). After a short descent, a new alarm threw all into confusion. When we asked the cause, they replied that we were surrounded by enemies; on examination, it proved that some twenty Caffres of a village which we had not seen, fearing lest we might plunder their provisions and burn their tents, were frightening us with cries and war drums. We were compelled to hurry away, and they made signs of following us, when a gun-shot, which wounded one of their number, compelled them to let us pass. Our Caffres could not believe that the Muizas feared them, and all that the enemy wished was to get rid of us as soon as possible.

Gonçalo Caetano Pereira was attacked by a severe fever, which caused us no little alarm; had he died, his Caffres would hold it a bad omen, and would have deserted with the rest of the Checundas, who doubtless would not have been slow to follow. To-day I could not dine, there being no time, and I could not sup, having only a single bit of roasted manioc, given to me by Lieutenant-Colonel Pedro Nolasco. As the Caffres would not carry me, I judged better to reserve the food for breakfast, so as to gain strength before the next march. My sufferings at night were great, but it proved a wise precaution, the journey being long and hurried. The flight of a slave with a large basket left me without any clothes, except those which I was wearing, together with a shirt, a short quilt (godrim),* and pillow-case.

7th.—We marched without accident, but in hot haste, seeking some village where provisions could be procured. The bush was so sterile that it did not yield a wild fruit. There were signs of game, but the Caffres of Tete, who are most vile and worthless in the bush, preferred hunger to the light work of hunting. This day, Lieutenant-Colonel Pedro Nolasco supported me by sharing his breakfast and dinner. To lighten a

---

* Godri is a Hindi word, meaning a coverlet quilted with cotton. The other words in the text are "lençol" and "fronhas."

Caffre, who was blaspheming under a camp-bed (barra),[*] I allowed him to break it up, reserving for bed-clothes a sail-cloth; and I already thought of cutting the quilt to pieces. The hammock-bearers let me fall, to see if, by so doing, they could induce me wholly to dispense with their services.

8th.—We struck out with more spirit, having now issued from the unknown bush, and having hit upon the road that led us to the Cazembe's country. Many slaves ran off to find food, thinking that without it we should die, and others were left behind unable to move. At noon we reached the camp (mussassa) of an elephant-hunter; he had nothing to sell, not even meat, our Caffres, who had preceded us having secretly bought up the little there was with the cloth of which they had robbed us on the 4th instant. All this day I had to walk with unutterable toil, and Pedro Nolasco again fed me, as I had absolutely nothing.

9th.—Before setting out, I sent off, in different directions, three Caffres, with pieces of the quilt-chintz, to buy food; I took this precaution to avoid a repetition of yesterday's affair: with much difficulty we made a start; weakness rendered the march heavy, especially in my case, having with great labour to make it on foot. Arrived at the banks of the Aruangôa River, we found vestiges of Mutumbuca † villages, and we sent our Caffres to buy provisions, which they always kept for themselves, declaring that none could be found.

To escape this cheat, I crossed the river and exchanged a little negress for a basket of unshelled ground-nuts (a kind of almond also found in the Brazil), another and a smaller basket of millet-heads (corn-cobs), and a "quissero" (a little vessel woven with thinned and scraped tree-bark) ‡ of ground millet (*Holcus sorghum*). With this purchase, I returned contented to my companions, and distributed to them a small part. As it was late, my dinner was raw ground-nuts (mandome crû), which I was able to beg: Gonçalo Caetano Pereira seeing me present, offered me, for ceremony, some of his, but it was not accepted, lest he might feel the want of it.

10th.—We advanced with more spirit towards the river ford, in order to escape from the country of the Muizas, whose memory to us was not grateful. Hardly had we reached it, when we were told that Muzaranba, a certain Mutumbuca

---

* What, in the name of goodness, were they doing with a bed? No wonder that the slaves and Caffres refused to carry them.
† See Diary of August 20, 1798.
‡ It resembles the quitundo or kilindi, which I have before described.

kinglet, was waiting to plunder us, whilst further on was the
Mucanda. The news made us take the precaution of marching
down the stream, till we arrived opposite the country of the
Sengas,* where we could ford the Aruangôa and march straight
upon Tete. This determination was not taken till the Caffres,
who were summoned to our council, had agreed to it. Some
opined that we ought to leave our actual camping-place at the
shortest notice; but, as it was late, the journey was reserved
for the morrow.

11th.—Right early we set out, flying from the new danger
which seemed imminent and nearest; this made us hurry the
pace still more. In the great confusion of the line of march,
sundry slaves fled, and some carried off their loads of ivory.
I was borne in my hammock by the extraordinary efforts of
Pedro Nolasco, who took pity on the wounded soles of my
feet.

12th–13th.—Already hunger was upon us, and at each
step the Caffres threatened desertion, when Providence threw
in our way, at the foot of the road, a freshly-killed she-buffalo.
By no means would I insinuate that this circumstance was
miraculous or mysterious, knowing that Providence is ever
directing its creatures to the ends which it purposes, by ways
which we may not comprehend. I have referred to it only to
show the delight with which we hailed the good event of the
present march. We ordered the Caffres to cut it up, but they
refused, fearing a "Muando," or palaver with the hunter; and,
to prevent our remaining near the buffalo-cow, they pressed us
to advance. We persisted in wishing to purchase the game,
and at that moment appeared the hunter, who sold it to us in
exchange for a negress. It was then divided, and the feast
somewhat appeased our people's hunger.

14th.—Having meat but no vegetables, we made for some
settlement where we could buy them. After half an hour's march
we found one: when, however, we wanted to purchase, a Caffre
came out and told us that his village had nothing for sale, but
that on the other side of the river provisions were abundant;
he ended by offering himself as guide. We accepted, and
presently we sent him, with our Checundas, to the place referred

---

* According to Monteiro and Gamitto (p. 47) the Sengas live to the east of the
Chévas (Shevas), and near the mouth of the Aruangôa River. Dr. Livingstone
('Second Expedition,' chap. ix. p. 198) says: "The country north of the mountains
here in sight from the Zambesi is called Senga, and its inhabitants Asenga or
Basenga, but all appear to be of the same family as the rest of the Manganja and
Maravi." In M. Erhardt's map there are two chief ferries over the fanciful lake,
and the northern, or the western, shore is called Zénga, answering to the Tsenga
of Dr. Livingstone's map. The inhabited island in the Bemba or Bangweolo Lake
explains, I have said, part of the "Mombas Mission Map."

to, that they might return and let us know the prices. Meanwhile the whole party proceeded to procure shelter in the bush, which the dry grass and the small tree-motts or clumps afforded on the river-banks, very distant from that village. At 5 P.M. our Caffres returned, saying that they had found plenty of provisions, for which the owners wanted ivory and slaves. This good news gave us courage, and we reserved our purchases for the next day.

15th.—Gonçalo Caetano Pereira and Pedro Nolasco sent two ivories; I, having none, despatched a pair of slaves, with whom the purchase was speedily effected, whereas the tusks were rejected as cracked (por ter raxa). We were kept waiting for some time as the grain was not husked, and the Checundas left things in this state, caring for little beyond their own investments. Seeing my small store of food gradually disappear, and fearing lest that just bought should not come till after a long delay, I sent a third slave and all my rags to be bartered for a supply from another place. Here I tore in strips the only sheet left to me.

16th.—The purchased provisions came; they did not suffice, the cause being the thieving of the buyers; so I sent to lay in more: at this same time dried flesh of elephants, buffaloes, and other wild beasts was bought and exchanged for slaves.

17th and 18th.—The Caffre purchasers having returned, bringing the provisions, we continued our journey without accident.

19th.—When about to leave our nighting-place, two Caffre hunters came up, shouting and saying that our people had robbed their medicines (mezinhas) and tobacco; and that if the stolen goods were not returned, they would maltreat and wound the whole party. With such threats those two Caffres halted a body of some three hundred people. We satisfied the complainants, there being no other remedy, and we continued our march, seeking a fit place for buying a new store of food.

20th.—At 10·30 P.M. three lions passed near our encampment, and threw everything into the greatest confusion with their terrible roarings. Though perceiving us, they granted us the immunity of guests, and glutting their ferocity by falling upon a camp of hunters, they carried off a Caffre.*

21st–23rd. — Having bought provisions, we continued our journey, and at noon we crossed the river, the Caffres being unwilling to march opposite the land of the Sengas, which they now found to be far off.

---

* The next "Cazembe Expedition" also suffered from lions.

24th.—At 9 A.M. we met a small herd of elephants that opened out, and allowed us free passage.

25th–27th.—Again we found ourselves under the necessity of laying in provisions, and here we resolved to buy up all, Gonçalo Caetano Pereira having met with a village Fumo, who was acquainted with him.

28th–30th.—The Caffres, knowing all about our journey, studied only the various ways of robbing us : for this purpose, every ridiculous little Fumo demanded his blackmail, or "dash" (chipata), which is paid only to the great chiefs or to the king. Our men, however, were so down-hearted, that any threat compelled us to disburse.

Oct. 31st and *November 1st.*—As we passed a village, a Caffro, protesting that we had frightened his herd, and that a bullock had broken its leg, made a prize of an ivory, and hid it. Gonçalo Caetano Pereira, to whom the tusk belonged, complained to the Fumo, who promised restitution.

Nov. 2nd and *3rd.*—The tusk not appearing, and another having been stolen during the night, we agreed that the Fumo's promise was a deceit, and that he probably had a hand in the plunder. We resolved no longer to wait for his justice, though he pressed us so to do, and, not wishing to lose another tusk in the same way, we set out.

4th–7th.—At 11 A.M. we reached the "Bar," or gold diggings of José Victor de Sousa e Vasconcellos, one of the inhabitants of Tete : we met the owner, who gave us hospitality, and informed us of the safe arrival of that part of the Expedition in which was José Rodrigues Caleja with his followers.

8th.—We left the "Bar," and marched towards Marenga.

9th–13th.—We arrived at Marenga, where Gonçalo Caetano Pereira has his abode and gold diggings, and here we halted to rest the people and to lay in stores.

14th–18th.—At 8 A.M. we left Marenga for Tete, and found no provisions in the way, where before they had been abundant and cheap.

19th–22nd.—I took leave of Lieut.-Colonel Pedro Nolasco Vieira de Araujo, who at once started for Tete, and I set out with Gonçalo Caetano Pereira for Bamba, where we dined. I waited till night-fall before entering the Villa de Tete, having a repugnance to appear by daylight without decent ecclesiastical attire. Finally, at 6 P.M., I entered and met various friends, who congratulated themselves on my return. They had hardly expected it, since José Rodrigues Caleja, besides taking away my credit, by depicting me as an object of public indignation, had assured them that I should never be

M 2

seen again. He certainly was persuaded that his outrages on
the road would suffice to cause my destruction.

(Signed)   FRANCISCO JOÃO PINTO.

LETTER OF THE CHIEF-SERGEANT PEDRO XAVIER VELASCO TO THE HOME GOVERNMENT.

"QUILLIMANE, *November* 14, 1805.

"MOST ILLUSTRIOUS AND EXCELLENT SIR,

" I already have had the honour through two channels and on several occasions of a personal interview with your Excellency. On these occasions I took the opportunity to place before you the part taken by me, under His Excellency the late Governor Dr. Francisco José Maria de Lacerda o Almeida, in the discovery of the African interior, and in undertaking to forward the communication of Angola with the kingdom of Portugal. This was an enterprise on which he was sent by our Sovereign, and in which he was efficiently seconded by your Excellency. I also reported the constant and singular zeal, activity, and honour in the Royal service displayed by me during the discovery referred to. Thus only, confiding solely in your Excellency's kindness, can I hope for a word of favour to His Highness the Prince Regent, who, seeing and appreciating my zeal, and knowing how to reward and encourage his faithful vassals, may be pleased to place me under an obligation by showing some proof that my humble services are recognised.

" Now, however, Excellency, four years have passed without any notice being taken of those papers, nor do I even know if they have had the fortune to meet your kindly regard, a circumstance which has discouraged and depressed me to the utmost. Still, supposing that perhaps my ill fortune may have caused them to be lost on the way by shipwreck, or by their carelessness to whom they were committed for the purpose of being laid before your Excellency, I have again resolved, after taking copies of the papers drawn out in an official form, to submit them to you, hoping that you will be pleased to remember me. On the other side, I see myself compelled to announce to your Excellency that having, in the course of our journey, arrived at the kingdom of the King Cazembe (as is proved by the said documents), it was announced to me in the month of October of the current year, by the natives, that the King Cazembe had departed this life, and that his son, after succeeding to the kingdom, had sent to inform me how much he wished and anxiously desired communication with us. In proof of this his sentiment, he favoured me with a present, accompanied by reliable assurances on the part of his messengers that he has also sent to the town of Tete an offering to His Highness and to sundry individuals there. Therefore, prompted by activity in the Royal service, I must say to your Excellency that His Highness's treasury suffers much by the want of such intercourse, since those roads which were discovered on the former occasion are now closed. Thus nothing more remains for me to inform your Excellency, except that your extreme goodness and incomparable rectitude may deign to cast upon me a compassionate regard, and support me with the powerful hand of your protection, in favouring what your Excellency better understands concerning my prayer—a favour for which I shall never find expressions capable of conveying a just proof of my grateful heart.

    " I am, with that respect which I submissively offer to the most excel-
        lent person of your Excellency, whom God guard for many years,
            " Of your Excellency the most obedient Servant,
                " PEDRO XAVIER VELASCO."

JOURNEY OF THE "POMBEIROS,"

FROM

ANGOLA TO THE RIOS DE SENNA
(RIVERS OF SENNA).

[*Translated from the Portuguese, by B. A. Beadle, Esq., Chancellier to the Portuguese Consulate, London.*]

This Journal is very disconnected, and is manifestly written by an illiterate man. Some of his phrases are most difficult to understand: however, I have given great attention to them, and have succeeded in all cases, I believe, in giving his meaning; the original being disjointed, the translation is necessarily the same, to some extent.—TRANSLATOR'S NOTE.

CONTENTS.

---

* (Note in Portuguese.) All these documents are published without the least alteration, either in their orthography or anything else.

(A.)

MOST ILLUSTRIOUS AND EXCELLENT SIR,

I have the honour to bring before your worthy notice the letters which were forwarded to me from Tette by the Governor of the Rios de Senna (Rivers of Senna), which came by land, in consequence of the discovery of communication between the two coasts of Eastern and Western Africa, so much desired. And on this occasion are embarked in the frigate 'Principe Dom Pedro' the *pombeiros* (bondsmen) Pedro João Baptista and Amaro José, of Lieutenant-Colonel Francisco Honorato da Costa, Director of the Fair of Mucary, to whose enterprise and labours is owing the happy result of this work. They take with them the note-books of the journey, to be presented in the Office of the Secretary of State for this Department. God keep your Excellency. St. Paul de Assumpção de Loanda, 25th January, 1815. To the Most Illustrious and Excellent Marquis d'Aguiar. (Signed) JOSÉ D'OLIVEIRA BARBOSA.

MOST ILLUSTRIOUS AND EXCELLENT COUNT DAS GALVEAS,

His Royal Highness our Lord the Prince Regent having, in the year 1799, determined to see the opening up of the route from his capital of Angola to these rivers of Senna completed, in order that his people, both in Western and Eastern Africa, may turn their commerce to more lucrative account than they have yet been able to do; and also that news may circulate from one coast to the other with greater speed than it could do by means of vessels, and having entrusted the opening up of the Eastern side to the late Governor of these rivers, Francisco José de Lacerda, and on the Western side to His Excellency D. Fernando de Noronha, Captain-General of Angola, the latter committing it to Lieutenant-Colonel Francisco Honorato da Costa, Commander of the Fair of Casange, it so happened that the former (Lacerda) died in the Cazembo's country, whilst the latter (Da Costa), by means of his slaves, succeeded in opening up the western road as far as the same point. These slaves, however, have been for five years at that place, without the means of reaching this town to give the above information. Observing this place to be somewhat destitute of trade, through the bad understanding that has existed with several of the petty kings surrounding it, and desiring by some means to extend its trade, I invited to my residential quarters, in May 1810, Gonçalo

Caetano Pereira, an aged man, and one experienced in these inner parts. Conversing with him about the extension I wished this captaincy to acquire in its commerce, I asked him to point out to me some place to which our traffic could be sent. He replied that formerly the subjects of the King Cazembe frequented this town, but that from the time when we attempted the opening up of communications with those interior places, they had ceased to come, and he said he did not know the reason of it. Some declared it was in consequence of the disorders our people created in the (lands of the) said Cazembe after the death of Governor Lacerda, and others that it was because that nation had carried on war with the Muize people ever since those days. I then requested Pereira to give me three of his slaves to send as an embassage to the said King Cazembe, in order to see if it would induce that nation to come and trade again with this town, as it had formerly done. He gave me them, and I sent them as envoys to the said King Cazembe; and he, seeing the said slaves on their arrival, decided to send me an embassage composed of a chief and fifty of his vassals, by which he sent me word that there had been in his kingdom for the last four years those two persons who had come from Angola, whom he ordered to be given up. They reached this town on the 2nd February of the present year, bringing me a letter from their master, of which letter I have the honour to enclose you a copy. On my asking the above men if they wished to return voluntarily by the way they had come, they replied yes; but that it was necessary the means required for their transport should be provided by me. I ordered for them 700 cloths with 250 reis fortes each. I reported everything to my Captain-General, and asked him whether the Royal Council of that capital would place that amount to my account, offering in case of their refusal to defray the expense myself. To this despatch sufficient time has not yet elapsed for me to receive a reply.

I might make some reflections to your Excellency on this discovery, as I do not find a large amount of intelligence in these explorers; but, at the same time, I admit that, according to their capabilities, they did a great deal. As they return by the same route, I have instructed them as to the way in which they should proceed on their journey, the inquiries they should make as to the mood in which they find some of the petty kings, as to whether they will really allow us to travel freely through those parts, and what are the presents we should offer them, on all of which points they have been tutored by me. They promise to carry out the above objects exactly, with all necessary clearness, and to deliver to His Excellency the Captain-General of Angola whatever they may come into possession of bearing on

the opening up of the country, all of which I acquaint your
Excellency with, that you may be good enough to lay it before
His Royal Highness our Lord the Prince Regent.

I have also the honour of remitting to Your Excellency the
Diary which the explorers have offered me, numbered 1; as
also a list of questions which I put to them, numbered 2; and a
letter which the Lieutenant-Colonel, the master of the above
explorers, wrote me, numbered 3. God keep your Excellency's
Illustrious and Excellent Person. Residential Quarters of the
town of Tette, 20th May, 1811. To the Illustrious and Excellent Count das Galveas, of the Council of H.R.H., Minister and
Secretary for Marine and Colonies. (Signed) CONSTANTINO
PEREIRA DE AZEVEDO, *Governor of the Rivers of Senna.*

No. 1.   (COPY.)

1806.

In the name of God, Amen.

The route which I, Pedro Joām Baptista, followed in my journey
from the Muropue to the King Cazembe Caquinhata, by order
of the Most Illustrious and Excellent Captain-General of the
Kingdom of Angola, for the opening up of the way to the East
Coast of Africa by the Rivers of Senna, a work entrusted to
Lieutenant-Colonel Francisco Honorato da Costa, Director of
the Fair of Casange, with goods worth two contos of reis, to
expend in gifts to chiefs on the way, in order to facilitate the
obtaining permission for the opening up of the road to Tette.

[1st.] *Sunday, 22nd of May of said year.*—We started at 6 A.M.
from the Muropue's great farm, having stayed in the house of
his son, named after country fashion Capendo hianva, or according to his post, Soano Mutopo do Muropue. We passed a river
called Ingeba, of four fathoms width, and a second river, Luiza,
which both run into the river Lunhua. During the journey
we came to the guide's place, whom the Muropue had given to
us to conduct us to the Cazembe, the name of this place being
Cutaqua. We paid the guide ten chuabos and gave him a glass
of "bixega." We arrived at the above place at nightfall. We
met many people going to the said farm of the Muropue,
carrying mandioca flour for their masters. We marched with
the sun in our rear.

[2nd.] *Wednesday, 8th of June.*—We got up at seven, and
started from the guide's place. We passed three narrow
running streams, whose names we do not know, which run into

the river Zniza (Luiza ?), and we came to the farm of the black named Caquiza Muegi, a slave of the Muropue, near a small stream, the water of which they drink. He sent us to lodge in his houses, and we gave him two "chuabos."* We arrived there at noon, and met no one, neither did we do anything. We marched with the sun as before.

[3rd.]   *Thursday, 9th of same Month.*—We got up at 2 A.M., and started from Caquiza Muegi's farm. We passed five small streams, and on the march we stopped at the farm of the Quilolo of the Muropue, named Muene Cahuenda, to whom we gave as presents six chuabos and two white twisted glasses with bell-shaped mouths. We arrived at our halting-place at four in the afternoon, and built our huts near the narrow stream, of which they drink the water, called "Izabuigi." We marched latterly with the sun on our left. We met with no one.

[4th.]   *Friday, 10th.*—We got up at dawn, and started from Muene Cahuenda's farm. We passed four streams—names not known—and continuing on our journey passed a river three fathoms wide, called Mue-me, and came to our desert halting-place, beyond and near the stream called Canahia, which empties into the said river Mue-me; on the other side of the river Canahia we found houses already made by the travellers of the country called Canoguesa, who were come to bring their tribute to their Muropue. We arrived at three in the after-noon. We travelled with the sun as before, and met ten blacks who had gone to buy salt at the Salina.

[5th.]   *Saturday, 11th.*—We got up at five A.M. and left our desert-lodging. We passed three narrow turbulent rivers on the way, and came to another desert halting-place, near the narrow stream called "Quipungo." The farm of some of Muropue's black people was near, but we did not speak to any of them. We arrived at the said halting-place at noon, having marched with the sun on our left. We made a halt there to get necessary provisions.

[6th.]   *Sunday, 12th.*—We left our desert-lodging, having got up at cockcrow. We passed three narrow rivers, which run into the river called Calalimo—the names of them we do not know—and came to another desert lodging made of thick bushes staked to keep off wild beasts, near the said river Calalimo,

---

* In page 237, the Chuaba, or Xoabo, is explained to mean an East-Indian cloth; in other places it appears to be a measure.—R. F. B.

which is ten fathoms wide, more or less; we arrived at the
said stopping-place at noon, and had a little rain. We met
no one.

[7th.] *Monday, 13th.*—At 2 A.M. we left the desert, and
passed over eleven small streams. We marched up the valley
of the before-mentioned river Calalimo, and during this journey
we came to a halting-place near a river called Camu-sangagila,
on the other side of which we reached our halting-place at nightfall, and passed the night out, although the rain was falling.
We marched with the sun on our left.

[8th.] *Tuesday, 14th.*—We started from our desert halting-
place, near the river Camu-sangagila, which we left at 8 A.M.
We passed five running streamlets, and during the march we
came to the farm of a black named Muene Cassa, near a rivulet,
name not known, on the further bank of which we talked with
the said black about this our journey, that we were going to
Cazembe, being sent by Muropue. The farm was at some distance from our halting-place. We gave a small mirror as a
present, and a chuabo of red "serafina" (a kind of tissue).
We arrived at three in the afternoon, and marched with the
sun as before.

[9th.] *Wednesday, 15th.*—We started from the farm of
Muene Cassa at 7 A.M., passed the (nine?) narrow streams, and
during the march we came to the halting-place direct,* still
near the river Calalimo. We arrived at the said place at 2
P.M., having met with no one. We marched with the sun as
before.

[10th.] *Thursday, 16th.*—We got up and started at early
dawn. We passed three narrow running streams by bridges,
and came to another desert halting-place near a small river.
We arrived there at mid-day, and built near the same river.
Some men were in our ¦rear belonging to Soana Mulopo, sent
by him to buy salt; we met no one.

[11th.] *Friday, 17th.*—We got up and started at 5 A.M.
from the lodging above named. We forded a running river
called Roando, two fathoms wide, which runs into the river
Lunheca. During our march we passed another narrow river
called Rova, which may be, more or less, thirteen fathoms wide.

* Diralto, direct, may be an error for deserto, desert, deserted.—R. F. B.

This also runs into the Lunheca. The farm of a black, called
Fumo Ahilombe of the Muropue, was some distance from us, but
that did not cause us any trouble. We arrived there at noon,
and built near the same river, meeting with no one.

[12th.] *Saturday, 18th.*—At 5 A.M. we got up and started
from the farm of Fumo Ahilomba. We passed six narrow rivers
which run into the Rova, and during the march we came to the
desert halting-place, beyond and near the river called Cazale.
This stream may be, more or less, twenty fathoms wide, with
water up to our waists. It runs into the river Lunheca. We
reached the said place about nightfall. We met several people
loaded with dry fish, which they were going to sell at the
Muropue's farm. We marched with the sun on our left, and
saw nothing of importance.

[13th.] *Sunday, 19th.*—We left our desert halting-place
above mentioned at 6 A.M. We passed no river, and, continuing
our journey, we came to the farm of the Luilolo (Quilolo) of the
Muropue, called Caponco Bumba Ajala, and we conversed with
him about the journey we were making by order of the
Muropue to the Cazembe. He answered that it was well, and
directly ordered us some eatables on behalf of his master the
Muropue. We gave him a present of four chuabos and a mirror.
We reached the said city at 4 P.M., near the river called Muncuzu.
We met no one.

[14th.] *Monday, 20th.*—We started at two A.M. from the
farm of Capomo (Caponco ?). We passed a stream, and during
our march crossed in a canoe a river, called Caginrige. The
pilots of the Quilolo Muene Mene, who is Lord of this port, took
us across. This river may be about fourteen fathoms wide ; it
runs into the Lunheca. We reached the farm of the said Quilolo
Muene Mene, and talked with him about the journey we were
making to Cazembe, by order of Muropue ; he also answered
that it was very good, that the road was quite clear. We gave
him for this a muzenzo, containing a hundred blue stone-
beads and five chuabos of assorted serafina, and further forty
other white stones, and for his pilots two chuabos of Indian
cloth. We made our kraal some distance from the farm to keep
out of the way of the thieves who rob at night. We reached
there at 3 P.M., and met no one. We stayed at this place six
days to collect provisions with which to proceed.

[15th.] *Tuesday, 5th July.*—We rose at the first cockcrow,
and left the farm of Muene Mene. We passed four narrow rivers

which run into the river Caginrige, and we came to the farm of
a black, known to our guide as Soana Ganga. We spoke with
him about our journey to Cazembe. We reached there at 2
P.M., having met no one. We gave him no present. We
marched with the sun on our left.

[16th.] *Wednesday, 6th.*—We started from Soana Ganga's
farm at 7 A.M. We passed two narrow running streams which
empty themselves into the said river Caginrige. We came to
the farm of the Quilolo of the mother of Muropue called Lun-
congucha, and the Quilolo is named Muene Camatanga. We
spoke with him of the journey we were making to the Cazembe,
to which he answered, that as many as liked could travel that
way. We gave him a present of five chuabos and a small
mirror, and fifty milkstone beads. We reached this place at
noon. We marched with the sun as before, and met no one.

[17th.] *Thursday, 7th.*—We started from Muene Camatanga's farm at 6 A.M. We passed three streams which run into
the said river Caginrige. During the journey we came to the
farm of the Quilolo, the same before mentioned as Muene
Casamba, whither Camatanga himself directed us, in order that
his vassal, who had given us the guide, might supply us with
necessary provisions for our journey to Cazembe, made by order
of the Muropue. In this same farm we made a month's stay, to
prepare the said provisions and allow the (manioc) flour, which
had been steeped in water, to get dry. We met no one. For
the above service we gave two chuabos of woollen stuff.

[18th.] *Friday, 9th of August.*—We started from Muene Casamba at 9 A.M. We again passed the river Caginrige, and
during the march we passed another narrow river, the name
unknown, which also runs into the said river Caginrige. We
came to a desert halting-place, near another small river, which
we reached at 4 P.M. We built our circle (kraal) during rain; we
met no one.

[19th.] *Saturday, 10th.*—We got up and left our desert
halting-place at half-past five in the morning. We passed a
running river, narrow, with stony bed, name not known, and
came to another halting-place, called Canpueje, near a running
stream, where we found houses already made by the travelling
Arúndas. We reached there at 2 P.M., and saw nothing.

[20th.] *Sunday, 11th.*—We left our desert halting-place,
from which we rose at 2 A.M. We passed three narrow rivers.

During the journey we came to another desert halting-place, near a stream, the name of which we do not know. We reached the said place at four in the afternoon; we met no one.

[21st.] *Monday, 12th.*—We left our stopping-place at 6 A.M. We passed a narrow running stream called Maconde, and during the march we came to another halting-place called Lunçaja. The farm of the Quilolo, called Anbulita Quisosa, was near, but we did not talk with him about our journey. We reached the said place at noon; we met no one, and marched with the sun on our left.

[22nd.] *Tuesday, 13th.*—We got up and left our desert resting-place at 5 A.M. We passed no river, and came to the farm of the son of the Quilolo Cutaganda, near the river called Reu. We spoke with him concerning the journey we were making to Cazembe. We gave as a present to the said Quilolo two chuabos of blue serafina and 200 cowries. We arrived at the farm at 3 P.M. We marched with the sun as before.

[23rd.] *Wednesday, 14th.*—We left the son of Cutaganda at seven in the morning. We forded the river Reu, which is about twenty fathoms wide. We came to the desert halting-place, near a stream, name not known. We arrived at 2 P.M., having met with no one.

[24th.] *Thursday, 15th.*—We started at 6 A.M. from our desert stopping-place. We passed three narrow rivers which run into the river Reu above named. We came to another desert stopping-place near a stream called Quabela (Quibanla?), which also runs into river Reu. The farm of the black, named Muconcota, a chief of Muropue, being far distant, he himself came to our lodging-place that we might give him something as a present. We gave him seven chuabos of serafina of different qualities. We reached there at three in the afternoon. We marched with the sun as before, and met with no one.

[25th.] *Friday, 16th.*—We left our desert halting-place at 5 A.M. We passed four narrow rivers which run into the river Quabela. During the journey we reached a desert-lodging near a running stream called Capaca Melemo. We arrived at the said lodging at noon without rain. We had in our company some blacks, who were going to buy salt at the Salina. We met with no one.

[26th.] *Saturday, 17th.*—We started from our desert-lodging near the river Capaca Melcmo at 6 A.M. We forded four small rivers, and continuing our journey we passed another river called Ropoeja, which may be about thirty fathoms wide. It runs into the river called Lubilaje. We came to another desert halting-place near the same river Lubilaje, on the other side of which we reached our lodging at three in the afternoon, without rain. We marched with the sun the same as before; we met with no one.

[27th.] *Sunday, 18th.*—We made a halt at the farm of a black named Quiabela Mucanda, which is near the above-named river Ropoeja. He stopped our road, in order that we might give him something because he was a potentate of the Muropue's. Besides this he also gave us food to eat on behalf of said Muropue, and brought for us as a parting gift a dead stag and three quicapos of green manioca flour for our use. We gave him as a present ten chuabos and a small looking-glass. He said that we might continue our journey, and that had we not given him anything, he would have taken our goods from us by force of arms.

[28th.] *Thursday, 31st of August.*—We started at cockcrow from the city of Quiabela Mucanda. We passed two running streams, which emptied themselves into the said river Ropoeja. During our march we came to another desert stopping-place, called Cancaco, on the other side of a stream. We arrived at said place at noon, without fear of any Regano (chief) like the above-mentioned. We marched with the sun on our left; we met no one on the way.

[29th.] *Friday, 1st of September.*—We halted in consequence the illness of our guide, who had his hand swollen from blows received from his own slave.

Saturday, 2nd of said Month.—We started from our desert-lodging at two in the morning. We passed a river called Quipaca Anguengua, of small width, and during our march we came to another desert near a river called Rupele of four fathoms width, which runs into the river Lubile. We arrived at three in the afternoon. We marched with the sun as before; we met with no one.

[30th.] *Sunday, 3rd.*—We left our desert lodging at 5 A.M. We passed no river, and came to another desert-lodging near a river called " White," because of its white sand; it discharges itself into the river Lububuri, a small river near. We reached

the said lodging at noon. We built our kraal on the other side
of the river, and met with no one.

[31st.] *Monday, 4th.*—We got up at 7 A.M., and started
from our desert halting-ground; we passed no river during the
journey. We came to another desert near the said river
Lububuri, which we did not cross. We arrived at two in the
afternoon, having marched with the sun as before, and having
met no one.

[32nd.] *Tuesday, 5th.*—We started from our desert-lodging
near the river Lububuri at six in the morning; we passed no
river. We reached the river Lububuri, which we forded, the
water being up to our waists; this river is about forty fathoms
wide, and has a stony bottom. We saw some people, the slaves
of the potentate named Cha Muginga Mucenda; we spoke to
these people, whose language is similar to that of the town of
Cazembe. We arrived near the said farm at 2 P.M., we said
nothing about our object, and built our huts on the other side of
the river, near it, but distant from the farm. We met with no one.

[33rd.] *Wednesday, 6th.*—At seven in the morning we
started from near the river Lububuri; we passed no river. During the journey we came to the farm of the said Cha Muginga
Mucenda; we treated with him regarding our object, that we
were on our way to the King Cazembe, to seek for a white brother
of our king, who had travelled by sea, and to see if he was in the
said Cazembe's dominions. This potentate is a chief of the
Cazembe, who renders obedience both to the Muropue and
to the Cazembe: the said Cazembe has left him to cultivate
all kinds of provisions, wherewith to supply all travellers coming
from the Muropue to Cazembe, taking tribute, and called by
them " Mulambo," as also for those who come from Cazembe
to Muropue, taking the tribute sent by the said King Cazembe
to his King Muropue. On the day of our arrival he presented
us with a murondo of pombe. This city of Cha Muginga Mucenda, being the boundary on that side of the territories of
Muropue, the territory on this side being those of Cazembe, we
gave him a present of ten chuabos and two small looking-
glasses. He answered that he was preparing some food for us
to take to Cazembe, because that, halfway along the road, until
we came to the Salina, we should get nothing to eat. At this
same place we halted six days, for the purpose of collecting
extra provisions. We reached this same farm at noon, and
we built some distance from it, near and on the further side
of a river called Camonqueje. We met no one.

[34th.] *Thursday. 7th.*—We arose at 6 A.M., and started from Cha Muginga Mucenda's farm; we left our huts, passed no river, and on the journey we came to a desert-lodging called Musula Aponpo. We arrived at this lodging-place at 2 P.M., and built our huts to the east of the river "Lubury." We marched with the sun on our left. After we had built, some slaves of Cha Muginga Mucenda, coming with salt from the Salina, passed and saw our lodging-place. We marched with the sun as before, and met no one.

[35th.] *Friday, 8th.*—Started at 5 A.M. from the desert lodging Musula Aponpo. We passed a narrow running river named the son of the river Lunfupa (Lufula ?). During our journey we crossed the said Lunfupa, the water up to our waists; this river is about fifteen fathoms wide, it runs into the river Luaba (Lualaba ?). We reached this at noon, and saw nothing to disturb us; we built our huts beyond and near the river's side, and met with no one.

[36th.] *Saturday, 9th.*—We set out at 2 A.M. from the desert lodging near the river Lunfupa. We passed a narrow running river, name not known, and came to another desert-lodging near a large river-plain called Quebonda, with a small stream in it: here we found some black hunters with the game they had arrowed; they were going the same way as ourselves, to the Salina to buy salt; they did not inform us whence they came. We met no one.

[37th.] *Sunday, 10th.*—We arose at the first cockcrow, and started from the Quebonda plain. We were till midday crossing this plain. During our journey we came to a halting-place on the top of a hill, called Inpume, near the river, two fathoms wide, called Camoa, which runs into the Lualaba. We reached the before-mentioned lodging at three in the afternoon; we built our huts on the further top of the same hill; we had no rain. We met some blacks of Cha Muginga Mucenda, coming from the Salina; they told us that the potentate Quebule, a relation of the Cazembe, governor of the salt district, was well.

[38th.] *Monday, 11th.*—We left our lodging on the hill Inpume at 5 A.M.; we passed no river. During our march we came to another desert-lodging, near the stream called Catomta, and the lodging called Muary Agoia, being in the lands of Casembe. We marched now with the sun in our front, and arrived at the above lodging at noon. We met some blacks coming from the salt districts, but saw nothing unusual.

N

[39th.] *Tuesday, 12th.*—We started from our desert-lodging
Catomta at 6 A.M.; passed a narrow stream. During the journey
we came to another desert-lodging, near a river two fathoms
wide, called Huita Amatete, which runs into the River Lualaba. The said lodging being a long way off from the farm
of a black named Muire, a potentate of Cazembe, this man
came to our lodging at nightfall: we conversed with him
about our journey to King Cazembe, made by order of Muropue.
He answered that the Cazembe was well, and also his relation,
the potentate Quibury, Lord of the Salina; he offered us no
provisions. We arrived at this lodging at 3 P.M., without rain.
We marched with the sun in our front; met no one and saw
nothing of note.

[40th.] *Wednesday, 13th.*—We started from the farm of
Muiro at 5 A.M. We passed a small stream called Mulonga
Ancula, which runs into the Lualaba. On leaving this place,
Muire obliged us to present him with something; we gave
him a chnabo of Indian cloth and twenty small Canádo
(Canudo, bugles?) beads; he went away contented. We continued our journey, and reached the desert halting-place called
Luíana (Quiana?) Acananga, near a running stream termed
the Son of the Abulonga (Mulonga) Ancula River. We halted
at 2 P.M.; marched with the sun as before, and met many
salt-buyers travelling to the Muropue. We built our kraal
near the same stream; had no rain, and met no one.

[41st.] *Thursday, 14th.*—We started at four in the morning
from our desert-lodging Luiana (Quiana?) Acananga. During the journey we crossed a narrow stream from the east,
called Luigila, which forms a large river-plain, where it discharges into the river Lualaba. In this river-plain they get
salt; in order to obtain which, they cut the grass which is
there found, and burn it; they then throw the ashes into small
pans which they make, and proceed to prepare "luada" water.
They make their general measure of a small pan, by which
they sell the salt at the rate of ten pans for a chuabo. We
reached this place at three in the afternoon, and built our
huts the other side of the valley. The sun was as usual;
there was no rain; we met with no one, and saw nothing
remarkable.

[42nd.] *Friday 15th.*—Halted; our guide being ill.
Saturday, 16th.—We got up at 7 A.M., and started from
the river-plain; we found ourselves descending into another
river-plain. Passing no river during the journey, we came to

the said river-plain; we reached the said lodging at noon; we went into the houses already made by the salt-buyers; we met with no one. The river Lualaba, where the potentate Quibnry was on the other side, being very distant, we had nothing to say with his chiefs there, We saw nothing remarkable.

[43rd.] *Sunday 17th.*—At 5 A.M. we got up, and started in the river-plain, and found ourselves descending it. Wo passed no river. During the march we crossed the River Lualaba in a canoe. This river is about fifty or more fathoms wide; it discharges itself into the Lunheca. We came to another chief of the same potentate, Quibury of the Cazembe. The guide sent and gave notice of our arrival. He (the chief) directed that we were to lodge near his walls. We did not speak with him. We arrived at said place at midday without rain, having marched with the sun in our front. We met no one.

[44th.] *Monday, 18th.*—We halted at the farm of the chief Quibury, at six o'clock in the day. He sent for us, and we conversed with him about our project; that we had come from Angola, sent by his friend our King, whom they call Mueneputo, to see his superior, the King Cazembe; also that we were sent by Muropue, with orders to the said King Cazembe to treat us without malice; that we were going to seek the brother of our said King, who had gone by sea, to find if he were in the territory of said King Cazembe; and that we should ask permission to go on to the town of Tetto to see if he was there, for which purpose Muropue had given us this his guide Cutaquaseja, that he might deliver the message entrusted to him by Muropue to King Cazembe. We so acted knowing that all the chiefs would not let travellers with merchandise going to the lands of others pass; that if travellers who came to their places did not trade with them, they would, little by little, rob them by false pretences just like thieves. The Chief Quibury answered that white men were to be found in Cazembe who had come there to trade; that he did not know whence they had come, or through whose dominions; that he heard a white soldier had been found who had left those white traders; and that when we saw King Cazembe it would be well for us to treat with him. He presented us with two handfuls of fresh-killed bush-meat. We halted with him eight days, arranging all this. We presented him with twenty chuabos, one hundred milk-stones, a small mirror, and a Portuguese musket. He then allowed us to proceed on our journey.

[45th.]   *Tuesday 19th.*—At 7 A.M. we started from the farm of Quibury, a relation to the Cazembe. We passed no river. We found ourselves going down in the same direction as the river Lualaba. During the journey we came to the halting-place near a stream called "Chafim," which runs into the said Lualaba. We arrived at the halting-place at noon. We marched with the sun in our front; and built near this side of the said stream. We met many common animals, and saw nothing rare or strange.

[46th.]   *Wednesday, 20th.*—At 5 A.M. we left our desert-lodging near the stream "Chafim." We crossed the "Chafim," and during the march we came to another desert halting-place near a stream called Bacasacala. Arrived there at two in the afternoon, without rain; we built our circle to the east of the stream; marched with the sun as before, and met with no one.

[47th.]   *Thursday, 21st.*—At 6 A.M. we left the halting-place near the stream Bacasala (Bacasacala?). We passed a narrow running stream, and came to the top of a hill, the farm of the slaves of Quibury. We arrived at the said halting-place at 2 P.M. We built our circle near a small stream, without rain. We met no one.

[48th.]   *Friday, 22nd.*—At five in the morning we started from the place of the slaves of Quibury. Passed three small rivers, narrow, whose names we do not know. During our march we came to the place of the Chief of Quibury, named Camungo. We did not find this chief at this farm, only his "sons," he having gone to the chase. They allowed us to enter into their houses; and we gave them a present of two chuabos of Indian cloths. We spoke with them about the journey we were making to Cazembe. We reached this place at noon, without rain. We marched with the sun in front. We met no one.

[49th.]   *Saturday, 23rd.*—We got up at dawn, and left the farm of the black, Camungo. We passed a small river, and came to the desert-lodging. We began building when rain fell, and we continued on in the rain to finish our circle near a small stream, the name of which we do not know. We reached the lodging at two in the afternoon. We marched with the sun as before. At midnight two lions came near our lodging, and kept us awake by their roaring all night. By God's will they did us no harm. We met no one, and saw nothing of importance.

[50th.] *Sunday, 24th.*—We got up at 5.30 A.M., and started from our desert-lodging, We passed three narrow rivers. We came to another halting-place, the farm of the potentate Anpala being distant half a league. We arrived at the lodging at two in the afternoon. We built on this side of a river called Ancula, without rain. We met some black salt-merchants, who were going to buy provisions at the farm of the potentate Anpala. We went with the sun in the same position as before.

[51st.] *Monday, 25th.*—We started at cockcrow from our lodging near the river Ancula. We found ourselves going up with the said river Ancula. We passed a narrow stream, and, during the march, came to another desert-lodging near and on this side of the river Ancula. We entered the hunters' circle. We arrived at midday, without rain. We marched with the sun in our front. We met no one.

[52nd.] *Tuesday, 26th.*—We rose at 6 A.M., and started from the river Anonla (Aucula?). We passed two small rivers, whose names we are ignorant of; and during the journey we came to the farm of a black called the son of the potentate Pande, by name Muana Auta, to whom we did not speak, as he had gone to his father's farm. They ordered us to go in the houses of the people of the said potentate Pande. We reached there at midday, near the river Ri Lomba (Rilomba?). We presented two chuabos and a hundred cowries. It being afternoon, I went hunting, and shot a deer. The slaves of our guide found a dead buffalo, which had been killed by a lion. We met no one.

[53rd.] *Wednesday, 27th.*—At two in the morning we started from the farm called Muana Auta. We passed a stream called Quimane. During the journey we came to the place of the potentate called Pande, whom we did not see there the day we arrived; and he only entertained our guide, who came to us with a demijohn of drink called "ponbe." The bearer brought in word that he was occupied with messengers from King Cazembe, and that he would see us when he had more leisure. We arrived in the said farm at two in the afternoon, and built our circle near a river called Murucuxy, on the other side of it. We marched with the sun in our front, and met no one.

[54th.] *Thursday, 28th.*—A halt, caused by the said potentate; as also on Friday, Saturday, and Sunday, in order to treat with him about our journey to King Cazembe, he being a chief. We told him we were going to King Cazembe, from Muropue, who had sent us with a guide capable of conducting us to the town of Tette, to deliver a letter to the Most Illustrious Governor of that town, sent by the king whom they call Muanepúto. We presented him with twenty chuaboes of good woollen cloths, and he offered us two quicapos of millet and thirty slices of dry buffalo flesh, and told us we might continue our journey, and go on prosecuting our plan.

[55th.] *Monday, 1st of October.*—We rose at 6 A.M., and set out from the farm of Pande. We passed two narrow streams during the journey. We came to the farm of a black named Cahiumbo Camara. We did not speak to him on the day of our arrival; only two blacks came to our lodging to see us. We gave them no present. We reached there at two in the afternoon, and were not persecuted for gifts. We went into the houses of the travellers who go to Cazembe. We marched with the sun in our front, and met no one.

[56th.] *Tuesday, 2nd.*—We left the city of the black Cahiumbo Camara at cockcrow. We crossed a river, near which we passed the night. During the journey we came to the desert halting-place called Quidano (Quidaxi ?), near a river, whose name we do not know. We reached there at midday. We built on this side of it, finishing our circle in the rain. We met no one. In crossing a large river-plain we saw numerous zebras feeding there; when we approached they fled.

[57th.] *Wednesday, 3rd.*—We got up at two in the morning, and started from our desert-lodging "Quidano." We passed a narrow river, and during the journey we came to the ancient farm of a black named Luncongi, now depopulated. We arrived at our lodging at four in the afternoon, without rain. We built our circle near a small stream, whose name we do not know. We journeyed with the sun in our front, and met with no one.

[58th.] *Thursday, 4th.*—At 7 o'clock A.M. we got up and started from the depopulated farm of Luncongi. We passed no river; and during the journey we came to the new farm of the same potentate Luncongi, on the other side of a river named Luvire, which we crossed by canoe—it may be about twelve fathoms wide, and discharges itself into the Luapula. We entered the houses of the farm, and spoke with the said black Luncongi about our journey to Cazembe. We presented him with a chuabo. He told us King Cazembe was well; that he was willing to get food for our guide who had brought us; and with this idea we remained all day on Friday. He brought for the guide four pieces of fresh meat, and for us twenty, saying that in his farm there was a great deal of hunger.

[59th.] *Friday, 5th.*—We started at 6 A.M. from the farm of Luncongi; passed two rivers, the names not known, which run into the river Luvira. During the march we came to the halting-place, near the same river Luvira. We came down with the same river, and arrived at the halting-place at three in the afternoon. We built our circle amid plenty of rain. We marched with the sun in front, and met no one.

[60th.] *Saturday, 6th.*—We started from the solitary halting-place at cockcrow, and without rain. We passed no river, and during the march, we came to the place of a small potentate named Muene Majamo Amuaxi. We told him about our journey, that we were going to King Cazembe, and presented him with nothing. We arrived at this place at two o'clock. We built our huts near and on the other side of the river called Musumba. We met no one, and saw nothing rare or important.

[61st.] *Sunday, 7th.*—At seven o'clock in the morning we left the city of the Muene Majamo. We passed no river, and came to the place of a potentate called Muaxy. We conversed with him, saying that we were going to King Cazembe, by order of the Muropue. He said that the heir to the state of Cazembe was well; and that he on his part entertained us on behalf of King Cazembe. We halted one day for him to give us provisions. We reached this farm at midday, and he sent us word to occupy the houses of his slaves. We journeyed with the sun in front, and met no one. Presented him with seven chuabos and a small mirror. He gave us five quicapos of small millet, and sixty pieces of flesh, telling us to continue our journey.

[62nd.] *Monday, 8th.*—At 5 A.M. we started from the farm of the potentate Muaxy. We passed a stream of narrow width, its name not known, and during the journey we arrived at the desert-lodging near a small narrow river, with stony bottom, name of it not known. We reached this place at 4 P.M., without rain. We built our circle on this side of the river, and we met three blacks who were going to buy salt at the farm of Muaxy above named, having come from the court of King Cazembe. We marched with the sun in our front, and saw nothing new.

[63rd.] *Tuesday, 9th.*—At 2 A.M. we started from our solitary lodging. We passed five streams—names unknown—and found ourselves ascending a hill called Cunde Irugo. In the course of the march we crossed a river named Cavulancango, at 6 A.M. we started from the said Cavulancango, which is about seven fathoms wide, the water being up to our waists when crossing; it runs into the river Luapula. We reached the said lodging at noon, and built our circle on the other side, near the river. We met six black slaves of Cazembe going to the city of Muaxy. We said nothing to them. Marched with the sun as before.

[64th.] *Wednesday, 10th.*—At 6 A.M. we started from near the river Cavulancango. Passed no river. Were ascending the hill Cunde Irugo. During the march we came to another stopping-place, near a narrow river called the Son of Cavulancango. On the top of the said hill we reached our lodging, at two o'clock, without rain. We entered the circle of the travellers on the other side of the river. Marched with the sun as before.

[65th.] *Thursday, 11th.*—We arose at 2 A.M., and left our desert-lodging. Passed two running streams, and on the march came to another desert-lodging on the top of the said hill. We arrived during rain at six in the afternoon, built our circle, and met no one.

[66th.] *Friday, 12th.*—At seven in the morning we got up, and left the top of the hill. We passed seven narrow streams which run into the Luapula. We came to another desert near a narrow river, where we found a circle made. We met nobody, and walked with the sun in our front.

[67th.] *Saturday, 13th.*—At 2 A.M. we left our desert-lodging. We passed two streams, and pushing on crossed a river called Lutipuca, five fathoms wide, running into the Luapula. During the journey we arrived at the place of a chief of Cazembe, named Sota. We did not find him in the farm, he having gone to pay tribute to Cazembe. We halted at two o'clock, without rain, and gave no presents.

[68th.] *Sunday, 14th.*—We started from Sota's farm at dawn. Passed the river Lutipuca a second time on foot. On the journey we came to a desert-lodging near a stream—name of it not known. Arrived at noon at said lodging. We now march with the sun on our right. We met with no one.

[69th.] *Monday, 15th.*—At 5 A.M. we left our desert-lodging. Passed no river on the march. We came to another desert-lodging near the river Lutipuca. We followed it downwards, and arrived at it at noon, without rain. Marched with the sun on our right. Met no one, and saw nothing now.

[70th.] *Tuesday, 16th.*—We got up and started from our lonely halting-place. During the march we came to the farm of a small potentate of Cazembe, named Munxaqueta. We talked with him concerning our journey to King Cazembe, and he sent word to us to stay in the houses of his people. We reached this place at two in the afternoon. We presented him with four xuabos of serafina cloth. He told us he was pleased with the present, and directed us on our road. We did nothing else.

[71st.] *Wednesday, 17th.*—We got up at cockcrow, and left the farm of Munxaqueta. We passed through a magnificent river-plain with little water, it is about ten leagues in length, full of zebras, buffaloes, deer, stags, and many other animals not known to us by name. We came to the farm of another potentate named Muaxies, and of his brother named Quiocola: we spoke regarding our journey to King Cazembe. We reached this place at 4 P.M. We presented the two potentates with twelve chuabos. They said King Cazembe was well. We met no one, and marched with the sun as before.

[72nd.] *Thursday, 18th.*—Got up at five in the morning, and left the farm of Munxaqueta. Had no rain. We crossed the said river-plain, and on the west of it canoe'd over the river Luapula. Gave the pilots or boatmen two chuabos of woollen stuffs. We came to the farm of a black named Tambo (Amtapo ?) Aquilala, and spoke with him about our journey to King Cazembe from the Muropue. We arranged our own matters, arrived in this place at 4 P.M. Built near the farm. The river Luapula is about fifty-seven fathoms wide. We do not know where it discharges itself. Met no one.

[73rd.] *Friday, 19th.*—Got up at 6 A.M., and started from the place of Tambo Aquilala. Passed no river, but followed down the course of the river Luapula, and came to the farm of Cazembe's sister, named Pomba,* near the same river. She directly sent us to lodge in the houses of her people. We did not speak with her on the day of our arrival. Reached the farm at two in the afternoon, having met no one.

---

* In the other journal it is also a sister. See page 217.—R. F. B.

[74th.] *Saturday, 20th.*—Halted in the Cazembe's sister's farm, by her own order. At two in the morning, she sent for us, and we went inside her walls. She asked whence we came. We replied, from Angola and the court of Muropue, who had given us the guide. That we had come to speak with her brother King Cazembe, to get permission to go on to the town of Tette. She replied it was very good on the part of Muropue to send white people to speak with her brother; that none of Muropue's predecessors had done so; that it was a very great fortune for her brother Cazembe's heir to the State. She offered us a large she-goat, forty fresh fish, two bottles of a drink called "pombo," and six quicapos of dry mandioca flour. We presented her with thirty-two xuabos, a blue glass, and a "mozenzo" of a hundred white stones. She said she was much pleased with our gifts. We waited there that she might send notice of our arrival to her brother, King Cazembe, as it is obligatory on her part when travellers come to report them to her brother. With this end we waited six days at her farm, when the carriers came in search of us.

[75th.] *Saturday 27th.*—Got up and left the farm of Cazembe's sister at 7 A.M. Had no rain. We followed down the course of the Luapula. Passed a river of two fathoms' width, name unknown, which runs into the Luapula. During the journey we came to the farm of a black named Murumbo: we reached it at midday. We met no one, and marched with the sun on our right. We lodged in the houses of the farm, and saw nothing rare or important.

[76th.] *Sunday, 28th.*—We got up at 2 A.M., and started from the farm of Murumbo. We marched down with the above-named river on our left. We passed two rivers, Lufubo and Capueje, which run into the above-named river. During the journey we came to the farm of a black named Gando, near a river called Gona, here we gave no presents. We reached it at six in the afternoon. We marched with the sun as before.

[77th.] *Monday, 29th.*—At 5 A.M. we got up and started from the farm of Gando, near the river Gona. We passed two rivers, one called Belenje, the other's name not known; during the march we came to the place of a black named Canpungue. We reached this place at three in the afternoon, and met a good number of King Cazembe's people carrying firewood. We presented this black, Canpungue, with a chuabo of "Zuarte" or Indian cloth; he told us to continue our journey, as the Cazembe was expecting us.

[78th.] *Tuesday, 30th.*—At seven A.M. we started from
the place of the black, Canpungue—had no rain; we passed
no river, and during the journey came to the place of a black
named Luiagamára, of the Cazembe. Reaching this place
at four in the afternoon, we lodged in the houses near a river
called Canengua, narrow, and running into the river called
Monva, near which Cazembe's city is situated. We gave no
present to the owner of this place; we halted there, and sent
forward a day's notice of our arrival; we waited a little time,
when the King Cazembe's messenger arrived, bringing us, as
guest-gift, four murondos of a drink called "ponbe," one hundred
pieces of fresh meat, with some manioc flour for our consump-
tion, and also a message from King Cazembe, asking us to
remain at present where we were, that he would send for us
later. Day breaking directly, and it being two o'clock in the
morning, he sent for us by his chief, with orders that on our
arrival near the walls of his chiefs (ancestors?), we should fire off
all our guns, as a signal that we had arrived at his capital. He
ordered us to lodge with one of his gatekeepers, named Fumo
Aquibery. We did nothing respecting our journey on this day:
he sent us for our people, however, some provisions, manioc
flour, fish, fresh meat, and "pombe," she-goats, and meats already
prepared; he said he would see us with great pleasure. When
morning broke, he sent word for us to come and tell him
what brought us there. We found him seated in the public
highway, where he was accustomed to deliver his judgments
to his people, surrounded by all the great potentates of his
councils. He was robed in his silks and velvets, and had beads
of various kinds on his arms and legs; his people surrounded
him, and he had all his instruments of barbarous grandeur
round about him. He sent to say that the guide who had
come with us from his Muropue should speak. The guide
said, "I bring you some white men here from the king they
call Muenuputo; they come to communicate with you, King
Cazembe; treat them well, without malice, and execute the
wishes entrusted to them: grant them, King Cazembe, permission, together with some guide, who you may see able to
conduct them, to go to the town of Tette, to deliver a letter to
the Most Illustrious Governor of that town, they being entrusted
with this mission in Angola, whence they came. Muropue also
strongly recommends you will do all necessary to despatch the
travellers where they wish to go, and afterwards send them
back to Muropue, in order that he may return them whence
they came." The King Cazembe said that he esteemed it much,
and not a little, his Muropue's having sent travellers from afar;
that for a long time past he had entertained the idea of opening

the road to Senna; that he was very pleased to see travellers from Muropue, none of whose predecessors had similarly acted before; that he would do all in his power—not only provide a guide, but go with us himself as far as the Warcamp, to fight the highwaymen and robbers who meet with and intercept people on the road coming to communicate with him, King Cazembe. We had gone with King Cazembo as far as a farm of his people, about half a league from Cazembe, with numerous troops to escort us on the road; after this, a perturbation spread among his people, who did not wish to fight, so the attempt was frustrated; we returned to the farm with him against his wish. He began to cast out his chiefs; he cut the ears of some, others he mulcted in slaves and manilhos (bracelets); and on the second month he handed us over to his chief named Mnenepanda to accompany us with more people. On our reaching a desert-lodging called Qnipire, he turned back, saying that the town of Tette was a long way off; that the force he (Muenepanda) had to oppose to the potentates he might meet on the road was very small; that he did not wish to run any risk. We returned with him, and after waiting another half month, the black, named Nharugue, belonging to Gonçalo Caetano Pereira arrived, and we started and marched in his company till we reached this town of Tette.

King Cazembe is very black, a fine, stout young man, with small beard, and red eyes; he is very well accustomed to white traders, who come to his court to buy and sell such articles as seed, manioc flour, maize, millet, haricot beans, a good many "canas" (sugar-cane?), and fish which the people catch in the river near there called Monva. Ivory comes from the other side the river Luapula, and is brought as tribute by the people; green stones (malachite) are found in the ground, called "catanga"; traders from the Muizas people come and buy ivory, in exchange for tissues and merchandise; another nation, named Tungalugazas, brings slaves and brass bracelets, cowries, palm-oil, and some goods which King Cazembe has, come from the Cola (Angola?), a land of Muropue, also fine large beads. There is a good deal of salt in that part, which they get from the ground; there is also another kind of rock-salt which is brought as tribute from the salt district, on the road to Muropue's territory, called Luigila, where he has a chief and a relation, named Quibery, who takes account of the Salina, and sends tributes of salt to his Muropue, besides buying it of the travellers who come from Muropue. I have made no entry of the rainy days we stopped, or of those when we were detained by sickness. I saw nothing more at the Court of King Cazembe which I have forgotten to write; I saw nothing but that already stated.

DOCUMENTS RELATIVE TO THE JOURNEY FROM ANGOLA TO THE RIVERS OF SENNA.

No. 1.

(December)—1810.

Route Journal which I, Pedro João Batista, made on my journey from Cazembe to the town of Tette.

[1st.]—Lodging at Casocoma, a farm of our "Cazembe of the Road" (guide), who led us; he is called, after country-fashion, Catara. This day we left the city of King Cazembe, at seven in the morning. We crossed a river called Lunde, not very broad, which runs into the other river Mouva, near which lives the said Cazembe. We marched with the sun in front, and met no one.

[2nd.]—Started from the farm of Catara Casocoma, at two in the morning; passed a stream, and on the march came to the place of a black named Quihono, slave of the daughter of the Cazembe, named Quitende. We lodged in their houses; we halted there, and waited for Cazembe's road-escort, which had stayed behind. A delay of three days was caused by the same. We met no one, and saw nothing new.

[3rd.]—Started from the farm of Quihono at five in the morning; crossed no river. During the march came to the desert-lodging near a narrow river called Capaco; and having crossed another river called Bengeli, four fathoms wide, which runs into the river Mouva before-mentioned, we met two blacks loaded with dry fish, going to the large farm of the said Cazembe. We saw nothing more.

[4th.]—Left our desert-lodging at eight in the morning; did not pass any river during the march. We arrived at a deserted farm of a black named Muiro, near the same before-named river we came down by. Reached this place at 4 P.M., marched with the sun in front; we halted in the old houses of the farm. We stayed at this place one day, waiting for an ivory belonging to Catara.

[5th.]—Left the deserted farm of Muiro at two in the morning.

During the journey we came to and passed a river named Luena, about seventeen fathoms wide: it discharges itself into the river named Carucuige. We arrived at the desert-lodging near the same river Luena, built our circle, and met with no one.

[6th.]—From the lodging in the desert near the river Benlengi, say Luena, we started at cockcrow, and came to another desert (lodging?) called Muchito Agumbo. We reached this at two in the afternoon, travelled with the sun as before; we did not meet with any one.

[7th.]—Left our lodging in the desert Muchito Agumbo at seven in the morning; passed three small streams. During the journey we came to the place of a black named Cangueli and to the lands of a potentate of Cazombe, named Muenepanda. We reached there at three in the afternoon, near a narrow river whose name we do not know, which runs into the river named Panpajo; there we halted by order of the said King Cazembe, who wished to send some provisions to Catara.

[8th.]—Rose at dawn, and, without rain, started from the place of the black Cangueli. During the journey we came to the desert-lodging near a narrow river named Muangi, on the other side of which we reached the said lodging at noon. Marched with the sun in front, and did not meet any one.

[9th.]—At 4 A.M. we set out from the desert-lodging near the river Muangi. We passed two streams, names unknown. During the march we came to another desert-lodging near a narrow river called Camicomba. We reached the same at two in the afternoon; built our circle near said river; met with no one; marched with the sun as before.

[10th.]—From near the river Camicomba we started at six in the morning. Passed no river. During the march we came to another desert near a running stream named Caquietatume. We arrived there at three in the afternoon. We made a stay of two days there, awaiting ivory from the Cazembo. We met with no one.

[11th.]—At cockcrow we got up and started from the desert near the river Caquila. Passed a river named Lufunbo, three fathoms in width. During our march we came to another desert near a river, the name of which we do not know. We reached there at four in the afternoon; built our huts near said river, whose further side we had followed down. No rain. Met with no one.

[12th.]—At six in the morning we set out from our desert halting-place. Passed no river, and during the journey we came to the desert-lodging called Luipiri. We reached the same at Ave-Maria (nightfall) without rain. We occupied the houses already built by the travelling Muizas. We met with no one.

[13th.]—At dawn we got up and started from the desert-lodging Luipiri. Passed seven small streams; names unknown. During the march we came to the village of a deceased potentate named Luibue, whom Cazembe had killed in battle, and to the place of a potentate named Muiro Aquito, relation of the deceased Luibue. We arrived at two in the afternoon. We spoke with him about the journey we were making to the town of Tette, and stayed there as his guests. He gave the Cazembe of the road (guide) two quiapos of maize and two fowls, and told us we could continue our journey; that the way was open. Catara gave, as a present, five blue stones. Nothing more passed between us.

[14th.]—At two in the morning we started from the place of the potentate Muiro Aquito. Passed three streams, names unknown. During the journey we came to the place of a potentate named Luiama Cabanba, with the soubriquet "Sapue." We reached there at midday, and built on this side of and near a stream, of which they drink the water. He came to visit us, but brought nothing to entertain us with.

[15th.]—At five in the morning we started from the place of Sapue. Passed five streams, and during the march arrived at the potentate Luiama's own farm. Arrived there at midday. Spoke with him regarding the journey we were making to Tette. He answered it was well. We built near a river called Lucuetue, and halted to buy some provisions, and, by order of King Cazembe, to receive from him various runaway slaves who had escaped on the last journey of Catara's. He, however, did not deliver them, excusing himself by saying they were in the lands of others of his subordinate relations, who were a long way off.

[16th.]—We started from the farm of Luiama at eight in the morning, without rain. During the journey we came to the place of a black named Lupupa. We reached there at two in the afternoon; built our circle near a river called Rungo. We marched with the sun as before; met no one. We did nothing with him. We made only half a journey, because they wished us to give something to the said Lupupa. We gave a "caputem," and they went away.

[17th.]—At five in the morning we got up and started from the place of the black Lupupa. Passed no river, and during the journey we came to the farm of the said people, whose chief is called, after the country-fashion, Camango. We spoke with him, telling him we were going to Tette in the company of Gonçalo Caetano's black. To him we gave nothing. We arrived at this farm about nightfall; built close to it, and near a narrow river, whose name we do not know. Had no rain. Marched with the sun in our front.

[18th.]—At 6 o'clock A.M. we set out from the place of Camango. We forded a river named Lunbanzenge, with water up to our waists. During the march we came to the farm of a black named Cacomba, on this bank of the river which we crossed. We arrived at noon, and built near the said black's farm. We halted there, waiting for Catara, who was staying behind. We met no one.

[19th.]—Started at six in the morning from the farm of Mobengi. Crossed the river Hiabenge on foot. During the journey we arrived at (the place) of a black named Quiota, who came and paid us a visit at our lodging in his own interest, thinking we would give him something, named Luipata. We gave him nothing = Halt.* Started from the farm of Cazembe, which we left at 5 A.M. We crossed a stream, and came to the city of a potentate named Mobengi Acalama. We spoke with him about our going to Tette. We presented him a hundred small milk-stones and a bag of salt. We reached this place at noon, and when we had begun building he sent us a she-goat and two alqueires of maize. We halted there a day, awaiting Catara. We met no one.

[20th.]—From our lodging at Mobengi's place we started at 6 A.M.; crossed the river Heabengi on foot. During the journey we came to the place of a black named Luiota, who came to visit us in his own interest at our lodging, that we might give him something, named Luipata. We gave him nothing. At nightfall we reached this place, not having passed any one. We marched with the sun in our faces.

[21st.] We started out from the place of Luiota at two in the morning without rain. We crossed three streams, names unknown. During the march we reached the place of a black

---

* Evidently this is a march (No. 20), but for some reason, possibly a clerical error, it is not counted.

named Muazabanba, with whom we treated concerning our journey to Tette, that they called Nhunqua. The Cazembe of the road gave him a "bixo" (slave-boy); he gave as presents two "alqueires" of maize. We reached this place at four in the afternoon, having marched with the sun in our front, and having met no one.

[22nd.] At early dawn we left the farm of Muazabanba, without rain; crossed three streams, names unknown. During the journey we came to the place of the potentate named Capeco, the farm of that barbarian being some way off. We presented him with two bags of salt, which he took against his wish, wanting cloth. We reached said place at three in the afternoon, and built near a narrow river, name unknown. The sun in the same position on our march, during which we met no one.

[23rd.] At 6 A.M. we left the place of Capeco Calubunda, crossing two streams during the journey, and thence we left the lowlands we were travelling through, and went on ascending hills of rock. We came to a desert-lodging near a stream. We got there at four in the afternoon; marched with the sun in our front, and passed no one.

[24th.] Started at 7 A.M. from the desert-lodging, crossed two narrow rivers; one named Benzi, the other Macala. We came to the city of the people of a chief named Muceba; we spoke not with them of any gifts. We reached this place at four in the afternoon, built near a stream named Ca Meguigo; travelled with the sun in our front, and met no one.

[25th.] From the farm of the people of Muceba we started at early dawn, crossed two streams, and during the journey we came to the farm of Muceba's head-wife; she is not in the place, only her "sons" are. We spoke to them about our journey to Tette. They begged something for Luipata (a present). We replied we had not brought anything to give as Luipata; they did not cease to oppose us. We reached this place at four in the afternoon, built our circle near a river, name unknown, whose water they drink; we met no one.

[26th.] We left the head-wife's farm at six in the morning. We crossed a river named Huombia, and came to the place of a slave of the said Muceba, named Luinhiba do Cazembe. We arrived with him at midday, without rain. In this place Catara gave a bixo de Luipata (negro boy as gift) to the said

o

black that the present might be passed on to Muceba, lord
of the lands. We met with two blacks, people of Muceba's, and
saw nothing that caused us trouble.

[27th.] From the farm of Luinhiba we started at six in the
morning, crossed a river called Quibanga, and during our march
we came to the great farm of the said Muceba. We conversed
with him about our journey to Tette, and presented him with
a "Caputim;" while the Cazembe of the road gave him a black
woman. We reached this place at three in the afternoon, and
we built near the river, of which they drink the water, having
met no one.

[28th.] Started from the farm of the chief Muceba at 8 A.M.;
crossed a river called Luvira. We continued our march till
nightfall, and slept at a desert-lodging near a stream, name
unknown.

[29th.] Left the desert-lodging at daybreak; passed two
farms, called Calembe and Capelebanda. We came to another
farm of a black named Muaza Muranga, where we arrived at
Ave-Maria time; built near a river named Roanga the Little.
We treated of nothing with them. Marched with the sun in
our front, and met no one.

[30th.] At first cockcrow we arose and started from the
place of Muaza Muranga; crossed no river; and during
the march we came to the river Aruangoa, which we crossed on
foot—this river is said to be thirty fathoms wide. We arrived
at midday, and we occupied the houses already built by the
travellers from Tette. Having a little time to spare, we were
found in the same place by a number of blacks, loaded with
tobacco, going to the other side (of the river). We met no
one, and journeyed with the sun as before.

[31st.] At dawn we left the river Aruangoa, and marched
down in the same direction as the river. During the march
we came to the farm of a black named Capangara; had a good
deal of rain. Arrived in this place at four in the afternoon,
and built our circle near a narrow river called Rubinba. We
marched last with sun on our left, and met no one.

[32nd.] Started at 8 A.M. from Capangara's farm, crossed no
river. Came to the chief, named Muazabanba, spoke with
him about our journey to Tette; Cataro, the Cazembe of the
road, gave a "bixo;" we two chuabos of red serafina. We

reached this farm at midday without rain; built our circle near
the river called Matize, of which they drink the water; met
with no one, and travelled with the sun on our left side.

[33rd.]   From Muazabanba's place we started at five in the
morning; passed a narrow river called Lucingi, came to
the farm of some blacks, whom we do not know. Arrived at
three in the afternoon, having met no one; we marched with
the sun as before.

[34th.]   We left the farm of the before-mentioned blacks at
six in the morning, passed two small streams, whose names we
do not know, and reached the farm of a black named Quiceres
Quiamorilo.   We arrived here at two in the morning (afternoon ?), without rain; built near a running stream, name not
known, met some blacks loaded with tobacco; marched with
the sun as before.

[35th.]   From Quiceres Quiamorilo's farm we started at
6 A.M., crossed one river, and during the march came to the
farm of the village of Capelema, belonging to two blacks, one
named Capanga, the other Quicuta.   We said nothing to
them, and built near the river called Camba, not very wide,
of which they drink the water.   Marched with the sun as
before, and met no one.

[36th.]   Left the farm of Capangara at dawn.   Passed a river
we are ignorant of the name of, and during our march came to
the farm of a potentate, Capelemena, whom we did not find
there, he having gone to his houses.   We only found there his
head-wife and also his "sons."   They began directly asking for
"Luipata."   The Cazembe of the road gave a "bixo."   We
reached this farm at noon, and built near a narrow river named
Lucunzie.   Marched with sun on our left, and met no one.

[37th.]   Left the farm of Capelemena at eleven in the
morning, and came to the farm of the sister of the before
mentioned; we reached this place about nightfall.   We treated
of nothing with her.   We crossed no river, met no one, and built
near a small stream.

[38th.]   At 7 A.M. we got up, and started from the farm of
Capelemena's sister; we followed down the course of the river
Lucunzie, and during the march came to the town of a potentate
named Mocanda Caronga, and place of the black named
Quitanga Quiamuomba.   We reached this place at midday,
without rain, built near it, and met no one.

[39th.] At cockcrow we started from the farm of Quitanga, passed no river, and during our march came to another farm of the people of said Mocanda. We spoke with them about our journey to Tette, and gave them nothing. Arrived at three in the afternoon; marched with the sun as before. Met no one.

[40th.] At two in the morning we left Mocanda's people; crossed the great farm of the same Mocanda, and during the journey came to another of his people's farms, which we reached at four in the afternoon, without rain; travelled as before, and did not meet any one. We gave no presents to the said blacks.

[41st.] At 6 A.M. we got up and left the place above mentioned; crossed one river, name unknown. During the journey we came to the farm named Ponda. We reached it at seven in the evening, built near a narrow river named Luca; marched with the sun on our left, and met no one.

[42nd.] We started from the farm of Ponda, at seven in the morning. We passed one stream, name unknown. During our march we came to the farm of the people of the potentate Gurula, which we crossed. We reached there with drizzling rain at noon. Built near a stream, and met no one.

[43rd.] Started from the people of Gurula at five in the morning, crossed a river named Bue, and continuing our march we crossed three narrow rivers, and arrived at the city of a black named Luiangue. We got there at three in the afternoon, built during a good deal of rain, and near a river named Daramenca. Marched with the sun as before, and met no one.

[44th.] From the farm of Luiangue we got up and started at dawn; passed a hill named Inamirombe, boundary of the chief Mocanda Caronga's lands. We came to the farm of a black named Cairaire; we arrived there at two in the afternoon. We said nothing to any of them about our journey, and met no one.

[45th.] Left the farm of Cairaire at six o'clock in the morning; crossed a narrow river, and during the march we came to the farm named Capata. We reached there at four in the afternoon. The people gave us houses to lodge in, so that we had not to build our circle. Marched with the sun on our left, and met no one.

[46th.] At six in the morning we left the farm Capata,

without rain; crossed five narrow streams, names unknown; passed the old farm of Gonçalo Caetano; during our march came to another old deserted farm. We arrived at midday, with rain; built near a stream, name unknown; met no one, and saw nothing of rarity.

[17th.] At two in the morning we started from the old farm; crossed a river called "Quiamuombo" the Smaller. During the journey we came to a desert, and built near a stream, whose name we do not know. We reached this lodging at noon, without rain. Met four blacks loaded with maize. We marched with the sun as before.

[18th.] At two in the morning we started from our desert-lodging; crossed a river four fathoms wide, name unknown, and, coming to another desert at five in the afternoon, we built near a stream, the name unknown. We met no one.

[19th.] Started from our desert-lodging at six in the morning, crossed a river three fathoms wide, name not known. During the march came to the farm of a black, whose name we do not know. We arrived there at two in the afternoon; built in the rain, near the "Lovras" (probably "Lavras," or gold-washings) of the said black. We marched with the sun on our left, and saw nothing rare.

[50th.] We left the farm of the black above-mentioned at two in the morning. We crossed three narrow rivers, whose names we do not know. During the journey we came to the farm of two blacks, named Catetua and Catiza; we reached there at two in the afternoon, with rain. We marched with the sun as before. We met no one.

[51st.] At two in the morning we started from the farm of Catetua, crossed three rivers, each three fathoms wide. We came to the farm of Dona Francisca, named Moxinga. We reached there at three in the afternoon, without rain, and lodged in the houses of the said blacks. We marched as before, and met no one.

[52nd.] From Moxinga we started at 6 A.M. without rain; crossed a river on foot, which had water up to our breasts; we do not know the name of it. During the march we reached the farm of some blacks, whose names we are ignorant of. We arrived there at midday, having met with no one; we lodged in the houses of the farm.

[53rd.] At six o'clock in the morning we left the farm of the blacks. We crossed a river, whose name we do not know, and came to the farm of Gonçalo Caetano, named Musoro-anhata. We did not find him there; only the father-in-law of the same Gonçalo, by name Pascoal Domingos, who ordered us to occupy the houses of the slaves of the above-named. We reached this place at two in the afternoon without rain; we met with no one.

[54th.] Started from Musoro-anhata at eleven in the morning; crossed two small streams, whose names we do not know. During the march we came to the farm of Manoel Caetano, whom we found at home; he gave us shelter. We reached there at three in the afternoon with rain; we met no one.

[55th.] At two in the morning we set out from Manoel Caetano's place, crossed two streams, and came to the farm of the said Gonçalo Caetano Pereira. We arrived at noon; met some blacks sent by him. We occupied the houses of his Caffres by his order. We stayed in this place twenty days to rest ourselves; marched with the sun as before.

[56th.] At dawn we started from Gonçalo Caetano Pereira's farm; crossed a narrow river, name unknown. During the march we came to the farm of a soldier named Macoco. We reached there at four in the afternoon; met a great many people.

[57th.] Left the farm of the soldier Macoco, at seven in the morning. We crossed no river. During the journey we came near the river Zambeze; we crossed it in a canoe to this town, which we reached on Saturday, the 2nd of February, 1811.

[No. 2.]

On summoning to my residential quarters the two men, discoverers of the road from Angola to this town, I put the following questions to them:—

I asked their names. One answered, his name was Pedro João Batista, and his comrade's Anastacio Francisco. Asked them whence they came, and by whose orders. They replied, they came from the interior of Angola, by order of His Excellency D. Fernando de Noronha, Captain-General of

Angola, who charged their master, Lieutenant-Colonel Francisco
Honorato da Costa, Commander of the Fair of Casanje, to send
them on a discovery, from that Western Capital to the Eastern
Coast, from which master they brought a letter for the Governor
of these Rivers.

On being asked when they set out from the inner regions of
Angola, they replied, they left the plantation named the Fair of
Casanje at the end of November 1802; but that on the
eighth day of the journey they met with resistance, not being
allowed to pass beyond the farm of the chief Bonba, where
they stayed till the year 1805, without being able to go
either forward or back, to advise their master at their starting-
place, that he might send them some goods, so that the chief
would allow them to pass freely. However, as soon as they
were able to give such information to their master, he assisted
them with goods, to allow of their passing; and that, pursuing
their journey, they made a digression and went into the
territory of another chief, named Moxico, which digression cost
twenty days. That in the said farm, people wished to make war
against them, and seize the goods they had with them, because,
previously to their arrival, a merchant of the same fair had
gone to this farm, and had taken, on credit, a certain number of
slaves, a certain quantity of wax, and some ivory, and had not
yet paid the said chief. However, they state that they contented him with a quantity of cloths, and he allowed them
to leave freely. Continuing their journey thence they went
to the farm of Catende, a petty king, now subject to the
Grand Moropo, in which eight days were occupied from the
previous farm; and going on from this they went to the farm of
Chaonbuje, distant from the preceding three days; thence
they proceeded to the town of Luibaica, distant four days
from the last; and thence they went to another farm, named
Banga - Banga, in which they occupied two days; thence
they went to the farm of the Moropo's mother, named Locon-
queixa, in which journey they spent two days; thence they
went on to the capital of the Grand Moropo, and it is from this
place that they began to keep the route-journal, which they
delivered to me, up to this town of Totte.

On asking them if, in this digression, since they had started
from the inner regions of Angola to their arrival at Moropo's,
they had found provisions and water on the road, they answered
that they had found everything, and had paid for such things
with their goods.

On asking them if, since setting out from Moxico's farm to
Moropo, as also from this to Cazembe, and afterwards to this
town, they had encountered any marauders, who had attempted

to rob them of the goods they were carrying, they answered no, that on the contrary, they had met with much liberality in many forms.

On asking them when they had arrived at Cazembe, and for what reason they did not continue their journey to this city, they answered that they arrived there in the year 1806, and that having no resources whatever to bring them on to this town, because of King Cazembe's being at war with the King of the Muizes, a country through which they would have to pass, they remained in Cazembe till the end of the year 1810, when they then came on to this town.

On asking them with what amount of hospitality the King of Cazembe had treated them, they replied, that during the whole of the four years he had supplied them with all they needed, both food and clothing, so that all the time they wanted for nothing.

On asking them if they wished voluntarily to return by the same route, or whether they would prefer going by sea, as I could send them to Mozambique, so that they might inform their master of their proceedings, they answered that they wished to go back by the same route, as they were desirous of making a more complete and circumstantial route journal than the one they had presented to me ; but that to enable them to do this, I should have to provide them with goods from His Royal Highness, to maintain them on their journeys, to provide and pay the chiefs for safe-conducts, whom they would have to pass, and also to purchase some slaves to accompany them on the route, and carry them should either of them fall ill on the road.

[No. 3.]   (Copy.)

Illustrious Sir,—The Most Serene Prince Regent, our Lord, strongly urged upon the Most Illustrious and Excellent Dom Fernando Antonio de Noronha, Actual Governor and Captain-General of this State and Kingdom of Angola, on which this Fair of Casanje is dependent, the exploration and opening up of the Eastern with this Western Coast. His Excellency also ordered me to penetrate, if I could, as far as the Cazembe, where it is known that the illustrious Lacerda, worthy predecessor of your Excellency, had died ; and suggested I should write and communicate to your Excellency this most important object, so interesting to the whole nation, and so much desired by His Royal Highness, to whom all his faithful subjects are, with the greatest consideration, so ambitious to render services, and to unite in working together for the glory of such an excellent Sovereign.

The importance of this communication led me to send all my slaves on so serious an enterprise, though I was obliged to be without them so far away in the interior, and distant from the capital of Angola. This will be delivered to your Excellency by my said slaves. I have striven in this matter since 1797 to obtain from Sucilo Bamba, Cambambi, Camaçaca, and Mujumbo Acalunga, potentate and ruler of all Songo, a passage into the interior, to negotiate with all in general, and with the potentate Jaga Caçanje, ruler of the lands in which this fair is situated. And for this reason, I turned to discover the means of communicating with your Excellency through the above-named potentate, Ruler of all the Songo, concerning the expenses it was indispensable for me to incur with him; although I dissembled with him as to the principal purport of this business, by explaining to him the grief in which I was living, through my ignorance as to the existence of one of my brothers, who having taken a different route at sea, it was reported had travelled by land to Senna, and thence had gone to Cazembe, where he died. That I was in doubt as to whether such was the case or not; that if it was as stated, it would at once remove all anxiety, and I should, after lamenting his loss, proceed to console myself for it, as is necessary in this life; and should then go on to inquire what had become of his property, and who had succeeded him in his rights. In this way, I succeeded in obtaining from him a passage through his dominions, and sent my slaves, accompanied by his own vassals, to a country named Louvar, in which the potentate Luinhame governs. *He informed*, I say, that he was corresponded with and amicably treated, and informed me that he had just sent to ask for a daughter as his wife, to unite more closely the bonds of amity with those of relationship. He offered to send and ask that friend (now father-in-law, said to be to the west of the river Luambeje, which I believe runs to the eastern coast, but am not certain of yet, and who is a relation of Cazembe's, and owes, they say, allegiance to Cazembe) to have my messengers passed safely and peacefully by his people, that they may reach Cazembe. I write to the latter, requesting him to let these men come on to your Honour with my letter, by means of which I expect to obtain an exact knowledge of my said brother's fate, and who has succeeded to his rights according to the means that appeared best to me to adopt. Persons who have been sent to that capital to get information, recom-

mend that these inquiries should be conducted with all care and
the greatest possible secrecy, so that the prejudices which the
blacks entertain against the whites may not be disturbed; they
imagine that the latter never do anything except for their own
profit, and to their (the blacks') prejudice, that the whites have no
sincerity, and only turn their actions to their own advantage
against them. Another great reason for the strife and jealousy
existing among the black nations is, that the whites endeavour to
profit by their superiority of situation and power, to subject to
them other nations inferior in force and position. They are
jealous lest the blacks should enjoy the same privileges, and thus
be able to remove the yoke in which they are bound. They supply
them, themselves, with some few things that they think necessary, adding whatever they think proper to their cost; prevent-
ing the others obtaining the same articles first hand from whence
they obtain them, and which they have thus the power of
supplying them with.

You will kindly credit the profound respect I entertain for
you, and honour me with your, to me, much esteemed corre-
spondence, to effect the long-coveted discovery, in pursuance of
the Royal orders given to the Most Illustrious Governor and
Captain-General of Angola, at whose suggestion and recommendation I decided to try and obtain those of your Honour
for the same end.

With all consideration, I most cordially kiss your Honour's
hands, whom God keep many happy years. Fair of Casanje em
Carmo de Quiriquibe, 11th November, 1804. The Most Illustrious Governor of Senna and Tette. Your most obedient
and respectful servant, (Signed) FRANCISCO HONORATO DA
COSTA, *Director of the Fair of Casanje.*

(B.)

MOST ILLUSTRIOUS AND EXCELLENT SIR,—I have the satisfaction of laying before your Excellency the letter from the
Governor of the Rivers of Senna, which came by land, in
consequence of the discovery of a communication between
the two coasts of Eastern and Western Africa, with copies
of the letter addressed to me by Lieutenant-Colonel Francisco
Honorato da Costa, Director of the Fair of Mucary, to whose
fatigues and exertions this discovery is due, and the diaries
of the journeys and other intelligence bearing on the same
subject. The Pombeiro slaves belonging to the above-men-

tioned director, named Pedro João Baptista and Amaro
Jozé, are embarked on board the frigate "Prince Dom Pedro,"
to be delivered to the Secretariat of State, so that they may
personally give any other information to your Excellency.
The above-said Lieutenant-Colonel, through my intervention,
prays that His Royal Highness will remunerate him for his
services to the extent that he deserves.   God keep your
Excellency.   St. Paul's of the Assumption of Loanda, 25th
January, 1815 = The Most Illustrious and Excellent Antonio
de Araujo de Azevedo = (Signed) JOSÉ DE OLIVEIRA BARBOSA
(*Captain-General of Angola*).

[No. 1.]

This is another copy of the letter of F. H. da Costa, tran-
scribed in Part A, No. 6, page 206, and translated in pp. 198–
202 of this Appendix.

[No. 2.] *

One thousand eight hundred and six.—In the name of God,
Amen.—Route Journal, which I, Pedro João Baptista, make on
my journey from Muatahianvo to King Cazembe Caquinhata.—
1st day of the march and lodging, whence we started from
the great farm of the said Muatahianvo, from his son's house,
named, after the land fashion, Capenda Hianva, where we were
lodging, or according to his post, Soana Mulopo of the Muatahianvo, from which we set out at six o'clock in the morning.
We crossed two rivers, one named Igiba, of four fathoms' width,
the other Luiza, both of which run into the river Luluá; during
the journey we arrived at the place of the guide whom the said
potentate Muatahianvo had given us to the Cazembe, named, after
the country style, Cutaguaseje.   We reached this place at dusk.
Met a number of people, who were going to the Banza (abode)
of the Muatahianvo, carrying to their masters provisions of dry
manioc flour, called "Bobó."   Marched with the sun in our
rear, and saw nothing unusual.

[2nd.]   Lodging of Cutaguaseje.   Set out at seven in
the morning.   Passed three narrow running streams, whose
names I do not know, which run into the river Luiza.   Con-

---

* This is the same Diary, with trifling variations, printed in pp. 169–188.—
R. F. B.

tinuing the journey, we again crossed the said river Luiza, and arrived at the place of the black named Caquiza Muexi, a slave of the Muatahianvo, near a river, the water of which they drink. He ordered us to lodge in the houses of the owner of the farm. We arrived at midday, without rain, and met with no one.

[3rd.] Lodging place of Caquiza Muexi. We started at two o'clock in the morning. Crossed five streams, whose names I do not know. During the march came to the farm of the Quilolo of Muatahianvo, named Muene Canenda. We reached this place at four in the afternoon, and built near the river Isabuigi, of which they drink the water. Marched with the sun on our left. We stayed here three days, the guide's female slave being ill. Saw no great variety of birds or animals.

[4th.] Lodging of the farm of the Quilolo Muene Canenda. Started at dawn, without rain. Crossed four streams, whose names I do not know. Continuing our journey, we crossed a river named Mué-me, and came to the end of the desert, on the other side and near the river Canaia, which runs into the river Mué-me: here we found the houses built by the travellers of the country, named Canonguessa, who were going to pay tribute to Muatahianvo. We reached there at three in the afternoon, having marched with the sun as before. Met some people who had gone to buy salt in the Salina, called "da Quigila."

[5th.] Desert-lodging, whence we started at five in the morning. Passed three narrow rivers, which were rough in crossing. Came to another desert, near the narrow river called Quipungo, the farm of some blacks, whose names we do not know, slaves of Muatahianvo, being a little way off. We reached this lodging at midday, without rain. Met no one, and had no dealings with those in the farm. We saw no rarity, and to procure provisions we halted here two days.

[6th.] Desert-lodging, whence we started at cockcrow. Crossed ten (three?) narrow rivers, which run into the river named Calalema, which rivers we do not know the names of, and came to another desert-lodging of thick bushes, staked all round, near the said river Calalema, which is about twelve (ten?) fathoms across. We reached this place about two in the afternoon, with a little rain. Met no one, and marched with the sun as before.

[7th.] Desert-lodging. Started from the same at cockcrow. Crossed eleven narrow rivers, names unknown, and followed up the course of the river Calalema. During the journey, we came to a desert-lodging near a stream named Camussanga Gila, on the other side of which we came to the said lodging at nightfall, and had not time to build our huts to sleep in. Met no one, and saw nothing unusual.

[8th.] Desert-lodging, near the river Camussanga Gila. Started thence at five in the morning, crossed six running streams, and, during the journey, came to the farm of a black slave of Muatahianvo, named Muene Cassa, near and on the other side of a stream, the name of which I do not know, the farm above-mentioned being situated a long way off from our lodging. We reached here at three in the afternoon. Met no one. Marched with the sun on our left side, built near the said place, and had no dealings with those in the farm.

[9th.] Lodging of the farm of Muene Cassa. Started from this place at dawn, crossed nine small rivers, and, during the march, came to a desert-lodging, still near the river Calalema; reached this river at four in the afternoon. Met no one. Marched with the sun, as before, and saw no beasts.

[10th.] Desert-lodging. Started from this place at seven in the morning. Crossed three running rivers by bridges. Came to another desert, near a small river, name unknown. We reached there at midday, and built near the same river. Some of Soana Mulopo's people came along in our rear, sent by him to buy salt. Met no one, and marched with the sun as before.

[11th.] Desert-lodging. Started from it at five in the morning. Crossed on foot a running river, named Roando, two fathoms wide, which flows into the river Lulúa. During the march we came to another narrow river called Rova, and arrived at the end of our march near the said Rova, which is about thirteen fathoms wide, and also runs into the river Lulúa, the farm of a black named Tumo (Fumo?) Ahilanbe, of Muatahianvo, being a long way off. We arrived at midday, without rain, and built near the said river. Marched with the sun on our left. Met no one, and saw no beasts.

[12th.] Desert-lodging. Started at early dawn. Crossed six narrow streams, which run into the river Rova. During the march we came to the desert-lodging, on the other side and near the river called Cazalle, which is about twenty fathoms in width, with water to our waists; it runs into the

Lulúa. We reached this river at dusk. Met several people loaded with fish, which they were going to sell at the Banza of the Muatahianvo. Marched with the sun on the left. Saw nothing new.

[13th.] Desert-lodging above named. Set out at six in the morning. Crossed no river, and, continuing our march, came to the place of Quilolo of the Muatahianvo, named after the country Capoco Bumba Ajala. We spoke to him about our journey, which we were making, by order of his Muatahianvo, to the country of the Cazembe Caquinhata; he answered it was well, and ordered us to lodge in his "sona'" houses; he gave us as guests four moitetos of flour and a mutete of fish. We reached this farm at four in the afternoon, near a narrow stream or river named Mucuza. Met no one, and marched with the sun as before.

[14th.] Lodging at the farm of the Quilolo Capoco, from which we started at two in the morning. Passed a dry stream, and, continuing our journey, crossed the river Caginrige by canoe, the boatmen of the Quilolo Muene Mene, who was lord of the port, having put us on the other side of it; this said river is about fourteen fathoms wide, and runs into the river Lulúa. We arrived at the farm of Mene, the said Quilolo of Muatahianvo, and treated with him regarding our journey to Cazembe by order of the said Muatahianvo: he answered nothing, and only said that the way was open. We made our circle there, far off from the farm, and paid the boatmen two beirames of Zuarte (Indian cloth), and gave the owner a small looking-glass with gilt papered edges, and fifty beads of roncalha. We reached this at three in the afternoon. Met no one, and marched with the sun as before.

[15th.] Lodging at the place of Muene Mene. Started at the first cockcrow. Crossed four narrow rivers running into the said river Caginrigi, and came to the farm of the black known as the owner, and named by our guide Soana Ganga; spoke with him regarding the journey we are making to Cazembe. We arrived at two in the afternoon. Met no one, saw nothing uncommon, and marched with the sun on our left.

[16th.] Lodging of the farm of Soana Ganga. Started at seven in the morning. Crossed two narrow rivers running into said river Caginrigi; came to the farm of Muatahianvo's mother, Luconquessa; found there his Quilolo, named, after the country-fashion, Muene Camatanga. We spoke with him about our journey, that we were going to Cazembe Caquinbata by order of the Muatahianvo; he replied, that people going from Angola to Cazembe was very gratifying; we gave him a beirame of linen and ten tile-colored beads, besides fifty small blue stones for his "quipata," which is a gift to the lord of the land. We reached this city at midday, without rain. Met a good many people going to buy salt. Marched with the sun as before.

[17th.] Lodging at the farm of Muene Camatanga, from which we started at six in the morning, crossed three streams, which run into the river Caginrigi. During the march we arrived at the farm of the Quilolo of said Camatanga, named Muene Cassamba, whither Camatanga had directed us to go, in order to obtain provisions for our desert march, by order of Muatahianvo. With collecting these provisions we were detained fifteen days. Met no one, and saw nothing unusual.

[18th.] Lodging at Muene Cassamba's farm. Started from this place at two in the morning, again crossed the river Caginrigi. During the march crossed another river running into the same Caginrigi. We came to the desert-lodging near another narrow river, the name unknown. We reached said lodging at midday; built our huts during rain. Met no one, and marched with sun on our left, and no beasts.

[19th.] Desert lodging. Started from it at half-past 6 A.M. passed a narrow river with stony bed, and came to another desert called Canpueje, near a running stream, where we found houses, built by the Alundas travellers. Arrived there at two in the afternoon; saw nothing uncommon.

[20th = 21st of former Journal, p. 174.] Desert-lodging, Canpueje. Started hence at cockcrow, crossed a narrow river named Maconde. During the journey came to another desert-lodging called Lunsaja, the "libatas" (settlements, villages) of the Quilolo Anibulete Quissosa, of the Muatahianvo, being a short way off. Did not speak with him about our journey. Reached this at four in the afternoon, and built near a narrow running river, name unknown. Marched with the sun on our left, and met no one.

'[21st.] Lodging of the desert, Lunsaja, from which we started at five in the morning, passed no river, and during the march came to the farm of the son of Cuta Ganda, near a river

called Reu. We spoke with him about our journey to
Cazembe. We reached the said city at three in the afternoon.
Met no one, marched with the sun as before, and saw no
beasts.

[22nd.] Lodging at the farm of the son of Cutaganda. Got
up at seven in the morning, crossed the river Reu on foot; it
is about twenty fathoms wide. We came to the desert-lodging
near a small stream, name unknown. We reached said stream
at two in the afternoon. Met no one. Marched with the sun
on our left side.

[23rd.] Desert-lodging. Started from it at six in the
morning, crossed three narrow streams, which run into said
river Reu, came to another desert near a river named Quibenla,
which also runs into the river Reu, the "libatas" of the Quilolo
Munconcota being very distant. Reached there at three in the
afternoon, and saw nothing unusual.

[24th.] Desert-lodging near the river Quibenla. Started at
five in the morning, crossed four narrow rivers which run into
said river Quibenla. During the march came to another
desert-lodging, named Capaca Melemo, close by a running
stream. Reached this at midday, without rain. Marched with
the sun as before. Met no one.

[25th.] Desert-lodging, Capaca Melemo. Left at six in
the morning, crossed four narrow rivers. During the march
came to and crossed a river named Ropoege, which is about
thirty fathoms wide, and runs into the river Lubilage. We
came to the desert-lodging close by the other side of said river.
We reached this at three in the afternoon, without rain, marched
with the sun on our left, saw no birds nor beasts worth
noting.

[26th.] Desert-lodging. Started at seven in the morning,
crossed two streams running into the river Ropoege, and continuing our march came to the desert-lodging called Cassaco,
near and on the other side of a running stream. Reached there
at midday, having met no one, and marched with the sun as
before.

[27th.] Desert-lodging, Cassaco. Started at cockcrow, crossed
a camping-place near a flowing river, very narrow, named
Quipaca Amgnangua, and during the journey came to another

desert-lodging, close by the river Ropelo, four fathoms wide, running into the river Lububury. Reached this at three in the afternoon. Marched with the sun on our left; met no one. Saw only some wild boars, who were feeding on this side of the said river.

[28th.] Desert-lodging near the river Ropelo, from which we started at first cockcrow, passed no river, and continuing our journey we came to the desert-lodging near the narrow river called White River, it having white sands, which runs into the river Lububury. We reached said lodging at midday, built our barracks near the other side of the said river. Met no one. Marched with the sun as before; saw neither birds nor boasts.

[29th.] Lodging near the White River. Started at seven in the morning, crossed no river. During the journey came to the desert-lodging near the river Lububury, which we did not cross. Reached this place at two in the afternoon. Marched with the sun on our left; built our huts on this side, and near the said river. A number of people going to buy salt in company with us. Met no one; saw nothing unusual.

[30th = 32nd in former diary, p. 176.] Desert-lodging near the river Lububury. Started at 6 A.M., passed no river, came to the river Lububury, which we crossed on foot, and which had water to our waists. It is about forty fathoms in width, and has a stony bed. We met with people and slaves there of the Quilolo of the Muntahianvo and Cazembe, named, after the land fashion, Chamuginga Mucenda. Reached said farm at two in the afternoon. Did not speak with them, and built our huts near and the other side of the said river, a long way from the farm. Met no one; saw neither birds nor reptiles; marched with the sun as before.

[31st.] Lodging of the Cio (Citio, a farm?), near the river Lububury. Started therefrom at seven in the morning, crossed no river. During the march came to the "libata" of said Quilolo Chamuginga Mucenda. Spoke with him regarding our journey; that we were going to Cazembe Caquinbata, by order of the Muntahianvo. He answered that the Cazembe was well. We reached this place at midday. He presented us as his guests with a Sunga of Aló and eight moitetes of (manioc) flour —four for us and four for our guide—also a small she-goat. We built some distance from the farm, close by the narrow river named Camonguigi, but on the other side of it. Met no one; marched with the sun as before; saw neither birds nor beasts.

P

[32nd.] Lodging of the farm of Chamuginga Mucanda. Started therefrom at six in the morning, passed two halting-places but no river, and continuing our march came to the lodging named Mussula Apompo; reached this at two in the afternoon, built our huts to the east of the said river. Marched with the sun on our left side; saw nothing uncommon. Met no one.

[33rd.] Desert-lodging Mussula Apompo. Started at six in the morning; passed a narrow stream, named Son of the River Lufula, and continuing our journey we came to the same river Lufula, which we crossed, with the water to our waists. It is more or less fifteen fathoms wide, and runs into the river Lualaba. We reached there at midday, having marched with the sun on our left. Met no one, and built on the other side of and near the said river.

[34th.] Lodging of the desert near the river Lufula. Started at five in the morning, crossed a narrow river, whose name I do not know, and came to another desert resting-place, near a large river-plain named Quibonda, with a small stream on this side of it. Here we saw some black huntsmen, with the wild cattle they had killed with arrows; they were going by the same route to the Salina, to buy salt. They did not inform us whence they came. Reached said lodging at two in the afternoon, without rain. Marched with the sun as before, and saw nothing rare.

[35th.] Desert-lodging near the Quibonda, which occupied us till midday in crossing. Having started at the first cock-crow, crossed a stream, and during the march came to a lodging on a hill called Jupume (Inpume?), near a narrow river named Camoa, of two fathoms in width, which runs into the river Lualaba. We reached this place at three in the afternoon, built our huts on the side of said hill at the top, without rain. Met no one; marched with the sun on our left side.

[36th.] Desert resting-place near the river Camoa, from which we started at five in the morning; crossed no river, and during the march came to the desert-lodging near the small stream named Catonta, the lodging being called Mucary Agoin. We are now in the Cazembe's dominions. We reached here at noon; marched this journey with the sun in our front. Met some blacks, who were coming to the salt districts; saw no birds nor animals of any rarity.

[37th.] Desert-lodging in the halting-place named Mucari

Agoia, from which we started at six in the morning; crossed a narrow running stream, and, continuing our march, came to the desert-lodging near the river, of small width, named Huita Amalote, which runs into the Lualaba. We found, some distance from the halting-place, some huts of the Quilolo of the Cazembe, named Muire, lord of the copper-mines. It is in this farm they make the bara. We reached said halting-place at two in the afternoon; spoke with them regarding our journey, that we were going to the King Cazembe, being sent by the Muatahianvo. He answered that the King Cazembe was well, and also his uncle Quiburi, lord of the Salina. He presented us with nothing. Marched with the sun in our front; met no one, and saw no birds nor beasts.

[38th.] Halting-place of the Quilolo of the Cazembe, Muire, from which we started at six in the morning; crossed a narrow river named Mulonga Amcula, which runs into the river Lualaba. On leaving the said farm Muire asked us for a present. We gave him twenty small white bugles (missanga de Canudo), with which he was contented, saying he could not press us for more as he had given us nothing. Continuing our march we came to the desert-lodging named Quiana Acananga, near a running stream, son or tributary to the said river Mulauga (Mulonga?) Amcula. Reached said lodging at two in the afternoon, without rain. Marched with the sun as before. Met several people coming from the salt district, going to Muatahianvo. Saw nothing new.

[39th.] Desert-lodging, Quiana Acananga. Set out from this at two in the morning; crossed no river, and during the march we came to another desert-lodging named Mabobela, near a very small stream. Reached this at four in the afternoon; built near the same streamlet. Marched with the sun as before. Met no people, and saw many zebras, who were pasturing on the plain.

[40th.] Desert-lodging of Mabobela. Started at cockcrow. Crossed no river. During the journey came to the place of a black named Buibui, chief "Mauta" of the Salina (salt district) Quigila; we arrived there at two in the afternoon; spoke with the people of the farm about our journey to King Cazembe Cuquinhata. They answered, it was very fortunate to see white people, whom they call Muzungoe, coming from Angola. We lodged in their houses. Marched with the sun in our front. Saw many birds named Hundas, a sort of duck.

[41st.] Lodging at the farm of the Quilolo Buibui, we

started therefrom at six o'clock in the morning; continuing our journey, we came to and crossed the river Lualaba by canoe; this river is about forty fathoms wide. We arrived at the great farm of the Quiburi, uncle of Cazembe, lord of the salt district (Salina) Quegila; he received us with great pleasure and consideration, lodging us in the houses of his Quilolos. We gave to Quiburi a present of blue "roncalha" and two beirames of ash-coloured beads; at the port we gave fifty beads of same blue "roncalha." We reached this place at four in the afternoon. Met several of Quiburi's people going to fish in the above river. Saw a great number of wild cattle and small game. He gave us as his guests a leg of wild bull, two quixinges of dough or paste, two sangas of Aló de Lucu, called Caxai; he informed us that there was in Cazembe a white man intending to go to Angola, with letters from the Governor of Tette, who had died in Cazembe.

(42nd.) Lodging at the farm of Quiburi of the Cazembe; left therefrom at three in the afternoon. Passed no river. We marched down the course of the Lualaba; during the march we came to the desert-lodging, its name not known, near a stream called Chafim, which runs into the Lualaba. We reached this place at midday, without rain. Marched with the sun in our front. Built on the other side, near the said river. Saw a great many animals,—zebras, wild-cattle, muquetes, &c.

[43rd.] Desert-lodging near the river Chafim. Set out from this place at five in the morning, and crossed no river. During the journey we came to another desert-lodging, near a stream named Bacassacala; reached this lodging at two in the afternoon, without rain. Built on the east of the same stream. Marched with the sun as before; met nothing.

[44th.] Desert-lodging, Bacassacala. Left this at six in morning. Crossed no river. During the march we came to another desert-lodging near a narrow stream, the name of it not known. Arrived there at noon, without rain. Marched with the sun as before in our front. Built on the other side of, and near said stream. Met no one; saw nothing rare.

[45th.] Desert-lodging. Started therefrom at six in the morning. Crossed a narrow stream. Continuing our march, we reached the top of a hill, the huts of the slaves of Quiburi being seen in the distance. Reached this lodging at two in the afternoon, with the sun as before. Built on the other side of the said stream, without rain. Met no one; saw no animals.

[46th.] Desert-lodging on the top of the hill. Left this place at five in the morning. Crossed three narrow streams, names not known. During the march we came to the place of the Quilolo of the Quiburi, named after the country Camungo. We did not find him in the farm, but only his "sons," he having gone to the chase; his "sons" made us lodge in their houses, under the countenance of the guide the said Quiburi had sent with us, and who came in the Cazembe's interest. We arrived in this place at noon, without rain. Marched with the sun in our front. Met two of Quiburi's blacks, loaded with provisions of millet and haricot beans for seed for the said Quiburi. Saw no birds nor animals of any novelty.

[47th.] Lodging at the farm of Camungo. Set out at seven in the morning. Crossed a narrow stream, name not known. Continuing our march we came to the desert-lodging, and when we began building rain fell; built close to the other side of a narrow river, name not known. We came to this desert-lodging at two in the afternoon. Marched with the sun as before in our front. At midnight two lions coming near the camp on the other side of the river roared through all the most blessed night, causing us to lose our rest; but with God's help, no harm came to us. Met no one, and saw nothing new.

[48th.] Desert-lodging, from which we started at cockcrow. Crossed three small rivers, names not known to me. During the journey came to the lodging of the ambassador of the Cazembe, who was going to take the Mulambo to the Muata-hianvo. We did not see him, as he took a different route. We put up at the lodgings of the said ambassador, named Cabuitu Capinda; the huts of the Quilolo of the Cazembe, named, after the land-fashion, Ampala, being distant half a league, and near the river Ameula (Ancula?) four fathoms wide, at the other side of which we arrived at 2 P.M. without rain. We marched with the sun in our front. Met with seven blacks, dealers in salt, who were going to buy provisions in the said Ampala's place. Saw eight animals named muquetes, who passed us one by one on the road. Saw no birds of any kind.

[49th.] Lodging at the ambassador's, Cabuita Capenda, and lands of the Quilolo Ampala, from which we started at six in the morning. Followed up the river Ameula (Ancula?). Crossed a narrow stream on foot. During the march came to another lodging of the said ambassador in the desert, on this side and near the river Ameula. We occupied said lodgings.

Reached there at noon without rain. Marched with the sun as before. Met no one, and saw nothing now.

[50th.] Desert-lodging, near the river Ameula. Started at six in the morning. Crossed two narrow streams, and during the march came to the farm of the son of the Quilolo named Pande, the same called, after the land-fashion, Muana Auta. We did not speak with him, he having gone to his father's " Banza." We occupied the old huts of the blacks, the Senzalas (negro quarters) being a short distance off, near this side of the river called Rilomba. We reached this place at noon without rain. Marched with the sun as before, and met no one. It being three o'clock in the afternoon, I went out hunting, and shot a deer. The guide's slaves, who came with him from the farm of the Quiburi, found a wild bull which a lion had killed, and had only eaten a part of the inside and the rump. Saw nothing else worthy of note.

[51st.] Lodging of the farm of Muana Auta. Left this place at five in the morning. Crossed the small river Quimana, and during the march came to the Banza of said Quilolo Pande, whom we did not see on the day of our arrival: he only sent a message to our guide, Cutaguaseje, saying he was occupied with Cazembe's messengers, and that when he was more quiet we should see him. We arrived at said Banza at two in the afternoon, and built near a narrow river called Murucuaxi, but on the other side of it. Marched with the sun as before, and met no one.

[52nd.] Lodging at the farm of the Quilolo Pande. Started at six in the morning without rain. Crossed two narrow streams. During the journey we came to the place of his Ngolla Dolle, named Cahiombo Camara, with whom we did not speak on the day we arrived. Only two blacks came to see us, but we treated of nothing with them : the huts were some distance off. We arrived at this place at two in the afternoon, and lodged in the lodgings of Cazembe's ambassador, Cabuita. Marched with the sun in our front. Met no one. .

[53rd — 56th in the former diary, p. 182.] Lodging at the farm of Cahiombo Camara. Started from hence at cockcrow. Crossed the river, near which we passed the night. During the march we came to the desert-lodging named Quidaxi, on this side of and near a river, whose name I do not know. We reached this lodging at midday, and while commencing to

build, rain fell. Marched with the sun in our front; crossed a
river-plain, and saw a very large herd of zebras. Met no one.

[54th.] Resting-place of Quidaxi. Started at 6 A.M.
Crossed a narrow muddy river, and, continuing our march,
came to the old farm of the Quilolo of Luceongi, without rain;
built near a narrow stream, name not known. Reached this
place at two in the afternoon. Marched with the sun as before.
Met no one; saw no birds nor beasts of any kind.

[55th.] Desert-lodging of the old farm of Luceongi, from
which we started at seven in the morning without rain. Crossed
no river, and during the march came to the new farm of
Luneongi, on the other side of the river Luviri, which we
crossed by canoe; this river is about twelve fathoms wide, and
runs into the river Luapula. We lodged in the huts of the
"Senzalas" (negro quarters). We reached this place at four
in the afternoon. We spoke with the owner of the said huts
about our intention of going on to King Cazembe, by order
of the Muatohianvo: the said Luneongi replied that it was
very good. Marched with the sun as before; met no one.

[56th.] Lodging at the farm of Luneongi. Started at six
in the morning. Crossed two rivers, their names unknown
to me, which run into the river Luviri. During our journey
we came to the desert-lodging near said Luviri, having followed
down its course. Reached said desert at three in the afternoon.
Built in the rain. Marched with sun in our front. Met no one,
saw neither bird nor animal of any kind.

[57th.] Desert-lodging. Started from this place at cockcrow, without rain. Crossed no river, and, continuing our
march, came to the farm of the Macota of the Quilolo Muaxi.
Spoke with him about the journey we were making to Cazembe.
We reached this place at three in the afternoon. Built near
and on the other side the river Mufumbe. Met no one; saw
nothing new.

[58th.] Lodging at the place of the Macota of Muaxi.
Started at six in the morning. Crossed no river, and came
to the farm of the said Quilolo Muaxi; talked with him about
our journey: he replied, that King Cazembe already knew of
our coming. Reached this farm at noon, without rain. We
lodged in the houses of his people, the Banza of said Muaxi
being a little distance off. Marched with the sun in our front.
Met no one, and saw neither bird nor animal of rarity.

[59th.] Lodging at the farm of the Quilolo Muaxi, left at five in the morning; crossed a narrow stream, name unknown. During the march we came to the desert-lodging near a small river with stony bed. Reached this desert at noon. Marched with the sun as before. Built on the other side near the said river. Met three blacks going to the farm of Muaxi to buy salt. Saw nothing new.

[60th.] Desert-lodging. Left this at cockcrow; crossed five narrow streams. We are approaching the great hill named Cundo Irungo. During the march we crossed the river named Cavula Cungo, which is about seven fathoms wide, with water up to our waists. It runs into the river Luapula. Reached said desert-lodging at noon, without rain. Built near and on the other side of the river before named. Met some people coming from Cazembe, going to the farm of the Muaxi; they gave us no news. Marched with the sun as before.

[61st.] Desert-lodging near the river Cavula Cungo. Started therefrom at six in the morning; passed no river, marched in the direction of the same hill, Cundo Irungo. Continuing our march we came to another desert halting-place near the river called the son (or tributary) of the river above mentioned. Reached this lodging at four in the afternoon, without rain. Lodged in the huts of the other travellers on the other side. Marched with the sun in our front. Met no person whatever.

[62nd.] Desert-lodging of Cunde Irungo. Started at seven in the morning; marched to the top of the hill Cunde Irungo, crossed two small streams. During the march we came to another desert-lodging near the streamlet and the hill before mentioned. Arrived at noon, in rain. Built by the side of the stream. Met no one; saw nothing at all new or rare.

[63rd = 67th in the former diary, p. 184.] Desert-lodging of the hill Cunde Irungo. Started at seven in the morning; crossed a river named Lutipuca, six fathoms wide. During the march we came to another desert-lodging near a stream whose name I do not know. We arrived at midday; marched last with the sun on our right side. Met no one; saw no birds nor animals.

[64th.] Desert-lodging. Started at cockcrow. Crossed no river. Continuing our march we came to the lodging near the river Lutipuca before named, and marching down with this

river we arrived at noon, without rain. Journeyed with the
sun as before. Met no one.

[65th.] Desert-lodging. Started at six in the morning.
During the march we came to the farm of the Quilolo Mucha-
quita, of the Cazembe. Spoke with him about our journey.
He said he was very pleased to see Muzungos from Angola.
He sent us to lodge in his people's houses. Reached this place
at two in the afternoon. Met no person whatever.

[66th.] Lodging at the farm of the Quilolo Muchaquita.
Started at cockcrow. We marched across a magnificent dry river-
plain, no water whatever. It was about ten leagues in length,
and was full of various animals, zebras, empacassas (wild cattle),
deer, stags, and many other animals whose names I do not
know. Continuing our march, we came to the farm of another
Quilolo, named after the land Muschico, near that of his
Macota named Quiocola, the latter being some little distance
from Muschico. We spoke with him about our journey, that
we were going to visit the King Cazembe. We reached said
farm at two in the afternoon, without rain. Marched with the
sun on our right. Saw no one.

[67th.] Halting-place at the farm of Muschico. Started
at seven in the morning. Crossed the river-plain before mentioned on the western side, and passed over the river Lunpula
by canoe. For the services of the boatmen we gave them a
piece (muconzo) of straw cloth, thirty-three beads of white roncalha, and one beirame of "patavur" beads. Said river is about
fifty fathoms wide, more or less. Having crossed this stream,
we came afterwards to the farm of the Quilolo, Lord of the
Port, named, after the land, Amtapo Aquilala. Arrived at this
farm at four in the afternoon. Met no one. Marched with the
sun on our right side, and built some distance from the farm.

[68th.] Lodging of the farm of Amtapo Aquilala. Left
this halting-place at 6 A.M.; passed no river, descended along
the river Luapula. During the journey we came to the farm
of Cazembe's sister, named, according to land-fashion, Pemba-
femia: she directly requested we would occupy the houses of her
Quiloloa. We spoke to her about our undertaking; that we
were proceeding to her brother, the King Cazembe. She said
Mustahianvo's sending messengers from Angola pleased her
much: similar messengers had never appeared in the Cazembe's
lands before. She presented us with four moitetes of flour
and four fresh fish. We arrived here at two in the after-

noon, having marched with the sun on our right. Met with no one.

[69th.] Lodging at the farm of the Cazembe's sister, Pemba. Set out at seven in the morning, without rain. Still marched down the river, crossed a narrow stream two fathoms wide, running into the same Luapula. During the march we came to the farm of the Quilolo named Murumbo. Arrived at noon. Met no one. Marched with the sun on our right. Lodged in the houses of the farm. Saw neither birds nor beasts.

[70th.] Lodging at the farm of the Quilolo Murumbo. Started at cockcrow, and, descending with the Luapula on the left, we crossed two rivers, the Lufubo and the Capueje, running into said Luapula. During the journey we came to the farm of the Catuata, who marched in our company, named according to land-fashion Quissacanhi, near the river, three fathoms wide, named Gonna. We went into the houses of said Catuata. We reached this place at 2 P.M., without rain. Marched with the sun as before, and met no person whatever.

[71st.] Lodging at the farm of Quissacanhi, near the river Gonna. Started at 5 A.M.; crossed two running streams of small width, and during our march came to the farm of the black named Capunque, near the river Belengi, four fathoms wide, which runs into the Luapula. Arrived at three in the after-noon. Met a great many people coming from the Cazembe's great farm. Marched with the sun as before on our right; saw no animals.

[72nd.] Lodging at the farm of Capunque, near the river Belengi. Started at six in the morning; crossed no river, and continuing our march we came to the city of the Quilolo of Cabola, near the river named Cannegoa, three fathoms wide, which runs into the river Mouva. Arrived at four in the afternoon, and halted two days by order of said Cazembe. Marched with the sun on our right. Met a great many people coming from Cazembe's great farm. Saw nothing of any novelty or importance.

[73rd.] Halting-place at the farm of the Quilolo Cabola, near the river Cannegoa. Started at eleven in the morning, crossed no river, passed Senzalas, and during the journey we came to the capital of King Cazembe. Having come down a stately river-plain called Mouva, near which is built the said Cazembe's city, we reached the Banza at midday, and occupied the house of the keeper of his gates, named Quibiry Quitambo Quiamacungo. Receiving word by his page that as a signal of our arrival in these dominions we should discharge what guns we could, as it was a great pleasure to him to see people in his lands from Angola, a thing of which he had not thought of, and which was very fortunate for him, as heir to the deceased Cazembe Ilunga Amuronga, we discharged three guns, and he replied from within his walls with one, all being astonished at our coming, and overjoyed among themselves. He sent us a quantity of (manioc) flour, meat, fresh and dried fish, and Aló, treating us with great hospitality all the time we remained there. He also enabled us to reach the Rivers of Senna. During the journey we were halted twenty-two days, and on the march seventy-three.*

(Signed)   Pedro João Baptista.
(Countersigned)   Antonio Nogueira da Rooha.

[No. 3.]

Route of P. J. Baptista from the Cazembo to Telte in 1811 has not been given here.

[No. 4.] Number of Days' Journey from the Muataiianvo to the Fair of Mucary :—

	Days.
From the Mussumba of the Muatahianvo to the farm of the Camata Camunga	1
From the Camata to Cacenda	2
From Cacenda to Gongo	3
From Gongo to the river Laiza	4
From the river Luiza to the farm of Quissenda	5
From Quissenda to Milemba	6
From Milemba to the Desert	7
From the Desert to the river Luigi	8
From the river Luigi to Cavenga	9
From Cavenga to Canasuida	10
From Canasuida to the farm of the people of Mouricapelle	11
From Capelle, crossing the river Luhia by canoe, and to the farm of the Fumo Campeo	12
From the Fumo Campeo to the farm of the Muene Canceze	13
From Cancezo to the deserted farm Malembo	14
From Mutembo to the farm of the Quilolo Quirungo	15
From the Quirungo to the Desert	16
From the Desert to another Desert	17
From the Desert to Dembue	18
From the Dembue to the Desert near " Quiana of the water "	19
From Quiana to the farm of the Muene Rifunda Garga (Ganga ?)	20
From the Muene Rifunda to near the river Cacamuca	21

* The former diary (pp. 169-188) gives seventy-eight days; but it includes various halts.—R. F. B.

NUMBER OF DAYS' JOURNEY FROM THE CHIEF BOMBA TO THE FAIR OF MUCARY :—

	Days.
From the Desert to the farm of a son of the Bomba, named Hiemba Munda	5
From Hiemba to the farm of the chief Pundi Hiabonga . . .	6
From the Pundi to the chief Motende	7
From the Motende to the Capacala	8
From the Capacala to the farm of the Quissoca, sister of the Bomba	9
From the Quissoca to near the river Jombo	10
From the Jombo crossed to the other side of it	11
From the Jombo to the farm Souvela of the Cabita Catempo . .	12
From the Cabita to the farm of the Mocampa	13
From the Mocampa to the Desert	14
From the Desert to the farm of Genzo, brother of the Banda Gongo	15
From the Gongo to the Desert	16
From the Desert to the Quilcculo and farm of the Quiboala . .	17
From the Quiboala to the farm of the son of the Cabunxi and Catambo, named Cuinhiba	18
From the Cuinhiba to the farm of the Camba, brother of the Quibenda	19
From the Camba to the farm of the Quibenda	20
From the Quibenda to the Marimbo	21
From Marimbe to the Fair of Mucary	22

    (Signed)   Pedro João Baptista.
    (Countersigned) Antonio Nogueira da Rocha.

[No. 5.]

In the name of God, Amen.

REMINISCENCES OF THE DEPARTURE FROM THE MUATAYANVO TO THE DOMINIONS OF THE CAZEMBE CAQUINHATA, and what transpired with the Quilolos whom we found on the road beyond the State and Kingdom of Angola; and the rest that I saw in these territories, until we reached the lands of Cazembe, by the mystery of the Virgin Our Lady; and of our costly departure from said Pumbo to the town of Tete, bearing a letter for the Governor of the said town, despatched by my master, Lieutenant-Colonel Francisco Honorato da Costa, Director of the Fair of Mucary, and arrival of a Pombeiro of the Chief Captain Gonçalo Caetano Pereira, named, after the country-fashion, Marungue, now come to conduct us from the Pumbo of the Cazembe, who brought goods to buy ivory, slaves, and green stones (malachite); how the same Marungue released us from said place, and with whom we started from thence, after being delayed there four years, having started for Tete and turned back twice; and it was in the year 1810 that we finally started for the town of Tete.

On Sunday, twenty-second of May of said year, we started from the Mufumba of Muatayanvo, and came to the farm of the Cacoata, named Cutaquacexe, who acted as our guide. We were detained in this place sixteen days, caused by his performing his rites, and on Tuesday, seventh July, we started, and on the march passed the Quilolos and peoples of the said Muatayanvo, until we came to the site of the Quilolo named, according to the land-fashion, Chamuginga Mussenda, who owns allegiance both to Muatayanvo and Cazembe, because, when the last Muatayanvo and Cazembe marched forth to subjugate the country in which the Cazembe's lands are situated, they left this Quilolo Chamuginga Mussenda near the river Luburi, to receive all persons coming from the Muatayanvo or the Cazembe, in procuring all kinds of provisions for the use of all people coming from either potentate. This farm is the boundary of the lands of the Muatayanvo on that side; crossing said river Luburi on the other side of it, are found the people of the Cazembe, who subject themselves to the Quilolo of Cazembe—Quibi, who was in the river-plain of the Salina called Quigila, who is recently dead. At the farm of Chamuginga Mussenda all travellers buy provisions of manioc-flour, in order to go and buy salt and mucongos of straw-cloth, a few made-up articles, and wax. When we started from this farm of Chamuginga Mussenda, we travelled across others with valleys and hills, and saw, on the summit of the hills, stones which appear true (green?), and where they dig the copper; in the midst of this country is where they make the bars. There are two proprietors of the "Senzalas;" the first is near the road we crossed, named after the land (in country fashion) Muiro, and the other is called Canbembe. Those owners are the head smiths, who order the bars to be made by their "sons" and their own "macotas" (slaves), and pay such bars as tribute to the Quiburi, or his successor, for that Lord of the Salina to send them to the Muatayanvo, or to whoever the Muatayanvo sends for them. These two proprietors were also at one time sovereigns of the lands, as well as owners of the mines left them by their predecessors. They were, however, acquired by Cazembe by force, so that the lands are now in subjection to both the Muatayanvo and the Cazembe, having been conquered by the late Quilolo Quiburi, Lord of the Salina. Quiburi was a maternal relation of the Cazembe's, who had appointed him to govern the Salina and have the management of sending the tribute of salt, and the goods of the Muatayanvo; also to receive visitors or travellers who go from the Muatayanvo to the Cazembe. He sent the mulambo by his Cacoata to the Muatayanvo, to arrange with the said Lord of the Salina, that, in addition to the tribute presents of stuff, beads, salt, and other things, which they buy from the salt-dealers, should be delivered to the Cacoata to take to the Muatayanvo.

The Salina Quigila is near the river Lualaba, on this side of it. On the further side of the said river is established the Lord of the Salina, and in this same country there are no provisions of manioc-flour to be obtained, and what little there

is is bought with the goods that come from the Muatayanvo.
In the Pumbo only millet, large haricot beans, large maize, and
Lucu, which they call Caixai, are to be obtained, and even
these come from such retired farms that it is difficult to obtain
a mouthful of meal or any description of food, and very costly.
One must be provided with good beads, or some other article
they value, to be able to get anything. They do not cultivate
manioc, it not being the custom of the country : the previous
sovereigns of this land did not grow this production, and this
became the general habit in the said Pumbo. There is nothing
they can make use of for dress; men clothe themselves in
Mussamba busts, and women buy straw-cloth from the people
before named in exchange for salt; that is, in the dry season.
In the rainy season, when the salt-traders do not come, they
are put to great straits, and the traders cannot obtain the salt
at such times, the river-plain itself being flooded. In order to
get the salt they cut the straw and burn it; after which they
dissolve the ashes in water, and throw the lye into small pans
which they make; then they boil it, and this they exchange
for what they consider wealth, namely, woollen cloth, Indian
tissues, beads, and straw-cloths. The smiths (Ferreiros) also
exchange their bars for flour and other provisions that are
valued. From the lands of the smiths and the Salina to the
other side of the river Lualaba, where the governor of the
Salina, and the other Quilolos on the route to Cazembe also
live, they cannot rely upon a sufficient quantity of provisions for
travellers. Only millet is to be had; and even at the proper
time for cultivation it is expensive to obtain this, there not
being sufficient men to carry provisions, manioc beans, and
necessary things, which come as far as the river Lualaba. Thus
they risk losing their lives from hunger.

After having crossed the Luarula we reached on the other
side of the river a farm of the sister of Cazembe named Pemba,
and this lady received us with much consideration. She was
much astonished to see us, and pleased with Muatayanvo for
having sent whites, called by them Mugungos (Muzungos),
to visit her brother the Cazembe, a thing the previous Muata-
yunvos had never done; that it was a blessing for her
brother, Cazembo's successor, as they had no recollection of
having been before visited by whites coming from the Muatayanvo to the Cazembe. On Wednesday, the 15th of December,
aho sent for us and told us that when her father, Cazembe
Ilunga, was living, a great number of white people, with much
goods, had come in company of the Governor, and requested
permission from the Cazembe to allow them passage to the
Muatayanvo, and from the Muatayanvo to the fair of Cassange.

The late Cazembe, however, did not grant the permission; and
it pleased God that he (the Governor before mentioned) should
die in the Cazembe's lands; the colonists and soldiers who had
come in the said Governor's company then returned. (She also
told us) that the Cazembe himself was well, and that in the
said mussumba (place) there was a soldier who had letters to
go to Angola. She sent directly to inform her brother Cazembe
of our arrival, as also that it was her duty to send word of the
arrival of any traveller going to the Cazembe, before such
traveller's being allowed to go into the presence. She treated
us with much kindness in supplying us with food. We presented this lady with a blue twisted glass cup, a muzengo de al-
mandrilho, and two beirames of lead-coloured beads. We waited
there five days, pending the arrival of her messengers; and on
Saturday, the sixteenth, the Cazembe's messengers came to
fetch us, bringing for our use a she-goat, five motetes of manioc
flour, a motete of fresh fish, together with a black woman and
her child, and with a message from the Cazembe that he
was very pleased at our arrival, and that as a mark of his love
he offered us the black woman. He was very gratified at
his Muatayanvo's having forwarded to him white men from
Mueneputo, as he had never seen any such before in his
dominions.   To the Cacoata (guide) who had brought us,
he sent food to eat. We stayed one day with the
said messengers, and on the next we started with them.
Sunday, thirty-first of December, of one thousand eight
hundred and six we arrived at the mussumba of the King
Cazembe, at six o'clock in the afternoon. On that day we
did not see him, and he only sent word for us to occupy the
house of his Quilolo Quiota. On Monday, first of January,
one thousand eight hundred and seven, he sent for us. We
went and saw him; but we said nothing about our undertaking.
Only our guide spoke, saying, "I bring you here by order of
the King Muatayanvo, messengers from Mueneputo, who have
come to seek a white brother of the Mueneputo, who it is
stated is to be found in your territory. Treat them well,
without malice." The said Cacoata then delivered the present
that Muatayanvo sent to the Cazembe and added nothing more.
The Cazembe himself replied that he was very gratified at
his lord the Muatayanvo's sending him messengers from
Mueneputo, and that it was a very fortunate thing for him.
We then retired to our houses. After doing so he sent for us
privately, without letting the Cocoata hear of it, and he told us
that he had for a long time known the object of our visit; that
he would treat of this wish of his friend the Mueneputo's more
at leisure. As a signal of our arrival in his country, he wished

us to fire off all the guns we could, which was a thing that pleased him very much. We discharged three guns, and he, within his walls, also fired one. On Wednesday, the third day of said month, he sent his two Quilolos, named, after the land-fashion, Quiota Mutemba and Quitamba Quiamaungo, with a message that we were to explain particularly what brought us there, and to deliver the present that his friend the Mueneputo had sent by us for him.

We delivered his present, which consisted of two quicapos of green serafina (cloth), two quicapos of yellow serafina, two ditto singelos or dresses of red tammy (durante), two small mirrors with gilt paper edges, a Portuguese fire-arm, and two blue cups, all of which we made over to his messengers, saying. "Here is the Saguate, or present, which your friend the Mueneputo sends to and offers you. He sent us also to visit you, King Cazembe, as he is always desirous of maintaining a good and reciprocal intercourse with you, which is equally useful and profitable both for you and us. He asks that you will allow his messengers and their Caccata to pass freely, so that he may conduct us on the road to Senna, seeing that the brother of your friend Mueneputo is not here. The latter desires and wishes to keep up terms of friendship with you, King Cazembe. I hand you here the letter which I bring you from Mueneputo himself, and which he sends you in a friendly spirit for you to have read, and grant what he asks therein, regarding the journey to Senna." This letter the Cazembe received in the sight of his people, and retained. He replied that he knew how honourable all white men were, and that he would order the letter to be read at his leisure. On the fourth day of the said month, Thursday, he sent for us, and at his doorway we found a white soldier, native of Quilhiman, named Paulo de Santiago e Silva, and three blacks belonging to colonists of Tete and Senna, waiting to receive us by Cazembe's orders. When they did see us they received us with great joy, because we had come from Angola. The soldier had been detained two years, trying to find the way to Angola in the service of the Crown, and asking to be allowed to go, but was never granted permission.

The Cazembe replied he was very pleased with the Saguate which his friend Mueneputo had sent him, and that he was quite ready to carry out all the wishes of his friend Mueneputo. That he desired not only to provide us with a guide, but that he would himself go with us as far as the river Aruangua, as there were enemies and robbers to be met with on the way, who were in the habit of plundering the whites who came from Tete and Senna, with the intention of transacting business of their

Q

own in the Cazembe's lands. That he was convinced all the
white people were children of Mueneputo, because the Governor
of Senna himself had come to his dominions, accompanied by his
regiment of soldiers and officers, as well as civilian colonists of
said town of Tete, and had asked permission of his dead
father, Cazembe Hunga Anmomgo (Amuronga), to pass through
and visit Mualayanvo, in order to discover if they could go on
to Angola. That the said Cazembe Hunga would not grant this
permission, but that he, the son and successor to the State, would
do all that in any way might be possible. When we saw he
was ready to put us on the way to Senna, to content him still
more we presented him two blue glasses, two muzongos of coral
with hollow stems like a pipe, two muzengos of white romalha,
two ditto of Bumbango, three ditto of Queta Calongo, a quizapo
of black serafina, and two small looking-glasses with gilt frames.
We told him that his friend Mueneputo had sent him a good
piece of fine red cloth, and some good stone-beads, but that his
King Muatayanvo had taken them all. He answered it did
not matter; that he would carry out the wishes of our king;
and that he would have as much as possible notwithstanding.

On Tuesday, the twentieth of April, we started for the war-
camp, with the Cazembe to take us to the before-mentioned
river Aruangoa, the way being stopped so that no traveller
should pass, it being the custom generally amongst all the
heathen chiefs not to allow any traveller whatever to pass through
their towns with goods to other chiefs without the strangers
first stopping and trading with them. When we reached the
war-camp a great disturbance took possession of them (the
Cazembe's people) for fear that the eldest brother of the Cazembe, named, after the land-fashion, Capaca, whom the deceased
father, Cazembe Hunga, had banished to the land called Cassange,
was coming to take the State from Cazembe. On account of
the treason that now prevailed amongst his people, the Cazembe
proceeded to examine who was the instigator of the disturbance.
Some threw the blame on to his mother, his mother accused
some of the Quilolos, and the Cazembe banished to other lands
his cousin Quibanba, chief Quilolo, and ordered his hands and
ears to be cut. Other Quilolos he fined in goods, and any thing
else he chose to ask for. He then returned from the road to
Senna, and went to carry on war in the land called Tanga, and
us he delivered over to his Ticara, who remained in his stead,
and to his sister Cananga to attend to us, and assist us with all
the things we might require.

He was occupied in this war two and a half months, when
we saw him again, and stayed with him two months longer.
On our telling him that, as the way was not open to Senna, he

should let us return to the Muatayanvo, he answered nothing.
He sent forces to join in war on the other side of the river
Luapula. When we tried to arrange about our journey, and
asked him to let us go to the Muatayanvo, he began to mis-
lead us with presents of "garapaa" (juice of sugar-cane) and
meat. For some days there appeared no means of escaping
from our persecution; we were compelled to stay with him
without being able to go either to the Muatayanvo or to Tete.
When he saw our need for going was very great, he chose as
our Cazembe of the road (guide) the oldest of all his Quilolos,
named, after the land-fashion, Muenepanda, and his relation
Soana Mulopo, named Tambo; also two Quilolos, his brothers-
in-law, named after the land Chabanza Mutemba, and another
Quilembe, and other Quilolos, to assist in escorting us to Tete.
We started with the Muenepanda and the others named, who made
stoppages on the way to pray, and to attempt to divine whether ·
they could proceed or not. On our reaching the farm of
Cazembe's Quilolo, where we halted two days, waiting for
our guide, the Muenepanda, two messengers from the Chiefs
Quiana and Quebue came in our search, bringing an ox to
induce the Muenepanda and his war-men to go back, to allow
Chabanza to come past with ivory and other things which he
had with him to buy goods for Cazembe at Tete; they said
the road was quite clear. In spite, however, of all these
attempts to deceive, we continued our journey, and, crossing
the river Lupulo, we met some other messengers bringing two
oxen, who tried to turn the Muenepanda back, with the same
false tale about the way to Senna being clear, and that there was
no one to interfere with travellers, who could come and go on
their journeys at any time, and in any direction. On the second
day from this, the Muenepanda accepted the two oxen, and, at
the lodging of Quipiri, which we were come to, he ordered all
the ivory to be collected, and presented it to Quianna's messengers. He then turned back, saying that the way was quite
clear, thus neglecting to carry out Cazembe's orders, which
were to escort us to the river Aruangua, as arranged, and
receiving private gifts from the above chiefs to induce him not
to make war in their countries. Muenepanda stayed at the
above halting-place Quipiri, and we went on with Chabanza
Mutemba, and all the guide's ivory, slaves, green stones, bars of
copper, and ounce skins. We arrived at the farm of the Chief
Quiana Cutanba, where we were halted fifteen days without
being able to get away; Quianna deceiving us by saying we must
wait for the floods in the rivers to retire before we proceeded on
our journey. This was an excuse to detain us till the arrival
of his friends, to attack us and seize all the guide's goods. These

robbers are brothers to those whom the Cazembe killed in the war which he carried on in the Tanga country; he met these Huzas (Huizas?) returning from the Chief Cassongo's lands with his ivory, which was intended to purchase merchandize. At Quiana's place all our slaves and green stones were hidden away by the people when they saw we wished to escape from their place. By the aid of the Virgin Mary we had been warned by another chief, named, after the land-fashion, Quirando, who sent our guide Chabanza notice that, being a friend of the Cazembe's, he knew that Quiana had ordered his fighting-men to this side of the river Hianbigi (Chambeze), intending to kill him (Chabanza), and advising him to retire from Quiana's place. We escaped thence, with the loss of many slaves and other things that the Cazembe had sent to purchase merchandize in Tete. By the help of our Lady of the Conception none of us died, although we were robbed of a great deal. We returned to the mussumba of King Cazembe a second time, troubled and injured as we were, marching day and night, so that the fighting-men might not overtake us. We found the Quilolo Muenepanda very comfortably settled at his farm, and the Cazembe much enraged with him and the other Quilolos. After a long time had elapsed, by a providential circumstance the pombeiro of the Chief-Captain Gonçalo Caetano Pereira, arrived with merchandise, having come to buy slaves and ivory, by order of his master. He brought a letter for the soldier Paulo Santiago, to join the pombeiros of the said Gonçalo Caetano, who were detained there through the way not being clear. We started with this pombeiro for the town of Tete, with the Caconta, or guide of the Cazembe, named, after the land, Catára Mirimba, and with other persons, taking ivory, slaves, green-stones, and copper bars, to barter for cloth, and to deliver us to the Governor.

The trade of the Cazembe's country consists of ivory, slaves, green-stones, and copper bars, which they sell to the travellers from Tete and Senna, and to blacks of the Huiza nation, who are established on the road to Tete. These Huizas are the first travellers who ever traded with Cazemba, long before any pombeiro from Senhor Gonçalo Caetano appeared. They call these pombeiros "Mucazambos," meaning faithful men who are responsible for all things. Gonçalo Caetano being the first trader who discovered the Cazembe's land, and the Huizas are the people who in former days went to Tete to buy Indian goods and Tanga cloths, which they call maxilas, a name also given to our Tipoias (hammocks); also quizengos of scrafina, good printed calicoes, and plates, to present to the said Cazembe. Some Tangas (loin cloths) are made by the Huizas themselves.

Colonist travellers from Tete and Senna give for each slave
they buy in Cazembe's land at the present time five Indian
sheetings, and for ivory six or seven sheetings and other
extra articles for every large tusk, as Cazembe's people understand that ivory is more valued in Tete than slaves. When
we took our leave, he presented us, in the presence of his
Quilolos, or chiefs, ten slaves, and a large green-stone for his
friend the Governor. He produced two ells of fine red cloth,
telling us that a green-stone is named Cazembe, and that fine
red cloth is an overseer or superintendent whom they call
Calama. We received his letter in reply to the one we
brought to him, Cazembe, and for ourselves his messengers
were given five slaves; four moleques (black boys), and a black
woman for me, Pedro; and to my partner Anastacio five slaves,
two moleques, two molecas (girls), and a black woman; and to
buy provisions from his place to the Muatayanvo, he gave us
six hundred "sambos," three hundred for me and other three
hundred for Anastacio. I asked him if he had by chance any
white rhinoceros-horns, when he sent directly to find some, and
then gave two small ones to us. And during all the four years
we were detained there, trying our utmost to get away to Muatayanvo, as there was no road open to Senna, he gave us, to
keep us patient, two slaves, one for me, the other for my comrade.
For three years he used all possible diligence to open the way
to the Rivers of Senna, it having been closed all that time. He
did not allow us to incur any expenses on behalf of his friend
Mueneputo, but took them all upon himself. He also carried
out the orders of his King Muatayanvo.

On the return from Tete to the Cazembe we were delayed nine
months, caused by his collecting mulanbo (tribute) by means
of his Quilolos, his mother, sisters, and brothers, and preparing
a Cazembe of the road (the guide) to take charge of us, and bring
us with the tribute into the Muatayanvo's presence. Cazembe,
through his eagerness to obtain cloth, had left us to return to the
Muatayanvo with only remnants; and the result of his acting
in such a way was that we left his country quite puzzled, not
having even a piece of stuff, and neither beads nor shells to buy
anything with on the road, except the "sambos" he gave us.
We set out with his Cacoata (guide), named, after the land-
fashion, Mimbage, at a time when there was a great scarcity of
food, and after losses from desertion and death on the way,
caused by privations and detentions brought about by the
Cazembe; we had no remedy, nor could we prevent it. We set
out for Muatayanvo's, in order not to displease him, and at the
wish of the Governor of the Rivers of Senna, who directed that
if the Cazembe should give us his ambassador to conduct us to

the Muatayanvo's, we should treat him well, and with all love, peace, and quietness on the way, in the general service that we are engaged in, as perhaps His Excellency might send some one from Tete with a letter on the general service. Cazembe entertains great friendship for the Governor. Every month and year he sends his Cacoatas with slaves and whatever is most necessary to the Governor's house, his messengers coming and going with us. And in the course of two years, if God does not see fit to prevent it, he entertains hopes that the Governor will send and repay him for his trouble in sending us on safely to Tete, a way that was very difficult to open and keep clear. It is now open, but at the present time he does not send his Cacoata, as he is waiting for the Governor's messengers to arrive and confer with him, and then his "Cacoata" would accompany us to the Governor. King Cazembe has tea-pots, cups, pans, demijohns, silver spoons and forks, plates of Lisbon earthenware, good hats, shoe-buckles, and gold money, doubloons and half doubloons. He has a Christian courtesy: he doffs his hat, and gives good day, good afternoon, or good evening. He keeps all the white man's furniture that belonged to the late Governor Lacerda, and other white people, inhabitants of the same town, who had come in Governor Lacerda's company, and which was left, as there were no porters to carry such things to Tete, through the flight of the Governor's people, which ensued on the alarm felt at his death; he having come there with about a thousand cruzados' worth of goods from the Royal Treasury, in addition to his own means and the means of the residents of Tete and other places, to expend in opening up the way to Angola. It is even now well remembered how he was supplied with all they had in their homes, and how for want of the means to transport their belongings to the Rivers of Senna, a great many of the colonist-travellers sold them. The only one who did not suffer any loss was Senhor Gonçalo Caetano Pereira, who had his men, and his son, an ensign in the militia, Manoel Caetano Pereira, who also took away some goods, in-including a sedan-chair which belonged to the Governor.

The Cazembe is powerful in his capital, and rules over a great many people. His place is rather smaller than the Muatayanvo's: his orders are harsh, and he is feared by all the great chiefs, who are also lords of their own lands; they fought with him, but they are now in his power. Away from his dominions there are other potentates, highwaymen, and robbers, who are settled on the other side of the two rivers Hianbege (Chambeze) and Aruangoa, on the route to Tete. Cazembe has not yet been there, but he intends to go and attack them.

When there are no travellers trading at his capital, he will order slaves and ivory to be collected, and will go with his ambassadors to chastise such chiefs as stop the way to traders coming from Tete to his country; and, whoever the chief may be who will not allow travellers to pass, he will proceed at once to array his fighting men, and march them to such pombos. The robbers now begin to pay tributes of cattle, wishing to convey the false impression that they are his vassals, and some petty chiefs are already escaping to other lands some distance away.

The territory of Cazembe is low and very cold. A disease is prevalent therein that is painful to the eyes. It is supplied with provisions all the year round and every year; manioc flour, millet, maize, large haricot beans, small ditto, round beans, which they call Misso a Cabandi, Massango, which they term Impondo, and Caxai, alias Lucu, fruits, as bananas; sugar-canes, potatoes, yams, gourds, almonds (ground-nuts), and much fish from the rivers Luapula and Mouva, which are near. He owns three salt districts—Cabomba, Mungi, and Carucuige—beside the Salina Quigila, which is on this border of the Muatayanvo. He possesses victuals, oxen, which the before-named chiefs pay as tribute, and some other oxen, which he sends and buys from the Huizas in exchange for slaves, small animals, and she-goats. He has neither sheep nor pigs; except at the present time, a few pigs that came from the country called Tanga: he also requested the illustrious Snr. D. Francisca and the chief-captain, Gonçalo Caetano, to send others by us on our return from Tete. The Cazembe was the slave of the son of Muatayanvo, named, after the country-fashion, Mutanda, who was formerly governor of the salt district, by order of the Muatayanvo Muncanza, who had appointed him. This Mutanda was king of the so-called Acosa nation. He afterwards went to take part in the wars, and left as his substitute his Quilolo and slave Quinhata, to send the salt tribute and other necessary things bought with the salt to his "father," the Muatayanvo. This same Quinhata began to send a more important Mulambo (tribute), muconzos, beirames, and cloths, big pans of salt, and other things much esteemed by the Muatayanvo, than that of Mutanda, the "son," after his campaigns. He collected all the slaves taken in the wars and other things there valued; and he also ordered salt to be prepared for the slaves to carry, and collected the Mulambo. These they took to his father, the Muatayanvo, giving him the news of the raids which he had been engaged in; adding that the Mutanda could not personally render obedience to his "father," because his feet were injured. On the arrival of the said Mutanda's messengers, who delivered the Mulambo, his father Muatayanvo Muncanza, refused it, saying that what his slave Quinhata had sent was larger than his "son's," who had neither love nor obedience for him. The Mutanda's messengers returned with the Mulumbo and the former was offended by his "father's" having returned it, while he accepted the assertions of his slave Quinhata. He ordered Quinhata to be captured, and to be thrown into the river Mucuregi. The messengers, returning to the Muatayanvo, told him that his "son" had ordered Quinhata to be killed because he had sent a good Mulambo. The "father," on hearing this, immediately sent and expelled his "son" from the government of the Salina, giving the same to the son of the deceased Quinhata, named, after the land-fashion, Ganga Abilondo, who was invested with the white clay, knife, shield, javelins, together with other Quilolos to maintain him in his domains. He ordered him to govern the Salina and conquer all the lands he could; that when he came to any country supplying good things, he should stay there, in order to go on conquering, little by little, as he might be able. He established himself in the Quixinga land, in which he now governs, sending tribute to his masters, the Muatayanvos, by his ambassadors, and by some of Muatayanvo's "Cacoatas" (guides), who go there to collect and buy slaves, goods, sambos dolos (counterfeit cowries), which they call "pande," a kind of large round shell, saracas, chintz, small plates, large cowries, brass basins, huartes, and borralhos. It is some years since the Cazembe went to visit the Muatayanvo in person. By the latter's own orders, when former Cazembes came to conquer the lands in which the present chief reigns, they agreed not to leave their lands because of the danger lest the people, in their absence, might rise and kill the persons they left to represent them (relations or friends), while the Cazembe went to visit the Muatayanvo. Therefore it became a general custom for the Cazembes not to go personally to the Mussamba of the Muatayanvo, but only to send ambassadors with their Mulambo. Some Cacoatas who come from the Muatayanvo's do not wish to return to him: these remain in Cazembe's lands, and if the Muatayanvo sends for them, the Cazembe laughs, and sends slaves in their stead. All the slaves we brought died of hunger; some fled from the Pumbo of the Cazembe, there being no prisons where we could secure them. When we were on this side of the river Luburi, with the men ill and dying on the road from the Salina Quigila as far as the said river Luburi, on Wednesday, 11th February, we had a great fright, and were all the night on the look-out, as the chief, Muene Sambu, wanted to attack our Cazembe of the Road (guide), and kill us travellers also, who were in his company, because the Muatayanvo had killed the messengers of his friends, Quinhama and Muchima, and took

their goods to him, the Muatayanvo. With the assistance of
the Holy Virgin Mary, we left there without sustaining any
harm, by the Divine Providence; and with these losses it became
necessary to stay two months at the river Laburi, to get the
people into condition, who had come in so pale, thin, and ill
from hunger, we as well as they not being able to walk a step
through the same cause. We saw nothing more in the territories of the Cazembe that I have omitted to note; neither on
the road was there anything nor any misadventure which I
failed to report. I continued to make my notes regularly, even
when ill.

(Signed) PEDRO JOÃO BAPTISTA.

(C.)

1811.

In the name of God, Amen.

The following relates to what passed between the Most Illustrious Governor
of the Rivers of Senna, on the East Coast of Africa, regarding our
arrival from the dependency and Kingdom of Angola, and of our
delivery to the Governor of the letter sent by my master,
Lieutenant-Colonel Francisco Honorato da Costa, Director of the
Fair of Mucari; of other matters current in that town, its trade,
and the conquered lands now subject to the same town; the discoveries I made in the territory, and the persons who assisted me to
make them.

On Saturday, the second of February, 1811, we arrived in
the town of Tette, at four in the afternoon, in the company of the
Chief-Captain Gonçalo Caetano Pereira, who was to bring us
into the presence of the Governor. On the day of our arrival,
however, we did not see him, and the same gentleman, Gonçalo
Caetano, placed us in the house of a native of the place, who
was away from the town, whilst he stayed with his son-in-law,
José Sebastião de Ataide. We passed two nights on the
road after leaving the Senhor Gonçalo Caetano's farm. On
Sunday, the third, the Governor sent a soldier to summon us.
I went with Gonçalo Caetano, and delivered the letter to the
Governor himself: he did not open it in our presence, but said
that the way by land being open from the West Coast of Africa,
at Angola, to the Rivers of Senna, was a very good thing. The

Cazembe's ambassador, with whom we were, named Catara Mirimbu, gave the following message:—"I bring to your Excellency these men, who come from Angola;" at the same time the ambassador offered the present which Cazembe sent to the Governor: it consisted of two ivory tusks and a large green stone, which he did not deliver. His Excellency then asked me for the diaries kept from the Fair of Cassange to the Muathianvo, from the Muatahianvo to the King Cazembe, and from Cazembe to the town of Tette. To write these diaries, I at once asked for paper, which was given me, and I stated with all clearness what passed between us and the Muatahianvo on the subject of our journey; how he allowed us to pass on, and gave us the guide, who brought us to Cazembe, and the presents we gave to the Muatahianvo; also about the potentates and peoples on the journey to the Cazembe, and in like manner about the Cazembe, and the long delay there; how we were compelled to return twice, because of the Huizas chief being engaged in war with the Cazembe; the latter having killed their "sons" in the fight on his return from the road to Senna. After resting twenty days, when I remained to write out the journal from Cassange to the Muatahianvo, His Excellency would give me no more paper, and said that from the particulars I had given him verbally about Cassange, he was well informed of all; that he wanted only the two journals from the Muatahianvo to Cazembe, and from the Cazembe to the Rios de Senna. On delivering our letter, he told us that on no account he could provide us with all things required for our journey to Angola without the sanction of His Excellency the Governor-General; but that he would send us to see the General at Mozambique, who might write to Rio de Janeiro, and request our Lord the Prince Regent to allow him (the General) to send us with all the necessaries for our transport. He added that when the last Governor, Antonio de Noronha, or Antonio Norberto Barboza de Villa (Villas?) de Boas, made disbursements, some persons of the general works proved that he repaid the Treasury, from which he had taken the means, from the factory of His Excellency at Mozambique, and he was condemned to make a general distribution of merchandise; that under no circumstances could he do anything without orders (or permission) from Mozambique, because of the great stir there had been in consequence of our Prince Regent having to leave his capital to escape being caught by the great Buonaparte. That in the state of ruin and confusion the Rivers of Senna were in, without protective means, he could do nothing, and did not even know who would govern these Rivers of Senna, whether they would be Portuguese or English; and, in consequence of this panic, he was deprived

of his control over the Royal Treasury; that it was only to
the late Governor, José Francisco de Araujo Lacerda, who died
in Cazembe, that His Royal Highness had confided the task of
exploring the route from the Western Coast of Africa (Angola)
by land: the deceased had the Royal orders and everything
necessary for the undertaking, but he did not reach Angola,
as it pleased God to take him to Himself, and he died in the
country of Cazembe. In Goa there are now two Governors, one
English and the other Portuguese; and, according to news the
traders bring, who come from Mozambique to the Rivers of
Senna with goods, I mean with cloth to buy money—the name
they give to gold-dust—and ivory, the English will come and
take this place also, and there will be two Governors in the
Senna rivers; but who can tell what truth there is in it?

In addition to the above declaration the Governor made to us,
he asked if we would wear uniforms: and, telling me to sit down
upon a chair, said no one would venture to do what we had done,
in crossing overland from the West Coast of Africa by Angola, to
the East Coast at the Rivers of Senna; that His Royal Highness
had always been seeking some one who could accomplish this,
but all in vain, as he had not met with any one who would undertake this important task; and that the six thousand cruzados,
which Governor Lacerda had taken with him on his enterprise,
had been lost. I replied, "I cannot be seated in your Honour's
presence; it may be seen from the letter we bring, who we are."
The Governor then said, we had executed the task as well as
the gentlemen themselves executed the orders of His Royal
Highness: much more did we, being slaves, and having the
patience and ingenuity to obey and carry out our master's
orders, deserve being rewarded for the amount of trouble and
work we had gone through for His Royal Highness; and as
Angola had its own Government, with full powers, we would be
assisted, and our master, Francisco Honorato da Costa, as author
of this undertaking, would not fail to inform them of what we had
done for the Royal service. The Governor dealt with all
these matters at his public residence, in the presence of two
officers of the staff, and his Adjutant Rodrigo José de Aboim,
the Captain of Militia Camello José de Lemos, Gonçalo Caetano
Pereira, José Sebastião de Ataide, Judicial Clerk, and two other
men whose names I do not know. We replied, we could not go
to Mozambique, as our guide, whom Muntubianvo had given us,
was waiting at Cazembe for us; and also that we had been away
from our country nearly ten years, the time we had been occupied in this enterprise, and we did not know whether he who
sent us was living or dead.

The Governor answered that it did not matter, but that it

would be impossible to provide means for our transport to
Angola; therefore he would ask them as an obligation to His
Royal Highness. He sent me with a soldier to the house of the
Illustrious Joaquim Corrêa Craveiro Sabarreiros, to keep and
clothe me; and my comrade Anastacio Francisco to the house of
the Illustrious Lady Dona Francisca Josefa de Moura e Menezes,
to feed and clothe him. They treated us with great kindness,
giving, as food every ten or twelve days for the black boys and
negresses, a measure of millet, and to us they gave prepared food
at both houses for dinner, &c.; my comrade, however, getting
much more and better food than I did. The said Craveiro gave
me a white fustian garment, and a wrapper or gown of blue
serafina ferret with copper buttons, a pair of boots, and two
plates of Lisbon earthenware for my use. While we were
lodging in these houses the Governor sent for us, and gave us
a piece of Zuarte to make trousers of, and "cutoes;" and
to the Cazembe of the road (guide) they gave cloth and
fine beads, to buy provisions with at Senhor Gonçalo Caetano's
farm. The merchandise, however, they gave direct to Gonçalo
Caetano, at his son-in-law's house, José Sebastião de Ataide,
sending it by a sergeant of the garrison, Luiz José Ferreira
Lima, from the Governor's, to give them to the Cazembe of the
road, to buy what they pleased. Senhor Gonçalo Caetano did not,
however, give these things to the Cazembe of the road, but only
supplied him with provisions from his Arimos (warehouses). After
having given all these orders, he drew up a list of the names and
dwellings of the inhabitants of that town, that they might, each
man and woman, as an obligation to His Royal Highness, give
fifteen or twenty pieces of cloth. The Governor himself con-
tributed one hundred and thirty pieces towards our transport to
Angola, and that we might carry letters very carefully to the
Illustrious and Excellent Senhor General of Angola, and to the
Director Francisco Honorato da Costa. They promised to give
us only six hundred pieces of cloth, to which we answered, "If
your Honour wishes to take compassion on us, and send us to
Angola, six hundred pieces of the stuff of this country would
not be sufficient for such a long journey, with presents to make
to the chiefs on the way, and the cost of provisions for our use
from the town of Tette to the Cazembe, from the Cazembe to the
Muatabianvo, whom they call Muropue, and from the Muatabianvo to the Fair of Mucary." He began to get out of humour
with us, saying that when we came from Cassange we brought
no cloth for the exploration of the road to the Rivers of Senna,
to which we replied that the Lieutenant-Colonel Francisco
Honorato da Costa had despatched us with three contos
(Rs.3000$000) worth of woollen goods of fine quality, besides

bugles, and stone-beads of various kinds; fine red cloths, crimson beaver and druggets to present to the chiefs of the countries on the way to allow us to pass through. On our giving this explanation, he said we must not make comparisons with the goods that came from Angola on the West Coast. So he sent us away with only four hundred and sixty-eight pieces, which they call Xoabos (chunbos), Indian cloths much damaged, given by the inhabitants against their wishes; they saying that there was no obligation on their part to subscribe, there being plenty of goods in the King's factory. These things were given to us already packed in two small bales, called by them Mutorea. We do not recollect the particulars of these articles, neither had we a list of them to know what they consisted of; and we only opened them at the house of Senhor Gonçalo Caetano at the recommendation of the Governor in a letter brought with us by a soldier named Domingos Sampaio, ordering Senhor Gonçalo Caetano to take account of the goods and deliver them to us when we started. Thus we were despatched wanting what was most necessary to give away on the road, they having supplied to us no cloth that would be appreciated by the two potentates, the Cazembe and the Muatahianvo: these two chiefs having done all they could to assist us to carry out the undertaking, and help us to cross. They gave us neither firearms nor gunpowder to aid us in our defence; only four hundred and sixty-eight pieces of cloth, ten packets of small white, black and blue beads, bought out of the said cloths, and four bags of salt.

By the help of God, without either muskets or powder, we started from the town of Tette on Friday, May the tenth, 1811, nothing else having been treated of in connection with our expedition; noting the state of the said town, not only in consequence of the fear and panic created by Bonaparte, but also by the want of union existing among the townsmen. Even the Governor himself they accuse—I say they accuse falsely—of having been proved to have been the cause of the death of two Governors, the Illustrious Governor Francisco de Arnujo e Lacerda, whom it pleased God to take to Himself at Cazembe, being engaged in the same task of exploring the route from Tette to Angola, and the other, Governor Antonio Norberto Barbosa de Villas Boas, whom the colonists, officers, and soldiers, abandoned in the wars in the country named Caririm, belonging to an imperial potentate named, after the country-fashion, Moanna Mutapa Amutua. The latter is now persecuting the Governor of the above town aided by another nearer, who is called Prince of the land of Tette, or in country-fashion Changám: he is also persecuting the Governor to render him vassalage, and send him monthly tributes as the Sovereign of the lands.

The conquered districts held by the Government of Tette are four, Senna, Quilhimar (Quillimane), Zumbo with Marissa (Marrisca?), and the country (of the) Maravez, on the other side of the Zambeze river, in which people live, and in which are the warehouses (arimos) of the inhabitants of the town, male and female.   There is also another country to the west of the river Zambeze, called Sofalla, territory of the Muana Mutupa, who is under the Government of Mozambique.

The trade of the town of Tette consists in ivory, gold dust called money, which the traders from Mozambique, Senna, and Quilhimar, come to buy with Indian stuffs.   There is not a large trade carried on there in slaves, the price not being good enough to pay the seller.   In former times they were worth more, but not at the present.   They give for a "molocote," or slave-boy of six spans in height, a piece of zuarte eight fathoms in length, averaging (or capable of being cut into) twelve or fourteen cloths, and a piece of white "samater" of eight cloths, to make up the number of twenty-two cloths, which they call a scoro (corja), the number they give for a slave.   The traders of Mozambique, Senna, and Quilhimar always try to get slaves who came from the Cazembe, as they do not run away so much as those from our conquered districts about Tette.

The town of Tette is built of stone, and it is with the same material found in the country that they build one-storied houses of stone and clay, and some ground-floor buildings thatched with straw: there are only four houses roofed with tiles, and they belong to Dona Francisca called Quibonda; Dona Paula Mascarenhas; Dona Philipa Antonia, sister of the Quibonda, and Senbor Craveiro.   Salt is extracted from the streets in the Cassibo (Cacimbo, i.e., cloudy) season, as far as the fortress where the soldiers are quartered, and where the Governor's house, and the quarters of all the principal inhabitants, are situated.   On the further side of the Zambeze lie the Arimos (warehouses) of the inhabitants, containing supplies of wheat, barley, rice, and oven apples and quinces; millet, called Maça Ambála, and maize, known as Massa Aquindelle, fruits of different kinds; canes, from which they make sugar, and "Gerebita," a liquor extracted from the dregs of the sugar. The climate is very hot, fevers and agues prevailing.

Nearly all the inhabitants have mines, whence they get gold dust, called money; they are near the small rivers, where they send their slaves to find it.   On this side of the Zambeze, every day, there are slaves going and coming, belonging to the inhabitants, who bring maize and wheat for making bread, besides other necessaries, and firewood.   The said river Zambeze is about four hundred fathoms wide: to Senna and

Quillimar (Quillimane) there are roads running down the river-valley.

In the said pumbo (town) there are only a few white Portuguese, whose names are, the Illustrious Senhor Joaquim Correia Craveiro Sabarreiros, Lieutenant-Colonel of Militia; Doctor in Chief Mathias José Rebello, native of Loanda; Alexandre de Araujo Laceria Coutinho Pereira, Town Major; Leandro José de Aragão, Ensign of the Garrison; Michael Joaquim, Ensign of Militia; Joaquim da Costa and João da Guarda, Lieutenant of Militia; Manoel Antonio, Captain of Militia; Vicente Antonio de Quadros; Antonio Vergolino de (?), Ensign of the Garrison; Caetano Benedito Lobo, Lieutenant of Militia; Camillo José de Lemos, Captain of Militia; Rodrigo José de Aboiim, Adjutant and Captain of Militia; Christovão Franco, Chief Captain of the Mixonga (bush-land); Luiz José Ferreira Lima, Sergeant of the Garrison; José Oias, Quartermaster of the Garrison.

Those born in the same town, João Vicente da Cruz, Lieutenant of the Garrison; Ignacio Gomes dos Santos, Major of Militia; Manuel José Cardoso, Chief Captain of the lands; Luiz Nunes, Captain of Militia; João Cardoso, Ensign of the Garrison; Miguel da Costa e Santa Maria; José Dias de Sousa; Dionizio Xavier da Costa, Ensign of Militia; José Vicente de Aquino.

Ladies of the same country: the Illustrious Senhora Dona Francisca Josefa de Moura and Menezes, who had been married to two Governors of the town of Tette; Illustrious Senhoras Dona Paula Mascarenhas; Dona Filippa Antonia de Moura and Menezes; Dona Leonarda Oitavianna dos Reis Moreira; Dona Thomazia Ritta de Moura and Menezes; Dona Izabel Pereira de Araujo, Dona Anna Sebastião de Sousa Bragança, Dona Anna de Mello Botelho, Dona Izabel Anna de Sousa Bragança, Dona Rita de Araujo Lacerda; Dona Maria da Costa, and Dona Anna da Costa.

Beside these, there are people of another nation called the "Canaris" (of East Indian derivation), viz., the Illustrious José Pedro Diniz, Colonel of Militia; Gonçalo Caetano Pereira; José Sebastião de Ataide, Judicial Clerk; João Caetano de Andrade Soccorro, Lieutenant-Colonel of Militia; Domingos Antonio Salvador Colaço, Commissioner of the Royal Treasury; João Salvador Colaço, and other persons, whose names I do not know. There are also three persons, whites, whom they call Gentaos (heathens), who do not profess the Catholic faith; they dress in white clothes every day, and wear on their heads red turbans, which they do not remove to make any salutation, as other people do; one is named Tocraus Norus, tailor; the second is a blacksmith, and the third a carpenter.

On Saturday, 24th May, 1811, the Lieutenant-Colonel, I say

the Governor, I say the Adjutant, Rodrigo José de Aboim, sent for us to receive the goods given by the ladies and gentlemen which they were deceitfully trying to rob us of. Senhor Rodrigo and Senhor Luiz José Ferreira Lima told us that some very showy pieces of white "botira," given us by Senhor Craveiro, Dona Francisca Quibonda, and Dona Paula Mascarenhas, which they much needed or coveted, must be changed for Indian calico. We said, that having received said pieces from the Governor's hands, it would not do to exchange them for two pieces only, as this "botira" would be useful to us to present to the Cazembe: the Governor having given us no cloth that would please the Cazembe, who had been the means of our coming here with his Cacuata, and who would be pleased with them, and let us go on to Angola. The before-named gentlemen replied yes (that it must be done as they said).

On Monday, 25th of the same month, a soldier came to fetch us by the Governor's order, to go and see the articles. I went with my comrade Anastacio, and we saw in the Governor's quarto (room) Rodrigo Camelo, José de Lemos, and Luiz José Ferreira Lima: and, looking over the goods, we saw, without moving them, that the pieces that were there with the rest of the things were missing. Luiz directly went away, and when the said Senhor Rodrigo came in we asked him about them; he answered us very roughly and coarsely, saying, that if we had the impudence to question him, he would send us to buy where the Senhor Honorato was; and taking hold of me, he tried to throw me out of the window to the ground: and, as he could not lift me, he began to kick me, shouting uproariously all the time. At last, Senhor Camelo declared in our favour, saying that it was very wrong to exchange goods from the Royal Service; he prevented my telling the Governor about it, as I wished to, because he was ill in bed, and his companion Luiz very much wished to prevent it, as it was he who had taken down on paper a note of the goods as he went from house to house; they were both at the bottom of this exchange, which all the inhabitants considered to have been a very bad proceeding.

Nothing else was done, neither did we witness anything more in the territory of Tette that I have forgotten to mention, except my involuntary neglect to carry out the orders of my master, Lieutenant-Colonel Francisco Honorato da Costa, on this task of opening the road from the State and Kingdom of Angola to the Rios de Senna. God be ever praised that we departed from this town without the inconvenience which might have resulted from robberies and other crimes, which cause peace and quietness to be valued. (Signed) PEDRO JOÃO BAPTISTA. (Countersigned) ANTONIO NOGUEIRA DA ROCHA.

(D.)

The Governor of Angola transmits from the Governor of the Rivers of Senna the despatches, arrived overland in consequence of the discovery of a communication between the two coasts of Eastern and Western Africa, made by the pombeiros of Lieut.-Colonel Director of the Fair of Mucary, Francisco Honorato da Costa, to whose diligence and exertions is owing the happy result of this important and much-desired object. The beforesaid Lieut.-Colonel prays that he may be justly recompensed for his services; for the outlay he made from his own means on account of the expedition, and for the loss of the slaves engaged in the undertaking, giving up all his rights or title to the survivors, that they may receive from His Royal Highness the reward of merit. He wishes also to be able to remunerate the native heathen chiefs who assisted him.

I charge Pedro João Baptista to seek out the Illustrious Senhor Treasurer-in-Chief of the Royal Exchequer, Francisco Bento Maria Targini, at Rio de Janeiro, and to assure that gentleman of my respects, and to beg him to intercede and promote the intercession with the Prince Regent our Lord, the Queen our Lady, and the other Royal personages their counsellors and illustrious ministers, to obtain a fair and due remuneration for my great services effected entirely at my own cost, without assistance from any person, or a "real" from the Royal Treasury; but on the contrary, with known opposition from those who have governed Ambaca, and who are undeserving the name of Portuguese vassals, when the Royal Treasury has, without any result, lost all it expended, as well as the men who were entrusted with this enterprise. And so nothing was effected; but if any of those who came from Senna and Mozambique had reached Angola, no person, no matter how subordinate his position, would have been unrewarded similarly in addition to what recompense I expect myself. I hope to obtain something on account of my slaves whom I employed, of whom some died, others deserted, while others accompanied and assisted me when seriously affected with diseases which I have had difficulty in escaping. With the careful application of remedies and proper treatment persevered in by them, by the mercy of God I am alive to remunerate those who remain, and I wish also to reward the native potentates who assisted me, and who would by the incentive of rewards be ready to aid with similar zeal any further object of interest to the Royal Service; I renounce entirely all my rights existing in them (the slaves), that they may be able

R

to enjoy any favours, honours or rewards of which they may be
worthy, and which the Royal graciousness may be pleased to confer on them. Fair of Mucary, district of the kingdom of Angola,
27th October of 1814. (Signed) FRANCISCO HONORATO DA
COSTA.

Legislative documents referring to these explorations:—

[1st.]

To José d'Oliveira Barbosa, Governor and Captain-General
of the Kingdom of Angola.—Friend, I, the Prince Regent, cordially greet you. Having had before my Royal presence your
despatch accompanying the result of the exploration with
which Francisco Honorato da Costa, director of the Fair of
Mucari had been entrusted, who by means of unremitting attention and at considerable personal expense, has at last succeeded
in proving the existence of communication between the two
coasts of Eastern and Western Africa, I could not allow such an
important service, rendered gratuitously, and so worthy of my
attention, to pass unnoticed. Having already in consequence
granted some rewards to the said Francisco Honorato da Costa,
as you will have known, I am equally pleased to bestow upon
him a life pension of eight hundred milreis annually, which
shall be regularly paid by the Board of Administration of my
Royal Treasury in that kingdom of Angola. I also ordain that
he shall remain, as long as he may wish to do so, director of
the before-mentioned Fair of *Mucari*, from which place he
can best continue to make journeys, which should be annually
repeated from that point to the Rivers of Senna, for which purpose I have resolved that a company of *pedestres* (pedestrians)
shall be formed there in any manner you may consider best.
After hearing the opinion on the subject of the said Francisco
Honorato da Costa, you will be able to determine the number of men required to form such company, and also the
persons best suited to fill such posts; bearing in mind however that I have already reserved the post of captain in it for
Pedro João Baptista, as a reward for the services he rendered
in the first expedition and for the knowledge he obtained in it,
which he will be able to make useful in the subsequent
journeys. The expenses connected with the same will be made
in future on account of my Royal exchequer, so long as I do not
order to the contrary. All of which I think fitting to communicate to you for your information, and that you may so act
upon it. Given at Our Palace of Rio de Janeiro, on the
twenty-eighth day of August, eighteen hundred and fifteen.
(Signed) THE PRINCE. To José d'Oliveira Barboza.

[2nd.]

The Prince Regent, my master, having been pleased to confer on Lieut.-Colonel Francisco Honorato da Costa the appointment of brigadier of militia, as an acknowledgment for the important services rendered by him in the exploration of the communication between the two coasts of Eastern and Western Africa with which he was entrusted, as has already been notified to your Honour, the said August Sovereign is pleased to order that notwithstanding the absence of his nomination (or diploma) you will facilitate his obtaining and enjoying all the advantages such appointment confers on him, both as regards his use of the proper uniform, and the honours and privileges annexed to the post of brigadier. I forward this to your Honour for your information. God keep your lordship. Palace of Rio de Janeiro, 31st August, 1815. (Signed) MARQUIS D'AGUIAR.

[3rd.]

By a decree, a copy of which is enclosed to your Honour, my master the Prince Regent was pleased to name Pedro João Baptista, captain of the company of pedestrians, which is to be raised at the Fair of Mucari, there not being now time sufficient to prepare the nomination (or diploma) of this officer. The same August Senhor orders that notwithstanding this deficiency your Honour will consider him as already in the enjoyment of all the advantages which the appointment just granted by H.R.H. confers on him. His pay of 10,000 reis per month is to commence, and he will make use of the proper uniform. I forward this to you for your information and execution. God keep your Honour. Palace of Rio de Janeiro, 31st August, 1815. (Signed) MARQUIS D'AGUIAR.

[4th.]

Desiring to give a proof of the value in which I hold the services just rendered by Lieutenant-Colonel Francisco Honorato da Costa, Director of the Fair of Mucari, in the interior of the kingdom of Angola, so worthy my Royal attention, having succeeded at his own expense, and by untiring diligence, in opening the communication between the two coasts of Western and Eastern Africa, I have been pleased to confer on him the rank of Brigadier of Militia, to continue there in charge of the same important undertakings. The Supreme Military Council, having so understood it, will transmit to him the

necessary documents.   Palace of Rio de Janeiro, 13th May,
1815.   (With the signature of the Prince Regent.)

[5th.]

Having by Royal decree, dated this day, ordered the formation of a Company of Pedestrians, to be employed in the
communication which has just been discovered between the two
coasts of Western and Eastern Africa, I am pleased to confer
the post of Captain of this Company on Pedro João Baptista,
who was employed on the first expedition.   And, considering
the service he therein rendered, I have also been pleased to
grant him, in the exercise of that appointment, the stipend of
ten milreis per month.   The Supreme Military Council, having
so understood it, will, in conformity, transmit to him the
necessary despatches.   Palace of Rio de Janeiro, 28th August,
1815.   (With the Signature of the Prince Regent.)

RESUMÉ

OF THE

JOURNEY OF MM. MONTEIRO AND GAMITTO.

By DR. C. T. BEKE, Ph.D., F.S.A., F.R.G.S.

RESUMÉ

OF THE

JOURNEY OF MM. MONTEIRO AND GAMITTO.

By DR. C. T. BEKE, Ph.D., F.S.A., F.R.G.S.*

THE second mission from the Portuguese Governor of the Rios de Sena to the Court of the Muata Cazembe, in 1831, was very different in character from that undertaken by the governor of the colony in person in 1798. It consisted of Major José Maria Corrêa Monteiro, in charge of the mission, Captain (afterwards Major) Antonio Candido Pedroso Gamitto, second in command, an escort of twenty soldiers and a drummer, of whom four only were whites, from the garrison of Tete, and a Creole interpreter, with 120 negro slaves as porters. In company with the mission, and as auxiliaries, went two Creole traders with fifty slaves. Of this party the only persons who could read and write were the two Portuguese officers. With the exception of one magnetic compass, they took with them no instruments, not even a telescope, neither were they provided with medicines of any sort or kind. Captain Gamitto, who wrote the narrative of the mission,† of which I am now about to make use, appears to have been an intelligent and observant man, perfectly honest and unassuming, making no pretensions to any scientific knowledge, and seeming to have deemed it an advantage to the mission that no man of science was attached to it.

The expedition left Tete, and crossed the river Zambesi on June 1, 1831, and, after a most disastrous journey, reached the frontiers of the Cazembe's dominions on October 27th following. The barrenness of the country traversed is almost inconceivable. Dr. Lacerda had mentioned in his diary the absence of animal life, observing in his sarcastic, but good-humoured manner, that he supposed the inhabitants, having exhausted their food, had declared war against the butterflies,

---

* Reprinted, with the permission of the publishers, from 'Illustrated Travels,' vol. ii. p. 114.
† 'O Muata Cazembe.' Lisbon, 1854.

and consoling himself for the absence of mosquitoes by the reflection that they were spared the torture of their sting and the annoyance of their "infernal music." On this second expedition numerous deaths are recorded as having been caused by sickness brought on by want of proper nourishment, if not from absolute starvation. When once within the territories of the Cazembe they met, however, with larger supplies, the country being partially cultivated and having a larger population.

On November 9th the mission halted at the residence of a petty officer, on a little hill named Chempire, to await the Mambo's permission to approach his capital. The treatment they experienced there, and subsequently during their stay in the country, was widely different from the welcome received by the former mission, under Dr. Lacerda, from the Muata Cazembe Lekéza, whose memory, Gamitto says, continued to be respected both at home and abroad, on account of his many estimable qualities; whereas his son, the reigning Cazembe, was on the contrary, deficient in everything that was good, and was, therefore, detested even by his own relations.

As manifesting the different treatment the two missions received, I may notice the Royal message sent to the Portuguese at the same time that permission was granted for them to proceed to Lunda, the capital. It was to the effect that things were then very different from what they had been in the time of the king's father, when the former Mozungos visited the country; that every negro who should bo caught stealing should instantly lose his head; and that every soldier or negro who should be found intriguing with any of the wives either of the Muata himself or of his kilólos (nobles) should have his ears and genitals cut off, but not his hands, because without them he could not be of service to the Mozungos.

It is indeed true that things were not the same as in the time of the Muata Cazembe Lekéza; for Father Francisco Pinto relates that before the arrival of the mission, that sovereign called his nobles together, and ordered them to look after their wives; for that if they neglected to do so, and anything improper occurred, they would have themselves alone to blame. And when, afterwards, one of the courtiers complained to him of the conduct of a Portuguese officer with respect to his wife, and demanded satisfaction, the Muata ordered him to chastise his wife for having gone and inveigled the Mozungo!

But so far was the politic and conciliatory conduct of the father from serving as an example to the son, that the latter ordered the Muaniancita, or interpreter, not to make the

" Geral "—as the Portuguese envoy was called, as being the
representative of the Governor of Rios de Sena—acquainted with
the ancient customs, because, as the Mozungos were all new
men, they should be made to give larger presents than formerly.
And, accordingly, they were subjected to all sorts of extortions
and ill-treatment.

However, it is not my intention to relate the history of the
Portuguese mission, but to describe the manners and customs of
the strange people whom they went to visit, and with whom, it
is to be hoped, we shall shortly be made much better acquainted
by our countryman, Dr. Livingstone.

On the road to Lunda the mission had to pass by the
Mashámos (by Dr. Lacerda called Massangas) or sepulchres of
the deceased Muatas. As they approached the spot, the
soldiers of the escort donned their uniforms, and put themselves in marching order; and on reaching the Mashámos
they were received with *lunguros*, or cries of joy, from crowds
of persons of both sexes and of all ages, smeared over with mud
from the waist to the crown of the head, some using instead, as
a mark of distinction, a white powder like chalk, called *impemba*.
On their encamping there, the soldiers forming the escort were
sent to the Mashámos, at the request of the chief commissioned
to accompany the mission to Lunda; and as a mark of greater
respect, and for the sake of order, Captain Gamitto himself took
the command.

They were first conducted to the Mashámo of the Muata
Canyembo III., the third sovereign of that name and of this
state. It consisted of a large quadrangular enclosure, about a
hundred paces on each side, constructed of branches of trees and
stakes, forming an impenetrable barrier. Near the entrance
stood a heap of human skulls, and outside the door, seated
cross-legged on a lion-skin, was the Muine-Mashámo (grave-
keeper or minister), smeared over with *impemba* from the head
to the waist.

The soldiers here fired three volleys of musketry, and the
captain and the interpreter made their offerings to the Muzimo
(spirit) of the Muata by placing them in front of the minister,
who said they were insufficient, and that unless an addition
was made, he would not be able to offer them. His demand
having been complied with, he took the presents with him into
the Mashámo, and shortly afterwards sent to desire the strangers
to enter.

They found the whole space inside in a state of the utmost
cleanliness, and in the centre they saw a large circular house,
thatched with straw, in front of the door of which stood another
heap of skulls. In the centre of this large house was a smaller

one, of a cylindrical form, made of plaited cane-work, perfectly
empty, and without any decoration, except two painted pillars
at the entrance. This was the tomb of the Muata, and here
they found the minister seated cross-legged, with the presents
before him. After he had so remained some time in silence,
and apparently in deep meditation, he was heard from time to
time to mutter a few words, and at length he exclaimed, with a
loud voice, "Averie!" (Hail!). Gamitto says that this excla-
mation meant "much obliged;" but, even, if the true meaning
of the expression were not known, the context shows that the
Muine-Mashámo was addressing himself to the spirit of the
Muata, and not to the offerers; for he then turned round to
them, and said, "The Muzimo is much obliged to the Mozungos,
and to the Cazembe Ampata for having brought them!"
On this there was a loud clapping of hands, and cries of
"Averie!" on the part of the Cazembes who accompanied the
detachment; and the ceremony being then over, they all
retired, the Cazembes resuming their arms, which they had
left outside the enclosure, for no armed person is allowed to
enter.

On the following morning the sepulchre of the Muata Lekéza
—the fourth sovereign, and father of the reigning one—was
visited in like manner. Here everything was found to be
similar to the other, with the addition only that there were
seen two skulls attached to a tree, which, they were told,
were those of two powerful Mambos whom Lekéza had van-
quished and slain, and that near the monarch's grave stood
thirty gun-barrels, some of which were in very good order; but,
as they could not be repaired, they were deposited here as tro-
phies, dedicated to the deceased conqueror.

The ceremonies performed here were a repetition of those of
the day before at the grave of Canyembo III., except only that
the offerings on this occasion had to be increased, for the
alleged reason that Lekéza was the first Cazembo who had ever
seen and conversed with the Mozungos, and it was his spirit
that still watched over and protected them; an argument
which there was no withstanding. All the offerings made at
the sepulchres of the deceased Muatas were, however, for the
benefit of the living one, by whom they were taken possession of.

On the following day, November 19th, the mission made its
formal entry into Lunda, the capital, by a road some fifteen
yards in width. On this occasion an incident occurred which is
deserving of notice.

Captain Gamitto relates that on the journey from Tete one
of the Creole traders had brought with him a donkey; but, the

owner having died on the road, he had appropriated the animal to himself, and had ridden on it, instead of using a litter like the other Europeans. As it happened, he was a great gainer by this; for, in consequence of the sickness and incapacity of the bearers, his companions, and even Major Monteiro himself, had often to go on foot. As there was no saddle nor bridle, Gamitto had to put up with the best substitutes he could, covering the little animal with a tiger-skin as a saddle-cloth. It was mounted on this charger that the gallant captain took his place in the procession on its entry into the capital. His uniform consisted of a jacket of blue nankeen and white trowsers, with a scarlet cord and tassels for a sash. He, as well as the other Europeans, had allowed the beard and hair to grow so long that the former reached to his chest, and the latter as low down over his shoulders. On his head he wore an otter-skin cap, and at his side hung his trusty sword, the scabbard of which had become the colour of the natives themselves, from exposure to the air. Thus magnificently equipped, and mounted on his little donkey, caparisoned as already described, he made his solemn entry into what he says is perhaps the largest city of Southern Africa.

The post occupied by the cavalier, who in his own person formed the cavalry of the escort, was immediately after the vanguard; and, as may well be imagined, the singularity of his appearance attracted universal attention, and gave rise to innumerable remarks among the spectators. The ass, like the horse, is an animal totally unknown in that part of the world; so that some of the natives said, "It is a man with six legs:" others, "It is an animal that feeds on iron;" others, again, "He is a great warrior," &c. The immense multitude assembled together, the clamour that was raised by them, and the difficulty of penetrating through the crowd, excited the captain's charger to such a pitch that it galloped on with its mouth open, as if it wanted to bite the people, every now and then giving utterance to a prolonged bray, to the intense amazement of the people. "Were any one to appear in this trim in any town in Europe," profoundly remarks Gamitto, "he would assuredly be an object of ridicule;" but here the donkey and himself shared between them the admiration and applause of the public—so much so, indeed, that the rest of the mission was without importance, and attracted no attention.

This mention of the first appearance of the ass in the country of the Cazembe induces me to refer to a subject that has of late much occupied the attention of naturalists and archæologists, both in England and in France, since the time of the visit to Egypt of the Prince and Princess of Wales. At the anniversary dinner of the Royal Geographical Society, on May 24th, 1869,

Professor Owen, who had accompanied their Royal Highnesses
on their interesting tour, drew attention to the fact that " to the
Arabian shepherds, Hyksos or Sheiksos, Egypt was indebted
for the horse as a beast of draught. Previously to this Philistine
or Arabian invasion, the manifold frescoes on the tombs of
Egyptian worthies show no other soliped but the ass." *   And
at the meeting of the Académie des Sciences of Paris, on
December 13th last, M. Milne-Edwards, whilst admitting that
the horse appeared to be originally a native of Central Asia and
of a part of Europe, considered it as being, at the present day,
perfectly demonstrated that the ass is a species essentially
African, which did not extend itself into Asia, except in the
domestic state.†   However this may be, it seems quite certain,
from the anecdote I have just related, that the ass is not a native
of *Southern* Africa.

On the morning of November 29th they were summoned
into the presence of the Muata Cazembe, who was waiting to
receive the principal members of the mission.   In pursuance of
the arrangements previously made, they proceeded to the court
with the greatest ceremony, the detachment being under arms,
with their officer at their head; and as they had received an
intimation that they were all to take something as a present to
the Muata, so that he might know how many persons there were,
and who they were with whom he had to communicate, each
one carried a piece of cotton cloth.

On arriving at the Mossumba, or residence of the Mambo,
they entered a spacious court, which was already filled with an
immense crowd, so placed as to leave a small quadrangular
space vacant in front of the east door of the chipango, as the
inner enclosure containing the residence is called, whether it be
of the prince or of a subject.   The soldiers stationed in the
court were the garrison of Lunda, consisting of about four or
five thousand men, all armed with bows and arrows and spears ;
the nobles and officers wearing in a leather scabbard suspended under the left arm a large, straight, two-edged knife or
sword, called pocué, about eighteen inches long and four
inches broad.   They were all standing apparently without any
military discipline.

The Muata was seated on the left side of the east door of
the Mossumba.   Several panther-skins, with the tails turned
outwards, so as to form a sort of star, served him as a carpet, on

* In the *Athenæum* of June 12, 1869 (No. 2172), under the head, " The
Prince of Wales's Visit to Egypt," are some remarks of mine on this most interest-
ing subject.
† See ' Comptes Rendus, tom. lxix., p. 1239.

the centre of which was laid an enormous lion-skin, and upon this was placed a square stool or ottoman covered with a large green cloth. On this species of throne was seated the Muata, clothed with an elegance and sumptuousness such as the Portuguese officers had never witnessed in any other native potentate.

On his head he wore a sort of conical mitre, upwards of a foot in height, formed of feathers of a bright red colour. Encircling this was a diadem of stones, which, from the variety of colour and their quality, presented a most brilliant sight. At the back of his head, and rising from the nape of the neck, was a fan-shaped ruff of green cloth, fastened by two small ivory pins. The neck and shoulders were covered with a sort of cape, the upper edge of which was composed of the bottoms of cowrie-shells; this was followed by rows of pretty artificial stones of glass; below which was a row of small circular and square mirrors, placed alternately in regular order, on which, when the sun happened to shine, it was impossible to keep the eyes fixed. These formed the lower edge of the cape, falling equally over the shoulders, the chest, and the back.

On each arm, above the elbow, was a band of blue cloth four inches broad, trimmed with very narrow strips of fur, of which the hair, black and white, was four inches in length, having the appearance of a fringe. This, being a badge of royalty, could only be worn by the Muata Cazembe and his near relatives. The forearm, from the elbow to the wrist, was covered with rows of light blue beads.

The monarch's body, from the waist to the knees, was covered with a yellow cloth, having two borders on each side a couple of inches in width, the upper one being blue and the lower one scarlet. This cloth was several yards in length, and the way in which it was worn was by placing one end of it on the body and then bringing the cloth round over it, and fastening it in front with a small ivory pin. The rest of the cloth was then gathered up in small and very even plaits, which were secured by means of a strip of raw leather, so that the plaits were formed into a sort of rosette or frill. They call this cloth *muconzo*, and the girdle *insipo*. This strip of leather is cut out of a cow-hide, the whole length from the neck to the tip of the tail, and is five or six inches broad. When the *insipo* is fastened round the *muconzo*, the end of the tail hangs down from the rosette or frill in front.

The Muata had hanging on his right side, fastened to the insipo, a string of beads, and at the end of this was a small bell which, when he walked, knocked against his legs, keeping time with his pace. On his legs, from his knees downwards, were rows of beads like those on his arms. Dressed and ornamented in this fashion, his face, hands, and feet alone were naked, all the rest of his body being covered, and, as it appeared to Captain Gamitto, with great elegance and good taste.

To protect the Muata from the sun there were seven large umbrellas, made of different coloured cloths of native manufacture, raised on large bamboos fixed in the ground. Round the umbrellas stood twelve negroes, plainly and cleanly clad, each holding in his hand a whisk made from a cow's tail, the handle being covered with beads of various colours. These whisks were all shaken at the same time, as if to drive away the flies, on a signal given by the Cazembo with a smaller one which he held in his hand.

At a short distance from him twelve other negroes with brooms moved about slowly, their eyes fixed on the ground, sweeping and picking up all the weeds or other objects, however minute, that they might find; and these were followed by two others walking at the same slow pace, each one having a basket at his back to hold whatever the others might sweep up. But so clean was the place, that none of them had anything to do, only the court etiquette would not dispense with these ceremonies.

From the back of the Muata's seat were drawn on the ground two curved lines, which met together in front of him at a distance of four or five yards. The line on the left was simply cut in the ground; that on the right was made with impemba, the white powder already mentioned. In front of the Cazembo, outside and along these curved lines, were placed in two parallel rows about two feet apart several images of coarse workmanship, representing half-length figures of human beings with negro features, having on their heads the horns of animals, and fastened upon sticks driven into the ground. Between these two rows of figures, at the end nearest the Cazembe, was a wicker basket in the form of a barrel containing a smaller figure. Close to those at the further end were two negroes seated on the ground, having before them a small earthen vessel filled with live coals, on which they kept throwing leaves that produced a dense aromatic smoke. These two men, as well as all the images, had their faces turned towards the Cazembo. From below the last image on the right, nearest to the foot of the fumigator, ran a cord reaching to the feet of the Muata, though for what purpose was not apparent.

The door of the chipango was open, and within the doorway sat the two principal wives of the Muata. On the left was the chief wife, who is styled Muaringombe, seated on an ottoman and wrapped in a large green cloth, having her arms, neck, and head adorned with stones of various colours, and on her head an ornament of scarlet feathers similar to that of the Cazembe, only smaller. The second wife, who bore the title of Inteména, was seated on a lion-skin spread on the ground, being dressed in a plain cloth without any ornaments. Behind these were more than four hundred females of various ages, all standing, and dressed in uhandas, or waist-cloths reaching down to the knees. These formed the establishment of the chipango, or the seraglio as it may be called, being divided among the four principal wives, whose servants they were.

Seated on a lion-skin laid on the ground to the left of the Cazembe, protected from the sun by two umbrellas, and dressed like the Muaringombe, or chief wife, sat a young negress styled Nincamuana, mother of the Muane, or Muata, which title devolved on her on the death of the Cazembe's real mother, as being her next of kin. Behind her stood about two hundred negresses dressed in uhandas, forming her state establishment.

Within the square left vacant by the guards, ranged in a semicircle round the Cazembe, according to their respective ranks, were the Kilólos or vambires (nobles), seated on the skins of lions or panthers, each with his umbrella, and all dressed like the Mambo, with the exception of the cape and the scarlet feathers. In the centre of the semicircle, and forming part of it, were two persons who attracted particular attention on account of their scarlet feathers and fur armlets, like those of the Muata, only smaller. These were his relatives, the one named Kalulua being his uncle, and the other his nephew, named Suana-Murópue.

Between the Cazembe and the kilólos were the musicians, playing on instruments of divers shapes and sounds, quite different from anything the strangers had seen among the other people they had visited. They were divided into bands; and, as each band played its own tune, the effect was anything but harmonious; but when one band was heard alone the music was not without sweetness and harmony.

Among the musicians, and near the Muata, were several buffoons, ridiculously dressed in panther-skins, hanging down from their shoulders, with the heads of the animals covering their own heads, the rest of their bodies being naked. Others had their heads decorated with the horns of animals, and wore a girdle of straw, professedly for the sake of decency, but so arranged as to be, in fact, indecent. Others had strips of leather hanging from the waist, but in other respects were quite naked, their bodies being painted all over red and white. And lastly, some went altogether naked, their heads and faces alone being covered with grass. Dressed up in this fashion, these buffoons made all sorts of grimaces, and put themselves into the most ridiculous postures, without, however, attracting much, if any, attention from those present.

The multitude of persons thus assembled, and the great variety of their costumes, presented a confused but most brilliant spectacle. The Muata Cazembe appeared to be about fifty years of age, but was said to be much older. He had a thick beard, which had already turned grey. He was stout and tall, and in possession of health and agility which gave promise of a long life. His manners were majestic and agreeable, and his state and style of living were, in their way, showy. Most certainly it was not to be imagined that so much etiquette, ceremony, and ostentation would be met with in the sovereign of a region so remote from the sea-shore, and among a people apparently so savage and barbarous.

When the Portuguese envoy and his escort had come into the presence of the Cazembe, and advanced between him and the Kilólos, they halted and presented arms, intimating to the Mambo that this was intended for him, it being the way in which they saluted kings and great personages, to which he responded with a deep bow and the expression of his thanks. As they were all standing, the Muata ordered a large tusk of ivory, covered with a tiger-skin, to be placed at the feet of the envoy, whom he desired to seat himself on it. But as he had not done the same to the rest of the party, so that they must either have remained standing or else have sat down on the ground, the envoy explained that he could not be seated whilst the other Mozungos remained standing, such being contrary to their custom, at which the Muata smiled, and sent a panther-skin for each of the party.

When they had all taken their seats in front of the Cazembe, close to the images, he made a slight motion of the head, and immediately there began a drumming and dancing quite different from anything the visitors had ever seen anywhere else, which entertainment lasted a considerable time. When the Cazembe Ampata—that is to say, the envoy from the Muata to the Portuguese Government—who had accompanied the mission from Tete, came forward and danced before the Cazembe, the latter stretched out both his hands towards him and said, " Uávinga," which means " Well done!" this being the greatest honour he ever showed to any one. On this, that officer and all his suite prostrated themselves before their sovereign, rubbing their bodies with earth from the waist to the head, and crying out repeatedly, "Averie! averie!" (Hail! hail!) The Mambo then, turning round towards his courtiers, made a sign to them, and immediately they all rose and went to salute the Cazembe

Ampata, who, as they approached him, fell down on his knees. All those of superior or equal rank went up to him, each separately, and took hold of both his arms, clasping the inner part of the elbow-joint with the hand, he doing the same to them. The kilólos of inferior rank, however, did not touch him, but merely approached him in front, raising both arms in the air with the hands open, to which he responded in like manner. During the whole time he remained on his knees, not rising till they had all gone through the ceremony of thus saluting him.

The Portuguese envoy then intimated to the Muata that he also would like to fire a salute, which he approved; and when this had taken place he desired that it might be repeated, which was done accordingly. The solemnity being thus brought to a close, the Muata dismissed the mission, sending a female slave as a present to its chief.

INDEX.

THE END.

www.ingramcontent.com/pod-product-compliance
Lightning Source LLC
Chambersburg PA
CBHW030346270326
41926CB00009B/982